AUDUBON GUIDE

to the National Wildlife Refuges

Southeast

AUDUBON GUIDE
to the National Wildlife Refuges

Southeast

Alabama • Florida • Georgia • Kentucky
Mississippi • North Carolina • Puerto Rico
South Carolina • Tennessee • U.S. Virgin Islands

By Doris Gove

Foreword by Theodore Roosevelt IV

Series Editor, David Emblidge

A Balliett & Fitzgerald Book
St. Martin's Griffin, New York

Cartography: © Balliett & Fitzgerald, Inc. produced by Mapping Specialists Ltd.
Illustrations: Mary Sundstrom
Cover design: Michael Storrings and Sue Canavan
Interior design: Bill Cooke and Sue Canavan

Balliett & Fitzgerald Inc. Staff
Sue Canavan, Design Director
Maria Fernandez, Production Editor
Alexis Lipsitz, Executive Series Editor
Rachel Deutsch, Associate Photo Editor
Kristen Couse, Associate Editor
Paul Paddock, Assistant Editor
Howard Klein, Editorial Intern
Scott Prentzas, Copy Editor

Balliett & Fitzgerald Inc. would like to thank the following people for their assistance in creating this series:
At National Audubon Society:
Katherine Santone, former Director of Publishing, for sponsoring this project
Claire Tully, Senior Vice President, Marketing
Evan Hirsche, Director, National Wildlife Refuges Campaign
At U.S. Fish & Wildlife Service:
Richard Coleman, former Chief, Division of Refuges, U.S. Fish & Wildlife Service
Janet Tennyson, Outreach Coordinator
Craig Rieben, Chief of Broadcasting & Audio Visual, U.S. Fish & Wildlife Service, for photo research assistance
Pat Carrol, Chief Surveyor, U.S. Fish & Wildlife Service, for map information
Regional External Affairs officers, at the seven U.S. Fish & Wildlife Service Regional Headquarters
Elizabeth Jackson, Photographic Information Specialist, National Conservation Training Center, for photo research
At St. Martin's Griffin:
Greg Cohn, who pulled it all together on his end, as well as Michael Storrings and Kristen Macnamara
At David Emblidge—Book Producer:
Marcy Ross, Assistant Editor
Thanks also to Theodore Roosevelt IV and John Flicker.

ISBN 0-312-24128-3
First St. Martin's Griffin Edition: March 2000

10 9 8 7 6 5 4 3 2 1

CONTENTS

SOUTH CAROLINA

TENNESSEE

Appendix

Foreword

America is singularly blessed in the amount and quality of land that the federal government holds in trust for its citizens. No other country can begin to match the variety of lands in our national wildlife refuges, parks, and forests. From Arctic Refuge on the North Slope of Alaska to the National Key Deer Refuge in Florida, the diversity of land in the National Wildlife Refuge (NWR) System is staggering.

Yet of all our public lands, the National Wildlife Refuge System is the least well known and does not have an established voting constituency like that of the Parks System. In part this is because of its "wildlife first" mission, which addresses the needs of wildlife species before those of people. That notwithstanding, wildlife refuges also offer remarkable opportunities for people to experience and learn about wildlife—and to have fun doing so!

The Refuge System was launched in 1903 when President Theodore Roosevelt discovered that snowy egrets and other birds were being hunted to the brink of extinction for plumes to decorate ladies' hats. He asked a colleague if there were any laws preventing the president from making a federal bird reservation out of an island in Florida's Indian River. Learning there was not, Roosevelt responded, "Very well, then I so declare it." Thus Pelican Island became the nation's first plot of land to be set aside for the protection of wildlife. Roosevelt went on to create another 50 refuges, and today there are more than 500 refuges encompassing almost 93 million acres, managed by the U.S. Fish & Wildlife Service.

The Refuge System provides critical habitat for literally thousands of mammals, birds, amphibians and reptiles, and countless varieties of plants and flowers. More than 55 refuges have been created specifically to save endangered species. Approximately 20 percent of all threatened and endangered species in the United States rely on these vital places for their survival. As a protector of our country's natural diversity, the System is unparalleled.

Setting NWR boundaries is determined, as often as possible, by the needs of species that depend on the protected lands. Conservation biology, the science that studies ecosystems as a whole, teaches us that wildlife areas must be linked by habitat "corridors" or run the risk of becoming biological islands. The resulting inability of species to transfer their genes over a wide area leaves them vulnerable to disease and natural disasters. For example, the Florida panther that lives in Big Cypress Swamp suffers from a skin fungus, a consequence, scientists believe, of inbreeding. Today's refuge managers are acutely aware of this precarious situation afflicting many species and have made protection of the System's biodiversity an important goal.

Clearly, the job of the refuge manager is not an easy one. Chronic underfunding of the System by the federal government has resulted in refuges operating with less money per employee and per acre than any other federal land-management agency. Recent efforts by some in Congress to address this shortfall have begun to show results, but the System's continued vulnerability to special interests has resulted in attempts to open refuges to oil drilling, road building in refuge wilderness areas, and military exercises.

The managers of the System have played a crucial role in responding to the limited resources available. They have created a network of volunteers who contribute tens of thousands of hours to help offset the lack of direct financing for the Refuge System. Groups like refuge "friends" and Audubon Refuge Keepers have answered the call for local citizen involvement on many refuges across the country.

I hope Americans like yourself who visit our national wildlife refuges will come away convinced of their importance, not only to wildlife but also to people. I further hope you will make your views known to Congress, becoming the voice and voting constituency the Refuge System so desperately needs.

—*Theodore Roosevelt IV*

Preface

Thank you for adding the *Audubon Guide to the National Wildlife Refuge System* to your travel library. I hope you will find this nine-volume series an indispensable guide to finding your way around the Refuge System, as well as a valuable educational tool for learning more about the vital role wildlife refuges play in protecting our country's natural heritage.

It was nearly 100 years ago that Frank Chapman, an influential ornithologist, naturalist, publisher and noted Audubon member, approached President Theodore Roosevelt (as recounted by Theodore Roosevelt IV in his foreword), eventually helping to persuade him to set aside more than 50 valuable parcels of land for the protection of wildlife.

Because of limited funding available to support these new wildlife sanctuaries, Audubon stepped up and paid for wardens who diligently looked after them. And so began a century of collaboration between Audubon and the National Wildlife Refuge System. Today, Audubon chapter members can be found across the country assisting refuges with a range of projects, from viewing tower construction to bird banding.

Most recently, National Audubon renewed its commitment to the Refuge System by launching a nationwide campaign to build support for refuges locally and nationally. Audubon's Wildlife Refuge Campaign is promoting the Refuge System through on-the-ground programs such as Audubon Refuge Keepers (ARK), which builds local support groups for refuges, and Earth Stewards, a collaboration with the U.S. Fish & Wildlife Service and the National Fish and Wildlife Foundation, which uses refuges and other important bird habitats as outdoor classrooms. In addition, we are countering legislative threats to refuges in Washington, D.C., while supporting increased federal funding for this, the least funded of all federal land systems.

By teaching more people about the important role refuges play in conserving our nation's diversity of species—be they birds, mammals, amphibians, reptiles, or plants—we have an opportunity to protect for future generations our only federal lands system set aside first and foremost for wildlife conservation.

As a nation, we are at a critical juncture—do we continue to sacrifice wetlands, forests, deserts, and coastal habitat for short-term profit, or do we accept that the survival of our species is closely linked to the survival of others? The National Wildlife Refuge System is a cornerstone of America's conservation efforts. If we are to leave a lasting legacy and, indeed, ensure our future, then we must build on President Theodore Roosevelt's greatest legacy. I invite you to join us!

—John Flicker, President, National Audubon Society

Introduction
to the National Wildlife Refuge System

He spent entire days on horseback, traversing the landscape of domed and crumbling hills, steep forested coulees, with undulating tables of prairie above. The soft wraparound light of sunset displayed every strange contour of the Badlands and lit the colors in each desiccated layer of rock—yellow, ochre, beige, gold.

Theodore Roosevelt was an easterner. As some well-heeled easterners were wont to do, he traveled west in 1883 to play cowboy, and for the next eight years he returned as often as possible. He bought a cattle ranch, carried a rifle and a six-gun, rode a horse. North Dakota was still Dakota Territory then, but the Plains bison were about gone, down to a scattering of wild herds.

The nation faced a new and uneasy awareness of limits during Roosevelt's North Dakota years. Between 1776 and 1850, the American population had increased from 1.5 million to more than 23 million. National borders were fixed and rail and telegraph lines linked the coasts, but Manifest Destiny had a price. The ongoing plunder of wildlife threatened species such as the brown pelican and the great egret; the near-total extermination of 60 million bison loomed as a lesson many wished to avoid repeating.

Despite the damage done, the powerful landscapes of the New World had shaped the outlooks of many new Americans. From Colonial-era botanist John Bartram to 19th-century artists George Catlin and John James Audubon, naturalists and individuals of conscience explored the question of what constituted a proper human response to nature. Two figures especially, Henry David Thoreau and John Muir, created the language and ideas that would confront enduring Old World notions of nature as an oppositional, malevolent force to be harnessed and exploited. The creation in 1872 of Yellowstone as the world's first national park indicated that some Americans, including a few political leaders, were listening to what Thoreau, Muir, and these others had to say.

Roosevelt, along with his friend George Bird Grinnell, drew upon these and other writings, as well as their own richly varied experiences with nature, to take the unprecedented step of making protection of nature a social and political cause. Of his time in the Badlands, Roosevelt remarked "the romance of my life began here," and "I never would have been president if it had not been for my experiences in North Dakota." As a hunter, angler, and naturalist, Roosevelt grasped the importance of nature for human life. Though he had studied natural history as an undergraduate at Harvard, believing it would be his life's work, Roosevelt owned a passion for reform and had the will—perhaps a need—to be effective. Rather than pursuing a career as a naturalist, he went into politics. His friend George

Barren-ground caribou

Arctic Ocean
Alaska
Bering Sea
Pacific Ocean
Washington
Oregon
Idaho
Montana
North Dakota
South Dakota
Wyoming
Nebrask
Nevada
Utah
Colorado
Kansa
California
Oklah
Arizona
New Mexico
Texas
Pacific Ocean
Midway
Hawaii
Pacific Ocean

New England Region
Middle Atlantic Region
Southeast Region
Northern Midwest Region
South Central Region
Southwest Region
Rocky Mountains Region
Alaska and Pacific Northwest Region
California and Hawaii Region
Migratory Flyway
Great Lakes
New Hampshire
Vermont
Maine
Massachusetts
New York
Rhode Island
Connecticut
New Jersey
Delaware
Maryland
Pennsylvania
Wisconsin
Michigan
nesota
Iowa
Illinois
Indiana
Ohio
West Virginia
Virginia
Missouri
Kentucky
North Carolina
Tennessee
South Carolina
Arkansas
Mississippi
Alabama
Georgia
Louisiana
Florida
Atlantic Ocean
Puerto Rico
Gulf of Mexico

Bird Grinnell, publisher of the widely read magazine *Forest and Stream,* championed all manner of environmental protection and in 1886 founded the Audubon Society to combat the slaughter of birds for the millinery trade. Fifteen years later, TR would find himself with an even greater opportunity. In1901, when he inherited the presidency following the assassination of William McKinley, Roosevelt declared conservation a matter of federal policy.

Roosevelt backed up his words with an almost dizzying series of conservation victories. He established in 1903 a federal bird reservation on Pelican Island, Florida, as a haven for egrets, herons, and other birds sought by plume hunters. In eight years, Roosevelt authorized 150 million acres in the lower 48 states and another 85 million in Alaska to be set aside from logging under the Forest Reserve Act of 1891, compared to a total of 45 million under the three prior presidents. To these protected lands he added five national parks and 17 national monuments. The NWR system, though, is arguably TR's greatest legacy. Often using executive order to circumvent Congress, Roosevelt established 51 wildlife refuges.

The earliest federal wildlife refuges functioned as sanctuaries and little else. Visitors were rare and recreation was prohibited. Between 1905 and 1912 the first refuges for big-game species were established—Wichita Mountains in Oklahoma, the National Bison Range in Montana, and National Elk Refuge in Jackson, Wyoming. In 1924, the first refuge to include native fish was created; a corridor some 200 miles long, the Upper Mississippi National Wildlife and Fish Refuge spanned the states of Minnesota, Wisconsin, Illinois, and Iowa.

Atlantic puffins, Petit Manan NWR, Maine

Still, the 1920s were dark years for America's wildlife. The effects of unregulated hunting, along with poor enforcement of existing laws, had decimated once-abundant species. Extinction was feared for the wood duck. Wild turkey had become scarce outside a few southern states. Pronghorn antelope, which today number perhaps a million across the West, were estimated at 25,000 or fewer. The trumpeter swan, canvasback duck, even the prolific and adaptable white-tailed deer, were scarce or extirpated across much of their historic ranges.

The Depression and Dust-bowl years, combined with the leadership of President Franklin Delano Roosevelt, gave American conservation—and the refuge system in particular—a hefty forward push. As wetlands vanished and fertile prairie soils blew away, FDR's Civilian Conservation Corps (CCC) dispatched thousands of unemployed young men to camps that stretched from Georgia to California. On the sites of many present-day refuges, they built dikes and other

Saguaro cactus and ocotillo along Charlie Bell 4WD trail, Cabeza Prieta NWR, Arizona

water-control structures, planted shelterbelts and grasses. Comprised largely of men from urban areas, the experience of nature was no doubt a powerful rediscovery of place and history for the CCC generation. The value of public lands as a haven for people, along with wildlife, was on the rise.

In 1934, Jay Norwood "Ding" Darling was instrumental in developing the federal "Duck Stamp," a kind of war bond for wetlands; hunters were required to purchase it, and anyone else who wished to support the cause of habitat acquisition could, too. Coupled with the Resettlement Act of 1935, in which the federal government bought out or condemned private land deemed unsuitable for agriculture, several million acres of homesteaded or settled lands reverted to federal ownership to become parks, national grasslands, and wildlife refuges. The Chief of the U.S. Biological Survey's Wildlife Refuge Program, J. Clark Salyer, set out on a cross-country mission to identify prime wetlands. Salyer's work added 600,000 acres to the refuge system, including Red Rock Lakes in Montana, home to a small surviving flock of trumpeter swans.

The environmental ruin of the Dust bowl also set in motion an era of government initiatives to engineer solutions to such natural events as floods, drought, and the watering of crops. Under FDR, huge regional entities such as the Tennessee Valley Authority grew, and the nation's mightiest rivers—the Columbia, Colorado, and later, the Missouri—were harnessed by dams. In the wake of these and other federal works projects, a new concept called "mitigation" appeared: If a proposed dam or highway caused the destruction of a certain number of acres of wetlands or other habitat, some amount of land nearby would be ceded to conservation in return. A good many of today's refuges were the progeny of mitigation. The federal government, like the society it represents, was on its way to becoming complex enough that the objectives of one arm could be at odds with those of another.

Citizen activism, so integral to the rise of the Audubon Society and other groups, was a driving force in the refuge system as well. Residents of rural Georgia applied relentless pressure on legislators to protect the Okefenokee Swamp. Many other refuges—San Francisco Bay, Sanibel Island, Minnesota Valley, New Jersey's Great Swamp—came about through the efforts of people with a vision of conservation close to home.

More than any other federal conservation program, refuge lands became places where a wide variety of management techniques could be tested and refined. Generally, the National Park system followed the "hands off" approach of Muir and Thoreau while the U.S. Forest Service and Bureau of Land Management, in theory, emphasized a utilitarian, "sustainable yield" value; in practice, powerful economic interests backed by often ruthless politics left watersheds, forests, and grasslands badly degraded, with far-reaching consequences for fish and wildlife. The refuge system was not immune to private enterprise—between 1939 and 1945, refuge lands were declared fair game for oil drilling, natural-gas exploration, and even for bombing practice by the U.S. Air Force—but the negative impacts have seldom reached the levels of other federal areas.

Visitor use at refuges tripled in the 1950s, rose steadily through the 1960s, and by the 1970s nearly tripled again. The 1962 Refuge Recreation Act established guidelines for recreational use where activities such as hiking, photography, boating, and camping did not interfere with conservation. With visitors came opportunities to educate, and now nature trails and auto tours, in addition to beauty, offered messages about habitats and management techniques. Public awareness of wilderness, "a place where man is only a visitor," in the words of long-time advocate Robert Marshall of the U.S. Forest Service, gained increasing social and political attention. In 1964, Congress passed the Wilderness Act, establishing guidelines for designating a host of federally owned lands as off-limits to motorized vehicles, road building, and resource exploitation. A large number of refuge lands qualified—the sun-blasted desert of Arizona's Havasu refuge, the glorious tannin-stained waters and cypress forests of Georgia's Okefenokee Swamp, and the almost incomprehensible large 8-million-acre Arctic NWR in Alaska, home to vast herds of caribou, wolf packs, and bladelike mountain peaks, the largest contiguous piece of wilderness in the refuge system.

Sachuest Point NWR, Rhode Island

Nonetheless, this was also a time of horrendous air and water degradation, with the nation at its industrial zenith and agriculture cranked up to the level of "agribusiness." A wake-up call arrived in the form of vanishing bald eagles, peregrine falcons, and osprey. The insecticide DDT, developed in 1939 and used in World War II to eradicate disease-spreading insects, had been used throughout the nation ever since, with consequences unforeseen until the 1960s. Sprayed over wetlands, streams, and crop fields, DDT had entered watersheds and from there the food chain itself. It accumulated in the bodies of fish and other aquatic life, and birds consuming fish took DDT into their systems, one effect was a calcium deficiency, resulting in eggs so fragile that female birds crushed them during incubation.

Partially submerged alligator, Anahuac NWR, Texas

Powerful government and industry leaders launched a vicious, all-out attack on the work of a marine scientist named Rachel Carson, whose book *Silent Spring,* published in 1962, warned of the global dangers associated with DDT and other biocides. For this she was labeled "not a real scientist" and "a hysterical woman." With eloquence and courage, though, Carson stood her ground. If wild species atop the food chain could be devastated, human life could be threatened, too. Americans were stunned, and demanded an immediate ban on DDT. Almost overnight, the "web of life" went from chalkboard hypothesis to reality.

Protecting imperiled species became a matter of national policy in 1973 when President Nixon signed into law the Endangered Species Act (ESA), setting guidelines by which the U.S. Fish & Wildlife Service would "list" plant and animal species as *threatened* or *endangered* and would develop a program for their recovery. Some 56 refuges, such as Ash Meadows in Nevada and Florida's Crystal River, home of the manatee, were established specifically for the protection of endangered species. Iowa's tiny Driftless Prairie refuge exists to protect the rare, beautifully colored pleistocene land snail and a wildflower, the northern monkshood. Sometimes unwieldy, forever politicized, the ESA stands as a monumental achievement. Its successes include the American alligator, bald eagle, and gray wolf. The whooping crane would almost surely be extinct today without the twin supports of ESA and the refuge system. The black-footed ferret, among the rarest mammals on earth, is today being reintroduced on a few western refuges. In 1998, nearly one-fourth of all threatened and endangered species populations find sanctuary on refuge lands.

More legislation followed. The passage of the Alaska National Interest Lands Conservation Act in 1980 added more than 50 million acres to the refuge system in Alaska.

The 1980s and '90s have brought no end of conservation challenges, faced by an increasingly diverse association of organizations and strategies. Partnerships now link the refuge system with nonprofit groups, from Ducks Unlimited and The Nature Conservancy to international efforts such as Partners in Flight, a program to monitor the decline of, and to secure habitat for, neotropical songbirds. These cooperative efforts have resulted in habitat acquisition and restoration, research, and many new refuges. Partnerships with private landowners who voluntarily offer marginally useful lands for restoration—with a sponsoring conservation group cost-sharing the project—have revived many thousands of acres of grasslands, wetlands, and riparian corridors.

Coyote on the winter range

Citizen activism is alive and well as we enter the new millennium. Protecting and promoting the growth of the NWR system is a primary campaign of the National Audubon Society, which, by the year 2000, will have grown to a membership of around 550,000. NAS itself also manages about 100 sanctuaries and nature centers across the country, with a range of opportunities for environmental education. The National Wildlife Refuge Association, a volunteer network, keeps members informed of refuge events, environmental issues, and legislative developments and helps to maintain a refuge volunteer workforce. In 1998, a remarkable 20 percent of all labor performed on the nation's refuges was carried out by volunteers, a contribution worth an estimated $14 million.

A national wildlife refuge today has many facets. Nature is ascendant and thriving, often to a shocking degree when compared with adjacent lands. Each site has its own story: a prehistory, a recent past, a present—a story of place, involving people, nature, and stewardship, sometimes displayed in Visitor Center or Headquarters exhibits, always written into the landscape. Invariably a refuge belongs to a community as well, involving area residents who visit, volunteers who log hundreds of hours, and a refuge staff who are knowledgeable and typically friendly, even outgoing, especially if the refuge is far-flung. In this respect most every refuge is a portal to local culture, be it Native American, cows and crops, or big city. There may be no better example of democracy in action than a national wildlife refuge. The worm-dunker fishes while a mountain biker pedals past. In spring, birders scan marshes and grasslands that in the fall will be walked by hunters. Compromise is the guiding principle.

What is the future of the NWR system? In Prairie City, Iowa, the Neal Smith NWR represents a significant departure from the time-honored model. Established in 1991, the site had almost nothing to "preserve." It was old farmland with scattered remnants of tallgrass prairie and degraded oak savanna. What is happening at Neal Smith, in ecological terms, has never been attempted on such a scale: the reconstruction, essentially from scratch, of a self-sustaining 8,000-acre native biome, complete with bison and elk, greater prairie chickens, and a palette of wildflowers and grasses that astonish and delight.

What is happening in human terms is equally profound. Teams of area residents, called "seed seekers," explore cemeteries, roadside ditches, and long-ignored patches of ground. Here and there they find seeds of memory, grasses and wildflowers from the ancient prairie, and harvest them; the seeds are catalogued and planted on the refuge. The expanding prairie at Neal Smith is at once new and very old. It is reshaping thousands of Iowans' sense of place, connecting them to what was, eliciting wonder for what could be. And the lessons here transcend biology. In discovering rare plants, species found only in the immediate area, people discover an identity beyond job titles and net worth. The often grueling labor of cutting brush, pulling nonnative plants, and tilling ground evokes the determined optimism of Theodore and Franklin Roosevelt and of the CCC.

As the nation runs out of wild places worthy of preservation, might large-scale restoration of damaged or abandoned lands become the next era of American conservation? There are ample social and economic justifications. The ecological justifications are endless, for, as the history of conservation and ecology has revealed, nature and humanity cannot go their separate ways. The possibilities, if not endless, remain rich for the years ahead.

—John Grassy

How to use this book

Local conditions and regulations on national wildlife refuges vary considerably. We provide detailed, site-specific information useful for a good refuge visit, and we note the broad consistencies throughout the NWR system (facility set-up and management, what visitors may or may not do, etc.). Contact the refuge before arriving or stop by the Visitor Center when you get there. F&W wildlife refuge managers are ready to provide friendly, savvy advice about species and habitats, plus auto, hiking, biking, or water routes that are open and passable, and public programs (such as guided walks) you may want to join.

AUDUBON GUIDES TO THE NATIONAL WILDLIFE REFUGES

This is one of nine regional volumes in a series covering the entire NWR system. **Visitable refuges**—over 300 of them—constitute about three-fifths of the NWR system. **Nonvisitable refuges** may be small (without visitor facilities), fragile (set up to protect an endangered species or threatened habitat), or new and undeveloped.

Among visitable refuges, some are more important and better developed than others. In creating this series, we have categorized refuges as A, B, or C level, with the A-level refuges getting the most attention. You will easily recognize the difference. C-level refuges, for instance, do not carry a map.

Rankings can be debated; we know that. We considered visitation statistics, accessibility, programming, facilities, and the richness of the refuges' habitats and animal life. Some refuges ranked as C-level now may develop further over time.

Many bigger NWRs have either "satellites" (with their own refuge names), separate "units" within the primary refuge, or other, less significant NWRs nearby. All of these, at times, were deemed worthy of a brief mention.

ABOUT THE U.S. FISH & WILDLIFE SERVICE Under the Department of the Interior, the U.S. Fish & Wildlife Service is the principal federal agency responsible for conserving and protecting wildlife and plants and their habitats for the benefit of the American people. The Service manages the 93-million-acre NWR system, comprised of more than 500 national wildlife refuges, thousands of small wetlands, and other special management areas. It also operates 66 national fish hatcheries, 64 U.S. Fish & Wildlife Management Assistance offices, and 78 ecological services field stations. The agency enforces federal wildlife laws, administers the Endangered Species Act, manages migratory bird populations, restores nationally significant fisheries, conserves and restores wildlife habitats such as wetlands, and helps foreign governments with their conservation efforts. It also oversees the federal-aid program that distributes hundreds of millions of dollars in excise taxes on fishing and hunting equipment to state wildlife agencies.

ORGANIZATION OF THE BOOK

■ **REGIONAL OVERVIEW** This regional introduction is intended to give readers the big picture, touching on broad patterns in landscape formation, interconnections among plant communities, and diversity of animals. We situate NWRs in the natural world of the larger bio-region to which they belong, showing why these federally protected properties stand out as wild places worth preserving amid encroaching civilization.

We also note some wildlife management issues that will surely color the debate around campfires and congressional conference tables in years ahead, while paying recognition to the NWR supporters and managers who helped make the present refuge system a reality.

■ **THE REFUGES** The refuge section of the book is organized alphabetically by state and then, within each state, by refuge name.

There are some clusters, groups, or complexes of neighboring refuges administered by one primary refuge. Some refuge complexes are alphabetized here by the name of their primary refuge, with the other refuges in the group following immediately thereafter.

■ **APPENDIX**

Nonvisitable National Wildlife Refuges: NWR properties that meet the needs of wildlife but are off-limits to all but field biologists.

Federal Recreation Fees: An overview of fees and fee passes.

Volunteer Activities: How you can lend a hand to help your local refuge or get involved in supporting the entire NWR system.

U.S. Fish & Wildlife General Information: The seven regional headquarters of the U.S. Fish & Wildlife Service through which the National Wildlife Refuge System is administered.

National Audubon Society Wildlife Sanctuaries: A listing of the 24 National Audubon Society wildlife sanctuaries, dispersed across the U.S., which are open to the public.

Bibliography & Resources: Natural-history titles both on the region generally and its NWRs, along with a few books of inspiration about exploring the natural world.

Glossary: A listing of specialized terms (not defined in the text) tailored to this region.

Index

National Audubon Society Mission Statement

PRESENTATION OF INFORMATION: A-LEVEL REFUGE

■ **INTRODUCTION** This section attempts to evoke the essence of the place, The writer sketches the sounds or sights you might experience on the refuge, such as sandhill cranes taking off, en masse, from the marsh, filling the air with the roar of thousands of beating wings. That's a defining event for a particular refuge and a great reason to go out and see it.

■ **MAP** Some refuges are just a few acres; several, like the Alaskan behemoths, are bigger than several eastern states. The scale of the maps in this series can vary. We recommend that you also ask refuges for their detailed local maps.

■ **HISTORY** This outlines how the property came into the NWR system and what its uses were in the past.

■ **GETTING THERE** General location; seasons and hours of operation; fees, if any (see federal recreation fees in Appendix); address, telephone. Smaller or remote refuges may have their headquarters off-site. We identify highways as follows: TX 14 = Texas state highway # 14; US 23 = a federal highway; I-85 = Interstate 85.

Note: Many NWRs have their own web pages at the F&W web site, http://www.fws.gov/. Some can be contacted by fax or e-mail, and if we do not provide that information here, you may find it at the F&W web site.

■ **TOURING** The **Visitor Center**, if there is one, is the place to start your tour. Some have wildlife exhibits, videos, and bookstores; others may be only a kiosk. Let someone know your itinerary before heading out on a long trail or into the backcountry, and then go explore.

Most refuges have roads open to the public; many offer a wildlife **auto tour,** with wildlife information signs posted en route or a brochure or audiocassette to guide you. Your car serves as a bird blind if you park and remain quiet. Some refuge roads require 4-wheel-drive or a high-chassis vehicle. Some roads are closed seasonally to protect habitats during nesting seasons or after heavy rain or snow.

Touring also covers **walking and hiking** (see more trail details under ACTIVITIES) and **biking.** Many refuge roads are rough; mountain or hybrid bikes are more appropriate than road bikes. When water is navigable, we note what kinds of **boats** may be used and where there are boat launches.

■ **WHAT TO SEE**

Landscape and climate: This section covers geology, topography, and climate: primal forces and raw materials that shaped the habitats that lured species to the refuge. It also includes weather information for visitors.

Plant life: This is a sampling of noteworthy plants on the refuge, usually sorted by habitat, using standard botanical nomenclature. Green plants bordering watery places are in "Riparian Zones"; dwarfed trees, shrubs, and flowers on windswept mountaintops are in the "Alpine Forest"; and so forth.

Wildflowers abound, and you may want to see them in bloom. We give advice about timing your visit, but ask the refuge for more. If botany and habitat relationships are new to you, you can soon learn to read the landscape as a set of interrelated communities. Take a guided nature walk to begin.

(Note: In two volumes, "Plants" is called "Habitats and Plant Communities.")

Animal life: The national map on pages 4 and 5 shows the major North American "flyways." Many NWRs cluster in watery territory underneath the birds' aerial superhighways. There are many birds in this book, worth seeing simply for their beauty. But ponder, too, what birds eat (fish, insects, aquatic plants), or how one species (the mouse) attracts another (the fox), and so on up the food chain, and you'll soon understand the rich interdependence on display in many refuges.

Animals use camouflage and stealth for protection; many are nocturnal. You may want to come out early or late to increase your chances of spotting them. Refuge managers can offer advice on sighting or tracking animals.

Grizzly bears, venomous snakes, alligators, and crocodiles can indeed be dangerous. Newcomers to these animals' habitats should speak with refuge staff about precautions before proceeding.

■ **ACTIVITIES** Some refuges function not only as wildlife preserves but also as recreation parks. Visit a beach, take a bike ride, and camp overnight, or devote your time to serious wildlife observation.

Camping and swimming: If not permissible on the refuge, there may be federal or state campgrounds nearby; we mention some of them. Planning an NWR camping trip should start with a call to refuge headquarters.

Wildlife observation: This subsection touches on strategies for finding species most people want to see. Crowds do not mix well with certain species; you

A NOTE ON HUNTING AND FISHING Opinions on hunting and fishing on federally owned wildlife preserves range from "Let's have none of it" to "We need it as part of the refuge management plan." The F&W Service follows the latter approach, with about 290 hunting programs and 260 fishing programs. If you have strong opinions on this topic, talk with refuge managers to gain some insight into F&W's rationale. You can also write to your representative or your senators in Washington.

For most refuges, we summarize the highlights of the hunting and fishing options. You must first have required state and local licenses for hunting or fishing. Then you must check with refuge headquarters about special restrictions that may apply on the refuge; refuge bag limits, for example, or duration of season may be different from regulations elsewhere in the same state.

Hunting and fishing options change from year to year on many refuges, based on the size of the herd or of the flock of migrating birds. These changes may reflect local weather (a hard winter trims the herd) or disease, or factors in distant habitats where animals summer or winter. We suggest what the options usually are on a given refuge (e.g., some birds, some mammals, fish, but not all etc..). It's the responsibility of those who wish to hunt and fish to confirm current information with refuge headquarters and to abide by current rules.

COMMON SENSE, WORTH REPEATING

Leave no trace Every visitor deserves a chance to see the refuge in its pristine state. We all share the responsibility to minimize our impact on the landscape. "Take only pictures and leave only footprints," and even there you'll want to avoid trampling plant life by staying on established trails. Pack out whatever you pack in. Ask refuge managers for guidance on low-impact hiking and camping.

Respect private property Many refuges consist of noncontiguous parcels of land, with private properties abutting refuge lands. Respect all Private Property and No Trespassing signs, especially in areas where native peoples live within refuge territory and hunt or fish on their own land.

Water Protect the water supply. Don't wash dishes or dispose of human waste within 200 ft. of any water. Treat all water for drinking with iodine tablets, backpacker's water filter, or boiling. Clear water you think is OK may be contaminated upstream by wildlife you cannot see.

may need to go away from established observation platforms to have success. Learn a bit about an animal's habits, where it hunts or sleeps, what time of day it moves about. Adjust your expectations to match the creature's behavior, and your chances of success will improve.

Photography: This section outlines good places or times to see certain species. If you have a zoom lens, use it. Sit still, be quiet, and hide yourself. Don't approach the wildlife; let it approach you. Never feed animals or pick growing plants.

Hikes and walks: Here we list specific outings, with mileages and trailhead locations. Smooth trails and boardwalks, suitable for people with disabilities, are noted. On bigger refuges, there may be many trails. Ask for a local map. If you go bushwacking, first make sure this is permissible. Always carry a map and compass.

Seasonal events: National Wildlife Refuge Week, in October, is widely celebrated, with guided walks, lectures, demonstrations, and activities of special interest to children. Call your local refuge for particulars. At other times of the year there are fishing derbies, festivals celebrating the return of migrating birds, and other events linked to the natural world. Increasingly, refuges post event schedules on their web pages.

Publications: Many NWR brochures are free, such as bird and wildflower checklists. Some refuges have pamphlets and books for sale, describing local habitats and species.

Note: The categories of information above appear in A and B refuges in this book; on C-level refuges, options are fewer, and some of these headings may not appear.

—David Emblidge

Southeast

A Regional Overview

Only 200 years ago, the American Southeast was a vast landscape of green. High rainfall fostered the abundant growth of wetlands. Lowland and mountain forests were dense with understory; the mossy hills of the Piedmont were carpeted in layers of spectacularly lush vegetation. Over time, however, encroaching civilization introduced deforestation, agriculture, and city-building to the southeastern terrain, crowding out wild areas and their habitats. But with the dawn of the 20th century came public conservation efforts, which pushed the development of parks, forests, and national wildlife refuges to preserve and restore remnants of the ancient landscape.

The movement to maintain the integrity of native wilderness is rooted in the American Southeast's struggle to conserve its resident wildlife. And if the refuge movement has a founding father, it would most likely be President Theodore Roosevelt, an avid hunter and outdoorsman, whose first act of conservation was to set aside Florida's 5.5-acre Pelican Island in 1903. Huge flocks of snowy and great egrets, herons, brown pelicans, and roseate spoonbills had almost disappeared in this region, lost to hunters who, in cahoots with milliners, shot the birds for feathers to adorn women's hats. The fledgling National Audubon Society—then known as the National Association of Audubon Societies—stepped in to hire wardens on Pelican Island and other protected areas to guard the region's birds and nesting areas. Being a warden in the early days of land preservation was sometimes perilous work—a few were even shot for their efforts. (Audubon members also worked to influence hat fashions, a telling example of the often creative and multipronged approaches to conservation issues.) Today, these beautifully plumed birds still nest on Pelican Island. From this controversial but humble start in 1903, the NWR system has protected untold numbers of wildlife species and habitats.

The national wildlife refuges of the Southeast can be divided into two types: *coastal refuges,* which protect barrier islands, sea turtle nesting beaches, salt marshes, and other wetlands; and *inland piedmont refuges,* which restore damaged lands and their habitats and wildlife. Both types of refuge offer food, shelter, and stopovers to migratory birds that summer in northern states and in Canada. Mountains of the southeast (even the Great Smoky Mountains, a botanist's paradise) have no NWRs but are well protected by national and state parks and national forests. Intense management on both inland and coastal refuges preserves species diversity in the face of myriad external pressures and previous damage (see "Management Priorities," below).

Such stark contrast is no surprise, with southeastern elevations ranging from sea level to 6,684 feet and with thousands of miles between its northernmost and southernmost parts.

Sea oats on the southern coast

The seven states and one territory that make up the southeastern region are bounded

SOUTHEAST

ALABAMA
1 Bon Secour NWR
2 Eufaula NWR
3 Wheeler NWR

FLORIDA
4 Arthur R. Marshall Loxahatchee NWR
5 Crystal River NWR
6 Florida Keys NWRs
7 J. N. "Ding" Darling NWR
8 Lake Woodruff NWR
9 Lower Suwannee NWR
10 Merritt Island NWR
11 St. Marks NWR

GEORGIA
12 Okefenokee NWR
13 Piedmont NWR
14 Savannah Coastal NWRs

MISSISSIPPI
15 Noxubee NWR
16 Yazoo NWR

NORTH CAROLINA
17 Alligator River NWR and Pea Island NWR
18 Mackay Island NWR
19 Mattamuskeet NWR
20 Pee Dee NWR
21 Pocosin Lakes NWR

PUERTO RICO AND U.S. VIRGIN ISLANDS
22 Caribbean Island NWRs

SOUTH CAROLINA
23 ACE Basin NWR
24 Cape Romain NWR
25 Carolina Sandhills NWR
26 Pinckney Island NWR

TENNESSEE
27 Reelfoot NWR
28 Tennessee NWR

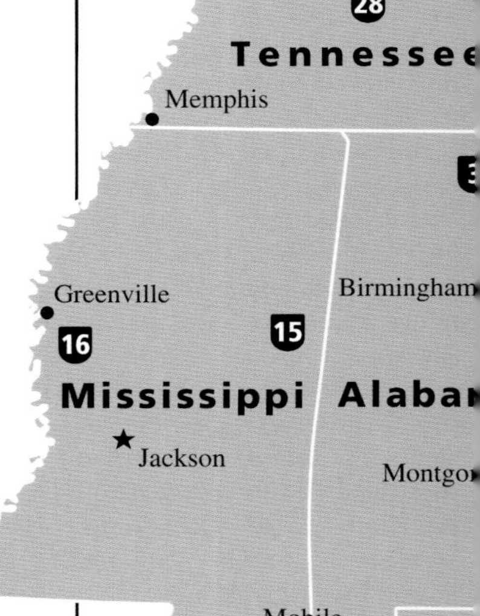

Frankfort
Lexington
Kentucky
Greensboro
Raleigh
Knoxville
North Carolina
Charlotte
Chattanooga
Greenville
South Carolina
Columbia
Atlanta
Georgia
Charleston
Macon
Columbus
Savannah
Puerto Rico
San Juan
Mayaguez
Ponce
Tallahassee
Jacksonville
Florida
Orlando
Tampa
St. Petersburg
Miami
18
21
17
19
20
25
24
23
26
14
13
2
12
22
11
9
8
10
5
4
7
6

on the west by the sinuous north-south trajectory of the Mississippi River and on the north by the straight line of the North Carolina–Virginia border. The region would be roughly a rectangle if not for the long, flat peninsula of Florida, which reaches down to the southernmost point of the continental United States.

More than 60 NWRs protect wildlife in the Southeast region. Some, which protect critical habitat for endangered species like the watercress darter, are closed to visitation. Others are enjoyed year-round by a steady stream of avid nature lovers. This book covers 29 refuges, each with at least some of the following attractions for visitors: walking, hiking, or canoe trails; Visitor Centers; nearby population centers with amenities; special habitat or wildlife not found elsewhere; an abundance of watchable wildlife; or special features (such as the beaches of Pea Island Refuge in North Carolina or the Florida Trail, which runs through St. Marks Refuge, Florida).

The 29 refuges in this book offer remarkable opportunities for recreation, solitude, and natural splendor: canoe trails, foot paths, and highly accessible autotour routes where abundant wildlife and beautiful scenery are close at hand. All beckon the curious visitor with an interest in the wild world.

Pocosin habitat, Alligator River NWR, North Carolina

GEOLOGY

An ancient shallow ocean once blanketed what is now the Mississippi Valley and the wide Mississippi and Atlantic floodplains. Corals and mollusk shells sank to the bottom, forming layers of limestone that now underlie the southeastern region. At other times, ice caps at the poles removed water from the oceans, and landmasses everywhere extended far beyond their present boundaries. Continental collision with Africa drove metamorphic granite, sandstone, slate, and quartz over the limestone to thrust the Appalachian Mountains upward. Erosion from heavy rains wore the mountains down and brought sand and minerals to lower areas. Thus, most of the inland National Wildlife Refuges, generally located in piedmont (mountain foothills) areas between the coastal plain and the mountains, have a limestone bedrock with other minerals mixed in, while the coastal refuges are based on former ocean sand, limestone, and collected organic matter.

CLIMATE AND WEATHER

The weather in the Southeast is usually humid; summers can be quite hot. Wildflowers generally thrive in a cooler spring, and certain extreme types of summer or winter weather can prove difficult for southern wildlife. When New England and Buffalo, New York, get blizzards, an Arctic cold front swings down as far as Florida and drives the endangered manatees deeper into the warm springs of Crystal River NWR. Summer droughts can cause dangerous fires in the peat layers of Okefenokee Swamp and the upland pine forests, while hurricanes and tornadoes can flatten red-cockaded woodpecker nesting trees. Hurricanes spawned in west Africa, tornadoes from updrafts, and windstorms from the plains and the ocean bring ferocious rain, snow, and changes to the Southeast, all a natural part of climatic cycles. Fire can be nature's way of providing varied habitats and new opportunities for wildlife. The northern part of the region enjoys four distinct seasons, while the southern part has cool, rainy winters and only an occasional freeze.

For most of the Southeast refuges, spring and fall are the best times to visit to see local wildlife and neotropical birds, and winter shows the best displays of migratory waterfowl populations.

HUMAN IMPACT

Humans moved into the Southeast more than 10,000 years ago. Even with modest demands on the environment, they may have unwittingly wiped out many native species of animals. Buffalo and elk once roamed the southeast, but were gone when Europeans arrived. The first European contact with continental Native Americans came when Ponce de Leon landed on the coast of Florida in 1513. There he met the peaceable Timucuan Indians near an area now occupied by Merritt Island NWR. Fellow Spaniards followed, looking for the Fountain of Youth, gold, silver, and other valuables. Later they established forts and settlements at St. Augustine, the Florida Keys, and St. Marks on the Florida Panhandle.

English settlers arrived on Roanoke Island, near the present Pea Island NWR (North Carolina), in 1587, sponsored by Sir Walter Raleigh. John White governed the first colony of 117 settlers, which was increased to 118 with the birth of Virginia Dare, White's granddaughter and the first English child born in America. White returned to England for more provisions for the struggling colony, but was delayed by interferences, such as bad weather and the Spanish Armada. By the time he got back to Roanoke Island, Virginia and all her fellow settlers had disappeared. Archaeologists and historians still search for signs of the Lost Colony.

Later settlers left plenty of signs of their presence. Europe, depleted by centuries of habitation, eagerly collected animal pelts and shipbuilding lumber. Settlers moved inland, built cities on the great rivers, cleared forests, and took Indian lands by treaty or conquest. After casting off British colonialism, southern Americans developed vast plantations of rice, cotton, tobacco, and indigo for profitable world trade. The gradual decline of the native population, the Civil War, and the subsequent Reconstruction period markedly changed the land and its economics. Intense logging and destructive agricultural practices damaged green hillsides and pristine rivers. Farmers drained swamps and other wetlands, destroying precious marine estuaries.

Wetland, Okefenokee NWR

The Piedmont suffered most from overexploitation. Forests were clear-cut, fields eroded into barren gullies, and species such as passenger pigeons, American chestnuts, wolves, and panthers, among others, were extirpated—or nearly so. Coastal areas fared a little better, but deforestation, swamp drainage, hunting and trapping, and urban development took their toll on wildlife species and habitats. New methods of hunting made it even easier to decimate populations. All of these factors forced a growing awareness that natural resources had limits.

More recently, habitat loss owing to urban and suburban development and pollution has begun to constitute the most serious threats to wildlife survival. Some species, such as red wolves, require large, uninterrupted habitats. Others, like nesting turtles and migratory birds, need several safe places for different parts of their life cycles. In many cases, the extent of habitat requirements for species at risk is not known. For other species, such as manatees and red-cockaded woodpeckers, biologists are discovering what they need just in time to save them.

Another recent threat to southeastern wildlife is the introduction of exotic plants and animals—fire ants, for example, in most of the region, or Brazilian pepper trees in Florida. These alien species aggressively displace native populations.

The purpose of conservation management and research—much of it carried out by the NWR system—is to minimize or reverse these dangers to wildlife before it is too late.

HABITATS AND PLANT LIFE

Upland and lowland forests, vast wetlands of swamps, marshes, estuaries, and river basins, a few natural lakes and some impounded lakes, and sandy beaches and dunes provide habitat for wildlife in the Southeast. In temperate parts of the region, northern and southern species came to live together as the result of advancing and receding ice ages. Along the coast, temperate, subtropical, and tropical species form the mix, and there is a trend for some species, like armadillos and anolis lizards, to expand their ranges north.

Most of the broad-leaved trees on the inland refuges drop their leaves, and many of the animals hibernate. On the coast, many trees keep waxy leaves all year, and many animals are more active in spring and fall than in summer. Most conifers remain green throughout the year, but swamp cypresses are an exception: Even in hot southern Florida, they observe winter by dropping their needles in late fall. Spring wildflowers abound throughout the region, with peak blooming times in February along the coast and March and April farther inland.

A few refuges have a special mission to protect threatened or endangered plants. Many of them are closed to visitation. Fern Cave, a satellite of popular Wheeler NWR in northern Alabama, protects the threatened American hart's tongue fern along with several species of bats. Lake Wales Ridge, a satellite of Merritt Island NWR in Florida, contains 19 rare endemic plant species. Established in 1990, Lake Wales is the first refuge designed to protect plants, many of which have become endangered because of the growth of citrus orchards and other farming on central Florida's sand ridges. Refuge managers at places like Wheeler or Merritt Island can tell you about these vulnerable beauties.

ANIMALS

Many threatened animals—such as scrub jays, manatees, cave fish, beach mice, indigo snakes, Ridley's sea turtles, wood storks, bald eagles, piping plovers, pine barrens tree frogs, watercress darters, and mangrove tree crabs—share living space on southeastern NWRs with thousands of other, thriving species. Wildlife conservation comes first on all the refuges; it is the mandate of each to protect and manage local wildlife species. To a lesser degree, the refuges are dedicated to providing opportunities for observation and nature-oriented recreation. The wildlife drives at Florida's J. N. "Ding" Darling NWR and Merritt Island NWR

Visitors admiring wildlife, J.N. "Ding" Darling NWR, Florida

Red-eared pond slider turtles

pass congregations of wading birds. Flocks of snow geese and tundra swans can be seen at Pea Island NWR in North Carolina, and hundreds of wintering sandhill cranes strut on the wet prairies of Georgia's Okefenokee NWR. Wood ducks and American alligators nest on most southeastern NWRs, and bald eagles feed or nest on many of them, though you may need a spotting scope or at least binoculars to find them.

Some refuges increase the populations of endangered species and help to reestablish the species in other places. Red wolves from Alligator River NWR in North Carolina have been reintroduced to places where they used to live. Sandhill cranes that winter in southeastern refuges have hatched whooping crane eggs in Maryland to save a species that was almost lost to extinction.

MANAGEMENT PRIORITIES

Most of the refuges established before the 1930s preserve a unit of undisturbed land or support specific animals. Pelican Island, the first refuge, harbors pelicans, egrets, and other birds that need isolated nesting areas. Small islands that are now part of Florida's Chassahowitzka NWR have played a similar role since 1908.

In the 1930s, it became clear to biologists that populations of migratory game birds were decreasing rapidly. The fate of the passenger pigeon throughout the United States and the bison on the prairie convinced them that these were serious threats and that animal populations would probably not recover on their own. Take-no-prisoners logging and widespread wetlands drainage to "improve" the land left too little habitat for migratory and residential wildlife.

For the inland refuges, it took real vision to look at an expanse of red, eroded hillside and predict that ducks, geese, and sandhill cranes could someday find a living there. Management of these lands nowadays consists of restoration, erosion prevention, planting, exotic pest control, and provision of nest sites or materials. As the system developed, emphasis shifted to considering the health of nongame species.

In the 1970s and 1980s, an increased awareness of endangered and threatened species grew, and refuges responded by managing their lands to help species at risk. For example, red-cockaded woodpeckers need mature pine trees to nest, and because logging had removed most of the suitable trees, the birds almost became extinct. Today, every refuge that has habitat for these small woodpeckers tries to help: They mark trees for preservation, install artificial nests that might attract the birds, and close nesting areas to hunting or other disturbances. These management strategies have been successful; many red-cockaded woodpecker colonies thrive. They seem to have escaped the fate of their larger relative, the ivory-billed woodpecker, which has not been seen for many years.

Special management strategies also help West Indian manatees, wood storks, and American bald eagles. In some cases, management policies change from day to day or season to season, and visitors should remember that this may change access to trails or other parts of a refuge. For example, a dike trail at Mackay Island NWR (North Carolina) may be closed to protect a bald eagle nest site.

For coastal refuges, beaches, dunes, and wetlands had to be saved from sprawling development, and destructive drainage projects needed to be reversed.

Another management tool on most southeastern NWRs is the once-

Pelican Island NWR, Florida

Cypress wetlands, Okefenokee NWR, Georgia

controversial use of fire in the form of controlled burns. Wildlife managers now realize that most habitats had natural fires from lightning and that the fires contributed to habitat renewal. Periodic small, controlled fires reduce the buildup of brush and other organic matter and, thus, reduce the severity of later fires. Some native species, such as longleaf pine in Florida, actually need fire to open their cones for seed germination and can't compete with hardwoods without fire.

Managed hunting occurs in some refuges, but only of abundant species, and often because some species, such as deer, could outstrip their environment and reduce the food supply to starvation levels for themselves or could destroy shelter for other species. In most refuges, special permits are required for hunting. Frequent studies monitor animal populations, and management strategies are shifted every year to maintain population balances. Feral hogs are also hunted to control damage they cause, and waterfowl are hunted for sport, but only when it is determined that their populations will not suffer from pruning. The refuges establish tight limits on all hunting.

Fishing is allowed on most refuges where appropriate but also with tight restrictions. Crabbing for blue crabs is allowed on many coastal refuges.

In many other refuges, water flow is managed. In Okefenokee NWR, early logging and attempts to drain the swamp reduced its ability to hold water. A sill was built on the Sewannee River that drains the swamp to control water flow and reduce catastrophic wildfires until the swamp vegetation is restored and can manage its own affairs. In Loxahatchee NWR (Florida), dikes and levees control water level because this is the only remaining piece of the northern Everglades, where draining has severely disturbed water flow. Many refuges have controlled impoundments (artificial lakes) that are managed to increase food for wildlife and to reduce mosquito populations.

Some refuges, such as Okefenokee and Pelican Island, have designated *Wilderness Areas.* This status requires the highest protection of any public lands and prohibits disturbance to wildlife or the environment.

Refuge management involves juggling many complex factors at the same time.

For example, in the impoundments at Pea Island NWR, water salinity must be considered as well as water levels to provide enough food for overwintering birds, so managers have to balance pumping and draining, measure evaporation loss, and count on accurate weather predictions.

PARTNERSHIPS

Many NWRs develop creative partnerships with community groups, such as Audubon Refuge Keepers (ARK), and many depend on friends' groups, other agencies, and research facilities. The Visitor Centers at Merritt Island and other refuges are staffed by volunteers. At Ding Darling NWR, on Florida's popular Sanibel Island, friends, groups have raised money to build a new Visitor Center. Volunteers lead wildflower and bird walks and help with environmental education programs for local schools. At Lake Woodruff, an ARK group built a viewing tower, providing visitors a better chance of sighting wildlife.

Canoe trail, Bond Swamp NWR, Georgia

At Mackay Island NWR in North Carolina, a university researcher came out to observe a new bald eagle nest and advise the managers about how to protect it from visitor disturbance. At Alligator River NWR, also in North Carolina, a local high school football team slogged through knee-deep swamp to build a boardwalk. A military base gave the same refuge funds to build a lake overlook, and in recognition the refuge put up a know-your-jets interpretive sign with aircraft silhouettes. Sea turtle vigilantes walk the beaches at night to protect nests and hatchlings.

ACE Basin, in South Carolina, is not a large refuge, but state forest and conservation lands surround it to form the largest estuarine preserve in the country. The refuge and The Nature Conservancy share a restored plantation house as offices.

Some refuges were formed or enlarged by partnerships, land easements, and bequests. The National Audubon Society, The Nature Conservancy, other conservation organizations, and public agencies have helped purchase refuge lands or additions. Merritt Island NWR came into being when NASA turned its buffer lands over to U.S. Fish & Wildlife to administer.

At Cape Canaveral (Merritt Island NWR in Florida) and on the Outer Banks (Pea Island NWR in North Carolina), the National Parks system and the NWR system cooperate in the administration of refuges and national seashores.

At one refuge, the local law enforcement agency even turned land seized in a drug bust over to an adjacent NWR.

GETTING UNDER WAY

The national wildlife refuges in the American Southeast provide varied and excellent habitats for native wildlife; they also restore natural populations. Refuges work primarily to preserve wildlife, but in most cases public recreation and education are consistent with their wildlife conservation mission. In fact, most refuges are moving toward more public use, with the development of trails, wildlife drives, boardwalks, and Visitor Centers.

National wildlife refuge employees are downright passionate about the wildlife and ecology of their preserves and always eager to assist visitors looking for specific wildflowers, bird species, and other points of interest. This is especially true at the wildest and least-visited refuges, where staff know just how special their place is and want the public to realize it, too. Ask for their help, and enjoy the benefits.

Bon Secour NWR

Gulf Shores, Alabama

Sunrise, Bon Secour NWR

The name Bon Secour—French for "safe harbor"—referred originally to the refuge's protection of the harbor of Mobile Bay; the refuge now also protects endangered species, migratory wildlife, coastal habitats, and fragile sand dunes. As the southernmost part of the Alabama coast, it may be the last (or first) United States stop for birds and monarch butterflies migrating across the Gulf of Mexico. Bon Secour NWR also attracts sunbathers and birdwatchers following the flocks of waterfowl that winter here before heading up the Mississippi Flyway in spring.

Bon Secour lies on a sand spit that stretches east across the mouth of Mobile Bay, opening onto the Gulf of Mexico. Traveling by water in the east-west direction hereabouts, hundreds of boaters use the Intracoastal Waterway passing through Bon Secour Bay. Not far off are the many islands and spits of Gulf Islands National Seashore, on the Florida, Mississippi, and Alabama coasts.

HISTORY

Established in 1980, the 6,500-acre refuge consists of five parcels of land tucked between developed beach communities. Archaeologists have uncovered shell-gathering sites and pottery shards indicating settlement between 1500 B.C. and 500 B.C. Spanish explorers traded with natives and repaired their ships here in 1519. Fort Morgan, on the tip of Fort Morgan Peninsula, guarded Mobile Bay (of which Bon Secour Bay is a part) during the Civil War.

In August of 1864, however, Admiral David Farragut entered Mobile Bay with a fleet led by two armored monitors. The first, *Tecumseh,* was blown up by a mine, and the other ships started to disperse in confusion. It was here that Admiral Farragut issued his famous order: *Damn the torpedoes; full speed ahead!* The ships regrouped and took the forts.

GETTING THERE

From Mobile, go east on I-10 to Exit 44. Turn south (right) on FL 59 to Gulf Shores and turn right on AL 180 for 8.2 mi. to the Visitor Center. From Pensacola, FL, go 35 mi. west on I-10 to Exit 44 and follow directions above.

■ **SEASON:** Refuge open all year.

■ **HOURS:** Refuge: Daylight hours; Visitor center: 7:30 a.m.–4 p.m., Mon. through Fri.

■ **FEES:** There are no fees.

■ **ADDRESS:** Bon Secour NWR, 12295 States Highway 180, Gulf Shores, AL 36542

■ **TELEPHONE:** 334/540-7720

TOURING BON SECOUR

■ **BY AUTOMOBILE:** There is no special wildlife drive, but the refuge roads pass through the major habitats. AL 180 connects four of the five parcels of the refuge.

■ **BY FOOT:** Pine Beach Trail is a 4-mile loop past Gator Lake and along dunes out to the beach. The wheel-chair accessible Jeff Friend Trail is a 1-mile loop. Various parking areas give access to the Gulf of Mexico beach.

■ **BY BICYCLE:** This is a sandy world. There are no bicycle paths in the refuge itself. However, biking is possible on AL 180 (between parcels of the refuge) during quiet traffic times.

■ **BY CANOE, KAYAK, OR BOAT:** Gator Lake, in the Perdue Unit, is open to canoeing and fishing from small boats, but access is only by a 0.8 mile portage. One flat-bottom rowboat is available for public use on Gator Lake. Canoes and kayaks are allowed in Little Lagoon.

WHAT TO SEE

■ **LANDSCAPE AND CLIMATE** This narrow sand spit is quite hot and

BARRIER ISLANDS

And everyone that heareth these sayings of mine, and doeth them not, shall be likened unto a foolish man, which built his house upon the sand: And the rain descended, and the floods came, and the winds blew, and beat upon that house; and it fell: and great was the fall of it.

—Matthew 7:26-27

Orville and Wilbur Wright made good use of a barrier island in 1903. The pirate Blackbeard used the tortuous thread of island inlets to hide his ships. General Billy Mitchell taught the U.S. Navy how to bomb ships from barrier-island sandbanks. But from the time of the Lost Colony of Roanoke Island (1587) to the modern era of beach houses that blow away like matchsticks in hurricanes, what has become clear is that permanent settlement on barrier islands is simply not a good idea.

Barrier islands are made of sand, all the way down, with no real bedrock. They protect the mainland from wave surges and the worst of hurricane winds. But the islands shift constantly; the ocean keeps the sand in constant motion. Plants and animals can shift; houses cannot.

Many refuges lie on barrier islands: Bon Secour, Merritt Island, Cape Romain, and Pea Island, among them. The best preservation of these islands may be in letting them be themselves.

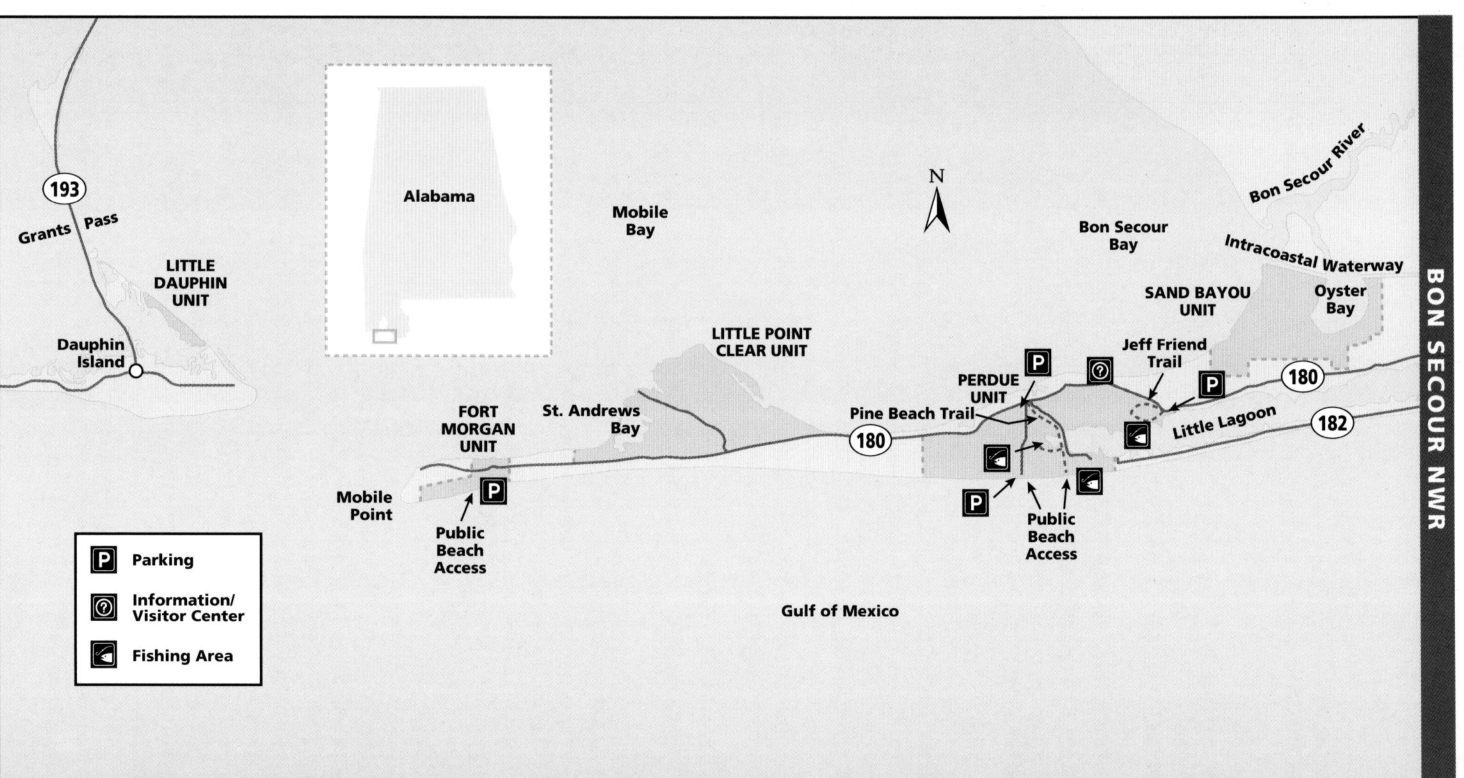
BON SECOUR NWR
193
Grants Pass
LITTLE DAUPHIN UNIT
Dauphin Island
Alabama
Mobile Bay
N
Bon Secour Bay
Bon Secour River
Intracoastal Waterway
SAND BAYOU UNIT
Oyster Bay
LITTLE POINT CLEAR UNIT
Jeff Friend Trail
PERDUE UNIT
180
Pine Beach Trail
Little Lagoon
182
FORT MORGAN UNIT
St. Andrews Bay
180
Mobile Point
Public Beach Access
Public Beach Access
Parking
Information/ Visitor Center
Fishing Area
Gulf of Mexico

buggy in summer, but come winter, early spring, or late fall and the weather is pleasant. Fragile barrier sand dunes up to 30 feet high are covered with sand-stabilizing plants, some taking root naturally, others planted. The dunes demand protection, and access is restricted—sorry, no rolling down these hills.

Though this spit of land is technically not an island, its geological history is much like that of barrier islands, and it protects inland areas from erosion caused by punishing Gulf waves and squalls.

■ PLANT LIFE Behind the refuge beaches and dunes lie forests, swamps, two freshwater lakes, and a brackish lagoon. Large live oaks, scrub oaks, myrtle oaks, and magnolias—all decorated with pendulous Spanish moss—are broadleaf trees with tough evergreen leaves. Conifers such as red cedar (which, amazingly, ranges from Quebec to the Gulf coast) and Choctawatchee sand pine (which, just as amazingly, ranges across only a few narrow miles of Gulf coast) live in the drier parts of the forest. Deciduous trees and shrubs are colorful here, including pond cypress, pignut hickory, persimmon, buttonbush, and beautyberry—the latter has clusters of mauve-to-violet berries. Palmettos, a low-growing, fan-leafed palm, root in both open and wooded habitats. Sea oats and vines help to maintain the dunes with their spreading root systems and low-lying growth above ground.

Wax myrtles and yaupon hollies grow behind the dunes. Yaupon holly, also called Christmasberry, has a curious Latin name: *Ilex vomitoria*. It is one of the few New World plants with caffeine in its leaves, and Native Americans made ceremonial "black drink" from it. A little black drink perks you up, and a little more makes you sick to your stomach.

Spoonbill

In spring, gopher apples, violets, fetterbush, coral beans, and blueberries bloom. Late summer and fall wildflowers, such as goldenrods, false foxgloves, beggarticks, and red basil, feed migrating hummingbirds and monarch butterflies. Yellow and purple bladderworts live in the swamps and trap small insects (in their "bladders") to get nitrogen.

Hurricane Frederic (1979) and, more recently, Hurricane Georges (1998) flattened parts of the Bon Secour forest and swamp. Much of the damage can still be seen, and most trees are new growth since the hurricane.

■ ANIMAL LIFE

Birds A dizzying array of colors and sounds makes this refuge a birder's paradise. Many species of wintering and migrating birds find food and shelter here. More than 300 other species of birds have been sighted at Bon Secour. Brown and white pelicans, oystercatchers, sandpipers, willets, curlews, and 12 species of gulls inhabit the beach and mudflats. Egrets, spoonbills, herons, geese, and ducks live in the marshes and lagoon. Flycatchers, warblers, wrens, martens, and hummingbirds migrate through the refuge to northern nesting areas, and some of these neotropical migrants stop here to nest.

For waterfowl, hawks, and many other large birds, the refuge is the gateway to the Mississippi Flyway, a lengthy migratory route that stretches from Bon Secour (where the birds winter) to the Northern Plains states and Canada (where the birds nest).

Mammals Most of the mammals on the refuge are nocturnal, including the endangered Alabama beach mouse, which spends its whole life on the dunes, eating sea oats and burrowing in the sand. Development and dune destruction have severely reduced its habitat. Bobcats, marsh rabbits, opossums, and foxes also live on the refuge. You will likely see a rabbit, you may spot a fox, but don't expect to catch a glimpse of the shy and elusive bobcat. Relative newcomers are armadillos, coyotes (more likely to be heard than spotted), and wild boars.

Reptiles and amphibians In May and September, threatened loggerhead and green sea turtles nest on the beaches. Refuge managers protect the nests with screens, which allow hatchlings to escape but keep foxes and raccoons from digging. Managers cover the nests with sand and use high-tech GPS satellite coordinates to record nest sites and later to check hatching success.

Alligators live in the lakes and in the lagoon, so if you're boating, don't dangle your feet over the gunwales. The prickly pear cactus provides food for gopher tortoises, whose presence can be spotted by long wide burrows in sandy soils. Racerunners and other lizards live in sandy parts of the forest.

At least 25 varieties of snakes have been reported at Bon Secour. Ribbon, garter, rat, and water snakes are most likely to be seen, while corn and hognose snakes stay underground most of the time. Coral snakes and their imitators, scarlet king snakes, are two of the most colorful reptiles on the refuge, but they also stay hidden. Five venomous snakes slither about here, but they rarely bother anyone except mice and rats.

Fish Bass, catfish, bluegill, and bream swim in the lakes; the Gulf and brackish lagoon support many other species.

Oystercatcher feeding at shoreline

Invertebrates Migrating monarch butterflies may stop at the refuge in fall on their way to Mexico and repeat the hazardous journey in spring. Then they breed, lay eggs on milkweed, and die. Their young will continue the migration; thus, a monarch butterfly in Maine is several generations removed from those that started the northward migration.

Many species of crabs inhabit the Gulf and the lagoon, and larvae of invertebrates start their lives in the lagoon and marshes.

Look for Portuguese man-of-war jellyfish on the beach after storms. These large jellyfish are recognizable by their purplish color and long stinging tentacles, which hungry seagulls don't seem to mind. Shells, egg cases, and other treasures also appear on the beach after high tides.

ACTIVITIES

■ **CAMPING:** There is no camping allowed on the refuge, but there is a campground with a lodge and rustic cabins 5 miles away at Gulf State Park, on AL 182 (334/948-7275).

■ **SWIMMING:** There are beaches with access points and parking on Mobile St. near Pine Beach Trail and at the Fort Morgan Unit (at the end of the peninsula). Pine Beach Trail also crosses dunes to the beach. Beaches on other units are accessible by boat.

■ **WILDLIFE OBSERVATION AND PHOTOGRAPHY:** The two foot trails and the beach at Bon Secour give access to all the refuge habitats for wildlife observation. Also, from Gulf Shores, AL 182 runs parallel to AL 180 along the Gulf side of the lagoon to the eastern end of the refuge and provides opportunities to see shorebirds and wading birds.

■ **HIKES AND WALKS:** Jeff Friend Trail (1-mile loop, handicapped-accessible with resting benches) crosses upland habitats beneath huge live oaks and wetlands where wood ducks, herons, alligators, and frogs reside. It passes the white sand beaches of Little Lagoon.

Pine Beach Trail also leads through uplands and wetlands, running from Little Lagoon to 40-acre Gator Lake, over sand dunes with wonderful views of the Gulf. From there you can walk down to the beach or back a dirt road to the parking lot, passing another pond with alligators and birds. The refuge plans to extend Jeff Friend Trail and connect it with Pine Beach Trail.

HUNTING AND FISHING
Hunting is not allowed at the Bon Secour refuge, but you may fish year-round at Gator Lake. Anglers most commonly find **catfish**, **bream**, and **bass**. You can fish from the shores, or take out the rowboat that the refuge keeps down by the lake expressly for fishing.

■ **SEASONAL EVENTS:** Seasonal events and environmental education programs are in the works at Bon Secour.

■ **PUBLICATIONS:** Bird lists, brochures, and a guide to Pine Beach Trail.

Eufaula NWR

Eufaula, Alabama

Wetlands with egrets, Eufaula NWR

Eufaula NWR protects valuable wetlands and bottomland forests and provides stops for birds flying on the outer edges of both the Mississippi and Atlantic flyways. Birdwatchers, like birds, flock to the refuge during migration and nesting seasons. Boating in a lovely setting, plus prime fishing and hunting, helps attract Eufaula's 300,000 annual visitors.

Eufaula NWR surrounds the northern part of Lake Eufaula (Walter F. George Reservoir), an impoundment on the Chattahoochee River. The Chattahoochee River rises just a few feet from the Appalachian Trail in northern Georgia, but unlike the famous footpath (leading to Maine), the river flows south, supplying Atlanta and other cities with water and then forming the border between Georgia and Alabama. Eufaula NWR straddles the state line, as well as the line between eastern and central time zones.

HISTORY

The refuge was established in 1964. The Army Corps of Engineers built the dam (creating the impoundment) during the late 1950s, and it started generating electricity in 1963. The Corps transferred the land around the northern part of the lake to the U.S. Fish & Wildlife Service.

GETTING THERE

From Eufaula, drive north on US 431 for 5 mi. Turn left on Old AL 165 and follow signs to visitor station. The Georgia side of the refuge can be accessed on GA 39 by driving 8 mi. north of Georgetown.

■ **SEASON:** Refuge open all year.

■ **HOURS:** Refuge: daylight hours; visitor station/office: 7:30 a.m.–4 p.m. (central time), weekdays. The Georgia part of the refuge is on eastern time.

■ **FEES:** None.

■ **ADDRESS:** Eufaula NWR, 509 Old Highway 165, Eufaula, AL 36027
■ **TELEPHONE:** 334/687-4065

TOURING EUFAULA

■ **BY AUTOMOBILE:** The 7-mile Wingspread Wildlife Drive has two loops that start near the refuge office. In summer, two extensions of the loops are opened. ATVs are not allowed anywhere on the refuge.
■ **BY FOOT:** Dirt roads, levees, and trails.
■ **BY BICYCLE:** Bicycles are permitted on gravel roads that are also available for hiking, and these may be shared by horseback riders. Stay alert. A levee trail in Georgia can be accessed from GA 39.
■ **BY CANOE, KAYAK, OR BOAT:** Canoes and motorboats are allowed on the lake, and there are boat launches on the refuge and at nearby state parks (see "Activities"). Open water, backwaters, and sloughs provide a variety of choices for wildlife observation from on or near the water.

WHAT TO SEE

■ LANDSCAPE AND CLIMATE

The Eufaula area is south of the Appalachian Piedmont and so is relatively flat. Woodlands, open fields, cultivated fields, marshes, and open water make up the easily recognizable habitats of the refuge.

In the summer many of the birds go north, and most animals are active only at night for a good reason: Southern Georgia is hot and muggy. However, fishing and watching wildlife in the cool morning hours are still attractive to many summer visitors. The real show is in winter, the best season for watching waterfowl; other birds migrate through the refuge in spring and fall.

■ PLANT LIFE

Hiking here, you will enjoy subtle shades of green in the sedges, grasses, and willows of the wetlands. Woodlands support oaks, hickories, maples, hollies, and gums, and the formerly cultivated fields show a successional growth of vines, briars, shrubs, and young trees. In time, the old fields will mature into forest; even now they provide shelter and food for wildlife.

American lotus

Among Eufaula's many spring flowers, you will find trillium, bloodroot, and violets growing in the woodlands, and yellow lotus blooming in summer on the marshes. Brown seedpods of the lotus persist into the next spring and look like small UFOs on stalks.

Local farmers lease cropland from Eufaula and leave 25 percent of their harvest (peanuts, corn wheat, soybeans, and sorghum) for wildlife. Crop fields and hay fields provide a combination of food and protective cover along the edges. Positioning yourself with binoculars near the edge of a field, you can watch the traffic on the ground and in the air.

■ ANIMAL LIFE

Birds Eufaula NWR ranks as one of the best places in southern Georgia to watch birds because of its location under two flyways and its variety of habitats. Ducks, geese, herons, and occasional sandhill cranes spend the winter here, and many birds, including wood ducks, bluebirds, and mockingbirds, stay to nest.

Six species of woodpeckers also nest at Eufaula, using trees of the maturing woods. Shorebirds, gulls, and terns—reminders that the Gulf Coast is near—find food in marshes and mudflats. Flocks of cedar waxwings strip hollies and other plants of their berries.

Prothonotary warblers reside in swampy areas, while brown-headed cowbirds, by contrast, cluster in the open fields. The latter species avoids the tough work of building a nest and feeding babies by laying eggs in smaller birds' nests. Smaller birds, mainly warblers, feed and raise the parasitic cowbird nestlings, often at the expense of their own broods. Refuges with large wooded areas protect many species of migrants because cowbirds live in open fields and grasslands. They parasitize other birds mainly near edges and rarely in deep woods.

Prothonotary warbler

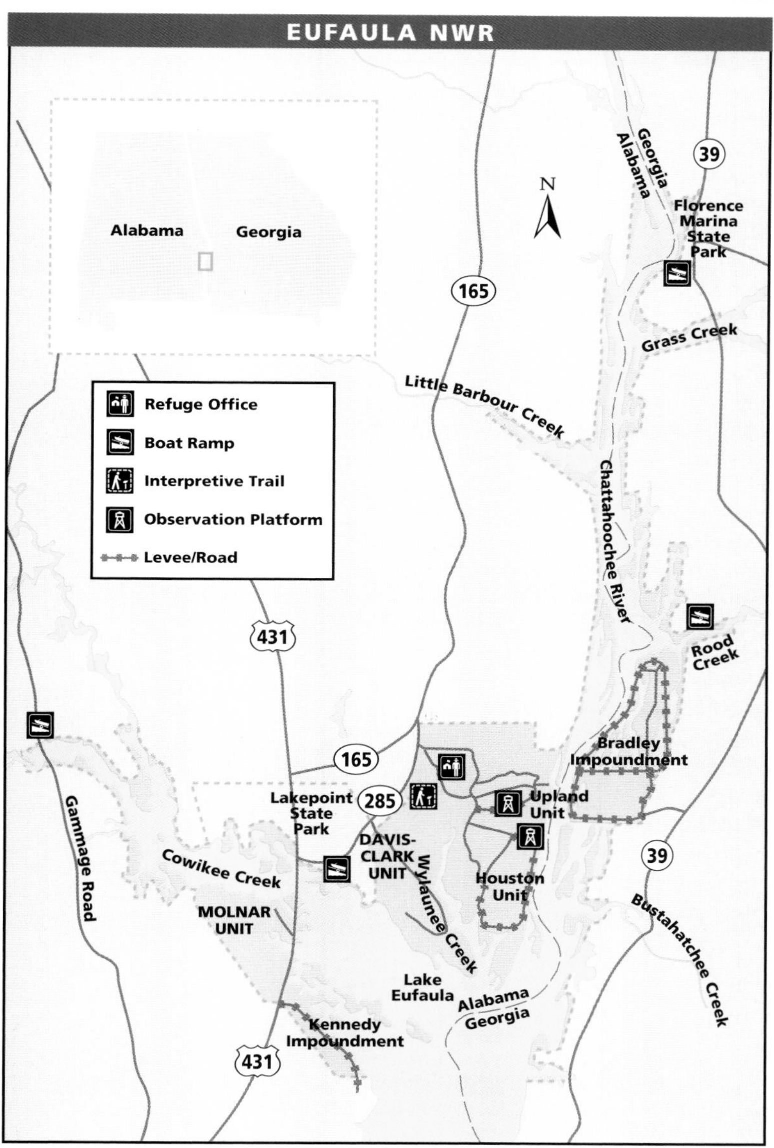

Mammals Bats, Eufala's most watchable mammals, swoop overhead in the evening to catch mosquitoes and other insects. Be nice to them—they're doing good work. Deer, raccoons, bobcats, and squirrels also call Eufaula home. In the fields, rabbits, mice, and rats become food for bobcats, foxes, hawks, and owls. Golden mice are present but secretive. You might spot their round leaf-and-grass nests in vines, shrubs, or sturdy meadow plants. Beavers and river otters feed in lake tributaries, and swamp rabbits jump in the water to flee predators. Coyotes and armadillos have moved in from the west.

Reptiles and amphibians Alligators live in the shallow waters of the lake and marshes; Eufaula is near the northernmost part of their nesting range.

ACTIVITIES

■ **CAMPING:** Camping is not allowed on the refuge, but Lakepoint State Park (on AL 431) and Florence Marina State Park (on GA 39) have campgrounds.

■ **SWIMMING:** Swimming is not permitted on the refuge.

■ **WILDLIFE OBSERVATION AND PHOTOGRAPHY:** There are two observation platforms on the wildlife drive with good views of marshes and other open areas where many birds might gather. Overlooks along the Chattahoochee River and canoe trips in backwaters should provide good opportunities for wildlife observation.

■ **HIKES AND WALKS:** Dikes and roads (even if gated) are open to hiking and give access to open water, marshes, open fields, old fields (former cultivated fields that are reverting to woodlands), and woods. The grassy dikes divide impoundments and may be hot at midday, but they provide excellent wildlife watching in morning and evening. Be on the lookout for fire ant mounds along the paths—these little critters can sting like mad!

■ **SEASONAL EVENTS:** Eufala Refuge celebrates National Wildlife Refuge Week in October with special events.

■ **PUBLICATIONS:** Mammal lists, bird lists, self-guiding wildlife drive leaflet, and the Eufaula NWR brochure.

HUNTING AND FISHING Hunting for small game such as **rabbits** is allowed in Feb. only. You may hunt **doves** in Oct. only, but **waterfowl** are in season from Nov. through Jan. **White-tailed deer** are in season from Oct. through Jan., and may be hunted with bows. An adult-youth deer hunt, in which only the youth may hunt, occurs on the Georgia portion of the refuge during this season as well. Firearms are allowed during this hunt. The adult-youth hunt and the waterfowl hunt are limited to a given number of hunters and are subject to a fee; contact the refuge for details. All other hunting is unlimited.

Fishing, on the banks or by boat, is allowed year-round. You will likely find **largemouth bass, crappie, bream, hybrid bass,** and **catfish**.

Wheeler NWR

Decatur, Alabama

Wintering waterfowl, Wheeler NWR

If you were any one of thousands of migratory birds—from sandhill cranes, ducks, geese, and hawks to scarlet tanagers and ruby-throated hummingbirds—you might well choose to rest and feed at Wheeler NWR. That's because much of Wheeler's 34,500 acres is underwater. The easternmost refuge of the Mississippi Flyway, the refuge extends along both sides of Wheeler Lake on the Tennessee River. To refuel for the remainder of their fall or spring journey, migratory birds have their choice of open water, marsh, mudflats, cypress and tupelo swamps, agricultural fields, or oak, hickory, and pine woodlands.

Many birds, mammals, reptiles, and amphibians use these same habitats for permanent residence and can be seen all year. A large Visitor Center, a well-placed waterfowl observation building (just feet from splashing waterfowl), outstanding fishing opportunities, and trails through each habitat type make Wheeler well worth a visit. The refuge is located near Huntsville, Alabama, site of the U.S. Space and Science Center and Space Camp (for young would-be astronauts).

HISTORY

President Franklin Roosevelt established Wheeler NWR in 1938 as the first refuge around an impoundment, the Tennessee Valley Authority's Wheeler Lake. It was named, perhaps incongruously, for "Fightin' Joe" Wheeler, West Point graduate, Confederate general, U.S. congressman, volunteer in the Spanish-American War, and father of Annie Wheeler, a Red Cross military nurse with Clara Barton. Sites of American Indian habitation and Civil War battles are protected in the refuge. Nowadays, an extensive bird-banding program monitors many species of ducks whose populations have steadily improved since the refuge system expanded in the 1930s.

GETTING THERE

From Huntsville drive west on I-565 about 10 mi. to I-65. Turn south, continue

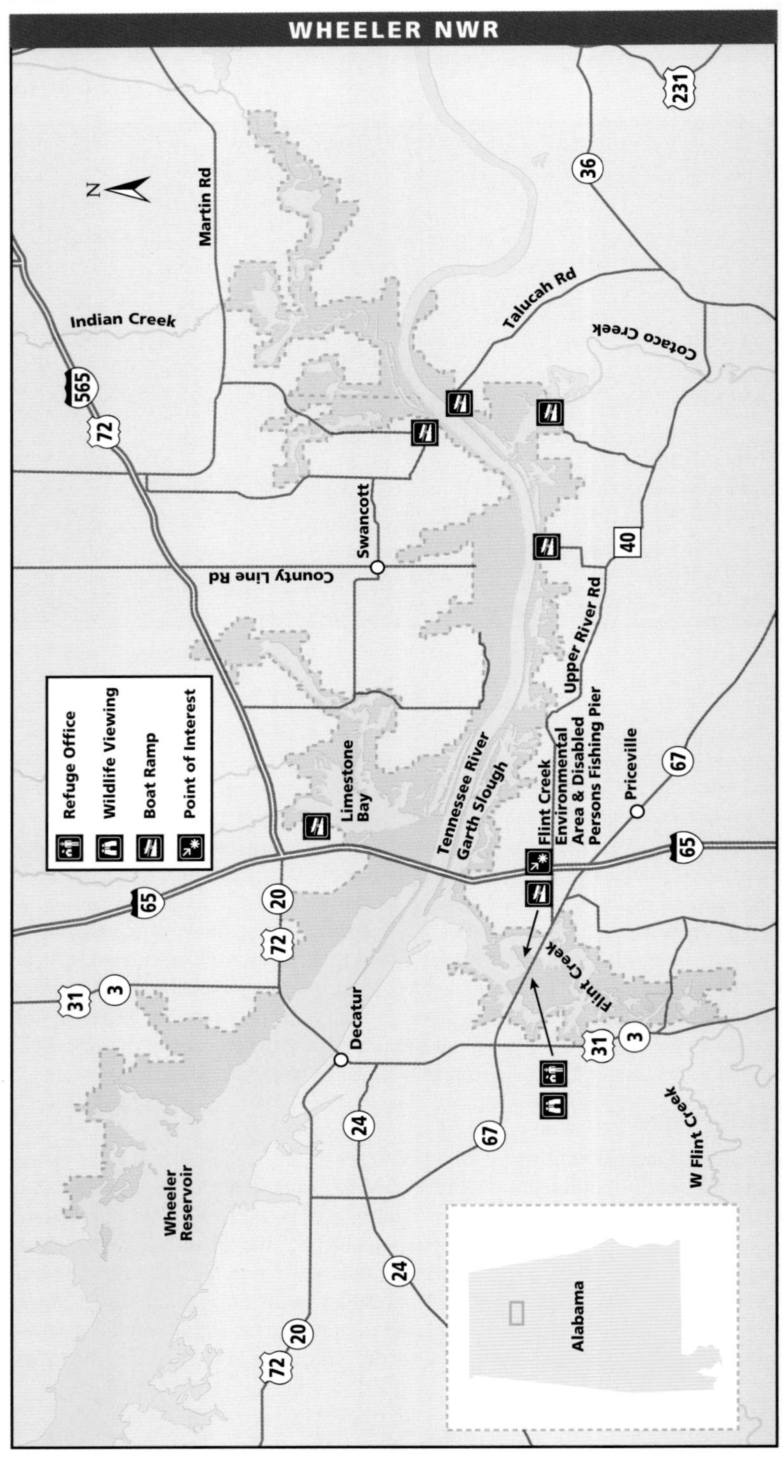
WHEELER NWR
N
Martin Rd
Indian Creek
565
72
Talucah Rd
Cotaco Creek
36
231
Swancott
County Line Rd
40
Upper River Rd
Refuge Office
Wildlife Viewing
Boat Ramp
Point of Interest
Limestone Bay
Tennessee River
Garth Slough
Flint Creek Environmental Area & Disabled Persons Fishing Pier
Priceville
67
65
20
72
31
3
Decatur
Flint Creek
24
67
W Flint Creek
Wheeler Reservoir
Alabama

about 2.5 mi. to Route 67 (Point Mallard Parkway), and drive 2 mi. to the Visitor Center entrance on the left. From Birmingham, drive north on I-65 to Rte. 67 and follow directions above. From Decatur, turn east at the intersection of Rtes. 31 and 67 and look for the Visitor Center entrance on the right in 1 mi.

■ **SEASON:** Open year-round.

■ **HOURS:** Visitors Center and Wildlife Observation Building, open daily Oct. through Feb., 10 a.m.–5 p.m.; March through Sept., Wed.–Sun., 10 a.m.–5 p.m.

■ **FEES:** None.

■ **ADDRESS:** Wheeler NWR, 2700 Refuge Headquarters Rd., Decatur, AL 35603

■ **TELEPHONE:** 256/350-6639

Trillium

TOURING WHEELER

Note: Use may be limited during managed hunts; call for current information.

■ **BY AUTOMOBILE:** Several main roads (including I-65) and gravel roads go through the refuge and must be used to get to the trails. Detailed maps and directions are available at the Visitor Center. The gravel road to Arrowhead Landing, going west from the Mooresville Exit of I-65, provides a good waterfowl observation opportunity. There are plans for an additional wildlife observation drive.

■ **BY FOOT:** Hiking trails include Atkeson Trail (0.3 mile), Environmental Trail (1.5 miles), Dancy Bottoms Trail (2 miles), and Beaverdam Swamp Boardwalk (0.5 mile), a good choice if you don't want to get your feet wet. Atkeson Trail starts behind the Visitor Center (which is on a gated access road) and is open only during business hours. Visitors may ride horseback on open gravel roads.

■ **BY BICYCLE:** Bicycles are permitted on open gravel roads.

■ **BY CANOE, KAYAK, OR BOAT:** There are six boat access ramps; canoes and motorboats are allowed for fishing. Water skiing and personal watercraft are prohibited.

WHAT TO SEE

■ **LANDSCAPE AND CLIMATE** From the long I-65 bridge across Wheeler Lake, you can see the expanse of water in the river valley, surrounded by forest and wetlands. The open water provides excellent fishing, and south of the Tennessee River channel is a slough and several backwater creeks where migratory waterfowl thrive. The backwaters also support mudflats, cypress and tupelo swamps, grassy marshes, and a few woodland ponds.

Wheeler has a temperate climate during fall, winter, and spring, though a freeze or a few cold days may occur. Summer is hot and muggy with abundant ticks, mosquitoes, and chiggers.

■ PLANT LIFE Plant diversity at Wheeler represents the natural landscape of northern Alabama, and the refuge protects vegetation needed for native animals. Much of the surrounding area is heavily farmed and, during the Great Depression, suffered from erosion and overuse. However, the refuge supports healthy stands of wooded and wetland habitat.

Marshes and mudflats In shallow water, American lotus, with round leaves more than a foot wide, has large yellow blooms in summer and flat-topped brown seed pods in fall. Sedges and tall grasses also grow here.

Swamps Cypress, one of the few deciduous conifers, has a swollen trunk and fernlike leaves and stands in quiet water. Its roots produce knobby "knees" that may help collect oxygen. In fall, mounds of bronze cypress needles cover the ground and boardwalks. Tupelo, a flowering tree, also grows in the swamps and shows brilliant red leaves in fall. Catalpa, sweet gum, persimmon, and sassafras trees grow on hammocks in the swamps. Hepatica and trillium are typical spring wildflowers, easily sighted along the footpaths.

Hardwoods Bottomland hardwoods include hickory, beech, maple, and several species of oaks. Witch hazel, grapevines, and spring wildflowers grow in the shade of the large trees, and resurrection fern sprouts from tree branches after a rain.

WHAT GOOD IS A SWAMP? Swamps get no respect. They have been drained, logged, "reclaimed," and reviled for their slimy denizens and mysterious depths.

However, swamps perform the important job of regulating water supply, and their slimy and "creepy" creatures are part of food chains that support good-press species, such as bald eagles and orchids. Most southeastern NWRs preserve swamps and help them get well-deserved appreciation.

Here's what some enlightened naturalists said of swamps while other folks were busy digging drainage ditches.

John Muir, founder of the Sierra Club, describes the first palmetto he sees on the edge of an intriguing swamp (writing in *A Thousand Mile Walk to the Gulf*, 1867):

[F]ew magnolias were near it, and bald cypresses. . . . They tell us that plants are perishable, soulless creatures, that only man is immortal, etc.; but this, I think, is something that we know nearly nothing about. Anyhow, this palm was indescribably impressive and told me grander things than I ever got from human priests.

John James Audubon often visited swamps to observe the birds of America. In his *Journal* (1820), he wrote:

One day at the swamp I saw a beautiful Mourning Warbler. It was within a few feet of me, but I was knee-deep in mud, and so, rather than alarm it, I preferred to gaze at it quite as innocently as it gazed at me.

Good advice.

Agricultural fields As with many refuges, fields are leased to local farmers who agree to leave 25 percent of their crops (soybeans, wheat, corn, and other grains) as wildlife food. These areas may provide good wildlife observation. Geese especially like the sprouts of winter wheat.

■ ANIMAL LIFE

Birds There have been some 285 bird species recorded at Wheeler, enough to keep most birders busy. About ten species of ducks migrate through the refuge and feed on the sloughs and mudflats, providing an interesting challenge to bird-watchers' attempts to distinguish one from another. Neotropical songbirds alight here in fall and spring. Canada geese stay all winter (you'll hear their familiar honking as they come in for a splash-down landing), and snow geese also appear at times. Sandhill cranes (with their surprisingly big wingspan), herons, grebes, ospreys, kestrels, bald eagles, and other raptors pass through or nest. The presence of raptors suggests that fish inhabit the shallow waters and small mammals live in the fields—all part of the avian food chain.

Refuge managers also attract wood ducks to nest here by setting out boxes near the water's edge. The female wood duck leaves the box as the ducklings hatch, and the baby birds (more fuzz than feathers at this stage) leap out to follow her.

Mammals The Beaverdam Trail leads through swamp to a large beaver dam, where patient, quiet visitors can see beavers feeding and working industriously on

Beaver building dam

the dam in cool mornings and evenings. Beavers are as enterprising at dam-building as the Army Corps of Engineers. Familiar mammals at Wheeler include white-tailed deer, rabbits, raccoons and squirrels, but ask for a list at the Visitor Center: Forty-seven species have been recorded here. A managed deer hunt, to trim the herd, is held every year.

Reptiles and amphibians American alligators were released at Wheeler when they became endangered elsewhere, and though rarely spotted here, they do bask in spring and summer sunshine. Not surprisingly for a watery place, snakes, turtles, frogs, toads, spotted salamanders, and red-spotted newts are all among the 47 species of reptiles and amphibians living here.

Fish If you come to fish at Wheeler, you're most likely to catch catfish, bass, and bluegill, all in the lake's open, relatively shallow water. Gar and the unusual paddlefish (a long, paddle-shaped snout) live in deeper water.

Invertebrates Two federally listed endangered mussels and one endangered snail live on the refuge. Many species of butterflies flutter around the waterfowl observation building and in the fields. Hikers may sometimes find crayfish building their excavation mounds right on a trail; the fish dig safety tunnels from water

Wood duck

level to dry land. Mosquitoes, alas, thrive in the wetlands. Fire ants build sandy mounds in open areas and should be left undisturbed.

ACTIVITIES

■ **CAMPING:** Camping is not allowed on the refuge, but Point Mallard Park in Decatur, approximately 10 miles away, has campsites (call Point Mallard Campground at 256/351-7772).

■ **WILDLIFE OBSERVATION:** The two-story waterfowl observation building near the Visitor Center overlooks a marsh and slough. Here you can watch animals close up without alarming them. Observers enter the back of the building along a fenced ramp and then gaze through one-way glass. Telescopes are available, and a whole class of schoolchildren can sit on bleachers. A microphone on a post in the water brings duck chatter to an inside speaker, and identification posters line the walls. "Less noise, more wildlife," a sign wisely suggests. A statue-still 4-foot-tall heron may suddenly catch a fish, and sandhill cranes may stride through the marsh. Waterfowl are most abundant in December, January, and February. In March, turtles, lizards, and snakes become active and bask on logs along the shore. Feeders and a wildflower garden attract smaller birds and butterflies.

During spring and fall, wildlife may be seen readily from the trails and boardwalks. In April and May, songbirds move in; some stay to nest and others fly north. Wood ducks, mallards, and black ducks are three of several types nesting on the refuge, and it's a sweet moment when ducklings appear with their mothers in May.

In fall, the migrating songbirds return from the north, with swallows and purple martins leading the way. By October, impressive and sometimes noisy flocks of waterfowl touch down again in the sloughs, and geese go out to the fields to see what the farmers have left for them.

■ **PHOTOGRAPHY:** The boardwalks and observation platforms provide the best setup for wildlife photographs. Sit quietly and wait until duck families, lizards, dragonflies, or hummingbirds approach. Early mornings and evenings will be best, but take insect repellent. Stay on the boardwalks; sitting on the ground invites ticks and chiggers.

■ **HIKES AND WALKS:** In addition to the short walk to the observation building, four trails wend their way through representative habitats. Atkeson Trail behind the Visitor Center has a boardwalk through a cypress swamp, an observation tower, and an open return path along cultivated fields. Environmental Trail, used by school groups, loops across two boardwalks and passes through quiet, shady oak-hickory forest. Resident ducks, turtles, and other animals live along the boardwalks, and many yellow lotuses bloom here in summer.

The other trailheads are several miles from the Visitor Center; ask for a map and more detailed directions there. Dancy Bottoms Trail is a pleasant, level 2-mile walk through oak, hickory, beech, and maple along Flint Creek, where fishing is good and waterfowl abound in marshes. Look and listen for woodpeckers, banging away high in the trees. Wildflowers in moist soils bloom profusely along the trail in spring.

Beaverdam Swamp Boardwalk is farther from the Visitor Center but worth the trip. The boardwalk (0.75 mile) enters the shade of huge black tupelo trees with swollen bases in dark swamp water. Benches along the way provide an opportunity to watch for birds, snakes, or lizards, and to gaze up into dense foliage. Tupelo was a valuable wood for furniture, wooden boxes, and railroad ties, and most stands were cut early in this century. The tupelos here are among the largest in Alabama. At the end of the boardwalk, look right for the beaverdam.

HUNTING AND FISHING Fishing is allowed year-round at the Wheeler refuge. Popular fishing spots are Wheeler Lake, where canoes and motorboats are allowed, and Flint Creek. The refuge even has fishing rodeos in March and Aug. You're likely to catch **catfish, bass,** and **bluegill** in the shallow waters of the lake, and may find **gar** and **paddlefish** in the deeper waters. You may hunt **squirrel, quail,** and other **small game** in Feb.; squirrel are also in season in Oct. **Deer** are in season from Oct. through Jan.

■ **SEASONAL EVENTS:** Wheeler refuge celebrates National Wildlife Refuge Week in October with special events. The refuge has fishing rodeos in March and August, a Day Camp for kids in summer, and a Wet and Wild Festival in October.

■ **PUBLICATIONS:** Bird and other wildlife checklists, refuge maps, brochures, and a pamphlet. The Decatur Visitor Information Center has brochures about other area attractions.

OTHER REFUGES

■ **Watercress Darter NWR, Blowing Wind Cave NWR, Fern Cave NWR, and Key Cave NWR** Wheeler NWR also manages these other four nearby refuges. Key Cave was recently opened to hunting. These small properties provide habitat for two species of endangered bats, the endangered Alabama cave fish, and the threatened American hart's-tongue fern. They are not open to the public, but Blowing Cave has facilities to let you watch bats leaving a cave. Evenings are best.

Arthur R. Marshall Loxahatchee NWR

Boynton Beach, Florida

Vast wetlands, northern Everglades, Loxahatchee NWR

Everglades. The word evokes images of vast wetlands and imperceptibly flowing waters, a landscape teeming with birds and all manner of tropical creatures. This "river of grass" is a labyrinth of channels and waterways only an experienced guide or a wise old alligator should attempt to navigate successfully. Indeed, the Everglades are glades, or open areas, that seem to go on forever. The 147,368-acre Loxahatchee NWR is a giant undeveloped section of the northern Everglades, a haven for wildlife and a buffer for the busy national park. Plans to restore the Kissimee River to its original course and to reduce agricultural runoff will further improve the habitats in this refuge. A boardwalk through a lush cypress swamp and trails along dikes surrounding productive wetlands make Loxahatchee well worth a visit. For visitors with time, energy, and paddling skills, there is a canoe trail within the refuge.

HISTORY

The eloquent and passionate natural-history writer, Marjorie Stoneman Douglas, published *River of Grass* in 1947. This landmark book showed that the biological health of the Everglades depends on clean water flowing south from central Florida. Douglas's heroic efforts helped to create Everglades National Park that same year and save it from draining and development. Unfortunately, most of the northern Everglades had already been converted to sugar plantations. Loxahatchee NWR protects a small northern portion of this "river of grass" and was established in 1969 by the Migratory Bird Conservation Act of 1929 for the purpose of protecting and managing the unique northern Everglades habitat and associated flora and fauna. The refuge was legally renamed the Arthur R. Marshall Loxahatchee NWR in 1986 for FWS employee Art R. Marshall, another dedicated environmentalist. Management of the refuge includes habitat protection for wildlife and freshwater conservation.

The Everglades became land only about 5,000 years ago; before that, the area was undersea. The limestone bedrock is covered by a layer of peat, which supports grasslands, cypress swamps, and hardwood hammocks. Peat beds in the refuge are 12 feet thick in places. The area was largely undisturbed by early European settlers—who preferred to live along the coast—but subsequent channelization and drainage to create land for suburban development and agriculture would have a serious impact on the land.

GETTING THERE

Enter from US 441, between FL 804 (Boynton Beach Blvd.) and FL 806 (Atlantic Ave.). From Florida's Turnpike (Exit 86) or from I-95 (Exit 44), take FL 804 west. Turn south (left) onto 441 and look for refuge sign, right, after 2 mi.

■ **SEASON:** All year.

■ **HOURS:** Refuge: daylight hours; Visitor Center: 9 a.m.–4 p.m. weekdays except Christmas; weekends, 9 a.m.–4:30 p.m. From May through mid-Oct., the Visitor Center is closed on Mon. and Tues.

■ **FEES:** $5 per car; $1 per pedestrian or bicycle.

■ **ADDRESS:** 10216 Lee Rd., Boynton Beach, FL 33437

■ **TELEPHONE:** 561/734-8303

TOURING ARTHUR R. MARSHALL LOXAHATCHEE NWR

■ **BY AUTOMOBILE:** The entrance road and the road to the wildlife-observation platform are open to cars.

■ **BY FOOT:** In addition to a designated marsh trail and a boardwalk near the Visitor Center, some of the dikes and levees are open to hiking for a more extensive view of the marsh. Closed areas are posted. Ask for a refuge map at the Visitor Center.

■ **BY BICYCLE:** The entrance road and the road to the platform are suitable for bicycles.

■ **BY CANOE, KAYAK, OR BOAT:** There is a 5.5-mile canoe trail, starting at a boat launch near the observation platform. The canoe trail may be closed in summer. Canals around the refuge allow 57 miles of boating, accessible from the main entrance and at the Hillsboro entrance on US 827.

Glossy ibis

WHAT TO SEE

■ **LANDSCAPE AND CLIMATE** The interior of Loxahatchee is closed to the public and reserved for water management. Saw-grass marshes and typical Everglades habitat form most of the southern part of the refuge that is available to visitors. Major habitats include sloughs (shallow open water), wet prairie, saw-grass marshes, tree islands, and cypress swamps. Many more trees grow here than in the southern Everglades because of the thicker layers of peat. Winter in the Everglades is usually pleasant but may be cool and rainy. Summers are intensely hot and often dry.

■ PLANT LIFE Taking in the panorama from the dikes, you will be able to distinguish sawgrass marshes containing tree islands with dense growth of wax myrtle, redbay, and buttonbush. Pickerelweeds, water lilies, and swamp potatoes bloom in the sloughs, whereas rushes and grasses grow on the wet prairie.

The impact of civilization on the Everglades is evident in various ways to a discerning eye. High levels of phosphorous from agricultural runoff promotes the growth of cattails, which crowd out other marsh plants. They provide less food and shelter for wildlife than other marsh plants and deplete dissolved oxygen. Exotic water lettuce and hyacinths have also invaded the wetlands.

Bald cypress shade the boardwalk behind the Visitor Center, along with maples, pond apple, and strangler figs. Royal, swamp, leather, cinnamon, and strap ferns (signs will help you tell them apart) grow on trees or on clumps of roots and soil near the water. Epiphytic bromeliads (relatives of pineapples) and orchids grow on tree trunks and branches. On many trees a bright red lichen, baton rouge, grows in irregular splotches.

■ ANIMAL LIFE

Birds Bring a bird field guide (or pick up a list at the Visitor Center), binoculars or a spotting scope, and some patience: There are scores of bird species to be seen at Loxahatchee. Egrets, anhingas, herons, and ibises—with their a long, slender, downwardly curved bills—nest here along with wood ducks and mottled ducks. Tall wading birds and rafts of migratory ducks can be seen in winter months, especially from the observation tower. Endangered or threatened birds include wood storks, snail kites (whose main food, apple snails, is found in the marsh), bald eagles, Florida sandhill cranes, and peregrine falcons. Use a field guide to spot fulvous—birder talk for "tawny"—whistling ducks, blue-winged teal, and green-winged teal. Limpkins, brown speckled snail eaters that are as tall as ibises, may be seen from the Marsh Trail, but they are well-camouflaged and shy.

Limpkin, Loxahatchee NWR

Mammals River otters, deer, bobcats, and raccoons call Loxahatchee home, along with the exotic armadillo, which migrated from Texas.

Reptiles and amphibians American alligators bask on the dikes or float like logs. Keep a respectful distance, and *never* feed an alligator. Far in the refuge's

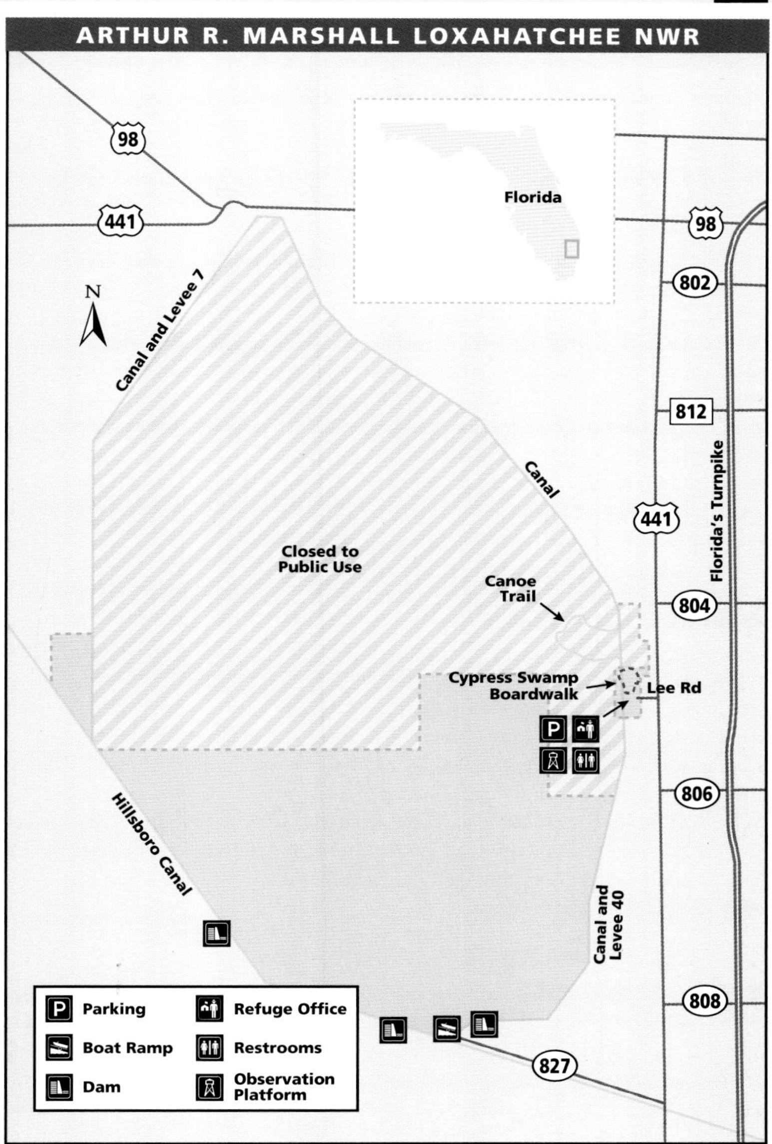

interior, alligators build nests and excavate deep pools when the water gets low. Fish congregate in the pools, and many other animals come to the pools for food and water. Florida peninsula turtles and water snakes enjoy the cover of the cypress swamp, but they also like to come out in the open. Less likely to be seen are pygmy rattlesnakes and coral snakes.

Fish Largemouth bass and bream nest here. Florida gars lurk in the mud, while mosquitofish swim at the surface and snap up mosquito larvae.

Invertebrates Butterflies actively feed on the wildflowers, shrubs, and native vines growing in the newly built Butterfly Garden at the Visitor Center. Say thanks to the dragonflies as they scoop up mosquitoes. Southern lubber grasshoppers can be seen on the dikes and roads. Watch for fire-ant mounds on the marsh trail but avoid touching them—the ants inside really sting!

ACTIVITIES

■ **CAMPING:** Camping is not allowed in the refuge, and the area east of the refuge is a crowded extension of Miami and Fort Lauderdale. Jonathan Dickinson State Park, about 40 miles north of the refuge on US 1, has a pretty campground; reservations are suggested. John Prince County Park, about 10 miles north of the refuge on Lantana Rd. and Congress Ave., in Lantana, has an in-town campground; reservations are suggested.

■ **WILDLIFE OBSERVATION AND PHOTOGRAPHY:** Winter has the most concentrated populations of wading birds and waterfowl, easily visible from the dikes (if you want privacy) and the observation platform (if you don't mind the presence of fellow birders and photographers). In spring, many species nest. Walking quietly on the dike is the best way to see turtles, alligators, and snakes. There's a sharp contrast between bright light and shaded areas here. Come prepared with appropriate film and lens filters.

■ **HIKES AND WALKS:** Cypress Swamp Boardwalk is a 0.4-mile boardwalk near the Visitor Center. Marsh Trail, a 0.8-mile pathway along an earthen square dike, has an observation platform at one corner for excellent views of wading birds, as well as interpretive signs and benches.

HUNTING AND FISHING Fishing is allowed throughout the year at the Loxahatchee refuge. The species most commonly found by anglers are **largemouth bass** and **bream**. You may hunt **waterfowl** from Nov. through Jan.

■ **SEASONAL EVENTS:** The refuge celebrates National Wildlife Refuge Week in October with special events. Also celebrated are International Migratory Bird Day (second Sat. in May) and National Fishing Week (first week of June).

■ **PUBLICATIONS:** Bird list.

SATELLITE REFUGE

■ **Hobe Sound NWR** Located on Jupiter Island, Hobe Sound Refuge comprises 967 acres of coastal-dune, mangrove, and sand-pine and scrub oak habitat. The 3.5-mile beach provides safe nesting areas for three species of sea turtles: leatherback, Atlantic green, and Atlantic loggerhead. Other endangered or threatened species here include indigo snakes, wood storks, manatees, gopher tortoises, Florida scrub jays, piping plovers, and least terns. Development from Miami to Palm Beach has destroyed most of the sand-pine habitat on the Atlantic coastal ridge and much of the beach area needed by the sea turtles. This refuge, established in 1969, is critical habitat, and management involves patrolling nesting sites that visitors should avoid respectfully.

Hobe Sound refuge is just north of Jonathan Dickinson State Park on US 1. Admission is $5 per car. Telephone: 561/546-6141. Interpretive museum hours: 9 a.m. to 11 a.m. and 1 p.m. to 3 p.m.; closed on weekends. Hiking: Sand Pine Scrub Trail (0.4 miles) and the beach. Activities: Summer camp for kids, ranger-led turtle watches, and environmental education programs.

Crystal River NWR

Crystal River, Florida

Crystal River NWR

About 20 percent of the entire American manatee population winters here in Crystal River Refuge. Critically endangered, these large, gentle aquatic mammals need this small refuge, with its warm, clear springs, to survive the winter months. More than 100,000 visitors every year seek out the almost mystical experience of swimming with the manatees. Refuge personnel enforce strict protection rules, rescue wounded manatees, conduct and encourage research, and coordinate their activities with the Manatee Education Center at Homosassa Springs State Wildlife Park. In summer manatees travel wherever the water is warm enough, either saltwater or fresh; one manatee, nicknamed "Chessie" for his foray over the Chesapeake Bay, has even made two sightseeing trips to Rhode Island.

Crystal River, on Florida's upper west coast, southwest of Ocala, is a part of Chassahowitzka NWR, a larger and older NWR (established in 1943) that receives less visitation because it is accessible only by boat and provides fewer visitor services.

HISTORY

Before 1983, this privately owned 46-acre parcel of land along Kings Bay and the Crystal River on Florida's upper west coast was just another piece of prime real estate slated for upscale home development. But conservationists made a case for preserving the land, claiming that building and unrestricted motorboat use would decimate the wintering manatee population, which was attracted to the warm water from 30 natural springs and the abundance of aquatic vegetation. The Nature Conservancy raised funds to buy the land and then sold it to the U.S. Fish & Wildlife Service in 1983. Waterfowl, otters, and other wildlife species also take advantage of the protection here.

GETTING THERE

From the town of Crystal River on US 98/19, turn west on Paradise Point Rd. (it

becomes Kings Bay Dr.) at the sign for the refuge. Follow signs for the refuge office on the right. To get to the Manatee Education Center, return to US98/19 and drive south for 7 mi.; the center is on the right.

■ **SEASON:** Open year-round; the best manatee observation times are from October to March.

■ **HOURS:** Refuge Headquarters: 7:30 a.m.–4 p.m., Mon.–Fri. Manatee Education Center: 9 a.m.–5:30 p.m. daily.

■ **FEES:** No fee for refuge or Manatee Education Center.

■ **ADDRESS:** 1502 Southeast Kings Bay Dr., Crystal River, FL 34429

■ **TELEPHONE:** Refuge Headquarters: 352/563-2088; Manatee Education Center: 352/628-5343

TOURING CRYSTAL RIVER

Crystal River is the only southeastern refuge with high visitation numbers but no foot trails, bicycle trails, or wildlife drives. There is a small picnic area behind refuge headquarters.

■ **BY CANOE, KAYAK, OR BOAT:** Small motorboats and canoes can be launched and/or rented in the town of Crystal River. Call or visit the refuge office or the Manatee Education Center for information about dive shops and marinas. Most visitors use the commercial tour boats.

WHAT TO SEE

■ **LANDSCAPE AND CLIMATE** Crystal River NWR consists of a few small islands within Kings Bay, the headwaters of the Crystal River. Though the weather may be cool in winter, swimmers can take advantage of the same warm-water conditions that the manatees require—water that is in fact warmer than the Gulf of Mexico. In cool weather, many observers wear wet suits. Warm springs pump millions of gallons of freshwater into the river channels.

■ PLANT LIFE Submerged freshwater aquatic plants include exotics, such as hydrilla and Eurasian watermilfoil, in addition to native eelgrass, pondweed, and naiad grasses. The islands' forests consist of oak, cedar, cabbage palm, and red maple overstory, a shrubby understory, and a fringe of saw grass. Many of the Chassahowitzka islands have mangroves as the dominant tree.

■ ANIMAL LIFE Manatees are royalty at Crystal River Refuge, but other wildlife species feed or visit here, of course.

Birds Birders could spend a challenging day spotting the 12 kinds of herons that use this property. Brown pelicans, cormorants, anhingas, and bitterns also catch fish here and nest on the islands. Boaters should look up from time to time between manatee sightings: Endangered wood storks and threatened bald eagles exploit the crowns of island trees to build their twig and branch nests. Kingfishers chatter as they swoop over the water looking for surface fish. Migratory birds—such as warblers, vireos, goldfinches, and thrushes—pass through in fall and spring. In all, 250 birds species have been recorded at Crystal River and Chassahowitzka NWR.

Mammals The manatees receive red-carpet treatment here. Refuge officers stay close by to watch the manatee watchers. Visitors may not approach manatees unless the big animals approach them first. People swimming in the bay must not

Great blue heron

Florida manatees

harass the manatees in any way, give them food or water, separate a cow from its calf, or disrupt their natural behavior. Seven sanctuaries closest to the springs are closed to public use and are marked with orange buoys. While most of the refuge manatees have propeller scars on their backs, they likely got them elsewhere.

A manatee may weigh as much as a small car, and babies weigh about 70 to 80 pounds at birth. They have front flippers with three or four fingernails and prehensile bristled lips to pull in aquatic vegetation, including grasses, broad-leaved plants, roots, and the sand that comes with them. Manatee molars wear down and are replaced much like those of their relatives, the elephants. The common ancestors of elephants and manatees lived more than 60 million years ago and diverged into three main groups—elephants, aquatic manatees, and dugongs (a.k.a. sea cow)—and the strange woodchuck-like African hyrax.

Manatees' rounded tail fins move up and down for energy-efficient swimming, and their lungs extend the length of their bodies, which allows increased air exchange and the ability to stay under water for several minutes. The extended lungs also increases buoyancy, so that rising for air takes almost no extra energy. Manatees sleep in short naps interrupted by breathing, and mothers push newborns to the surface for their first breaths. Mother and calf stay together for about two years, communicating with chirps and squeaks.

While swimming or boating, visitors should study the water surface for trails of chewed-up grasses or lines of bubbles (not exhaled breath, as you might think, but methane gas from digesting all that grass). You can also watch the manatees stick their noses up for a breath-their nostrils have valves that look like upside-down eyelids and open with a soft snort.

River otters get second billing here and may be sighted on shore or out catching fish. Dolphins jump farther out in the bay, so you may need binoculars to see them well.

Reptiles and amphibians Forty species of amphibians and reptiles have been reported at Crystal River, the largest being alligators and turtles.

Fish Jacks, snapper, and redfish are good for sport fishing in Kings Bay, and an occasional 6-foot-long tarpon puts up a fight when hooked. Smaller fish flash by in vividly colored schools, to the delight of manatee watchers in boats or under water.

Invertebrates The brackish, fresh, and salt water of Kings Bay supports crabs, hatchling fish, and larval clams, oysters, shrimp, and other important invertebrates. Barnacles attach themselves to manatees in salt water but die in the freshwater springs, leaving splotches on the skin of the manatees.

ACTIVITIES

■ **SWIMMING:** There is no better refuge for swimming with manatees; in fact, it may be the *only* one. Snorkels, fins, and wet suits help, but use of scuba equipment is discouraged because the noise alarms the manatees.

■ **WILDLIFE OBSERVATION AND PHOTOGRAPHY:** The best ways to observe manatees are while boating and swimming. While underwater cameras will often provide good shots of manatees, flashes can be disturbing to the animals. From a quiet canoe, photographers might get good pictures of birds, manatee faces breaking the surface, and other animals near a refuge island. The state park, which holds captive manatees that have been injured or cannot be released, and the Manatee Education Center also provide some observation and photography opportunities.

Fish & Wildlife staff members maintain an observation platform on an inlet of the bay at the edge of the state park. Manatees surface to breathe near the platform, and cormorants, ospreys, and other birds catch fish here.

HUNTING AND FISHING
Fishing is allowed year-round at the refuge, most often at Kings Bay. Anglers are in search of **jacks, snapper**, and **redfish**. You may hunt for **waterfowl** in Chassahowitzka only. Contact the refuge for further details.

■ **SEASONAL EVENTS:** Crystal River Refuge celebrates National Wildlife Refuge Week in October with special events. There are several special events at the Education Center.

■ **PUBLICATIONS:** Brochures, bird lists, and manatee information are available at the refuge office.

SATELLITE REFUGE

■ **Egmont Key NWR** This refuge is accessible only by boat and has walking trails, beaches, and turtle nesting areas.

Florida Keys NWRs

Big Pine Key, Florida

Key deer, an endangered species, Florida Keys NWR

Heavenly weather, multicolored coral reefs, and sparkling waters bring beach people and nature lovers to the Florida Keys, at the very tip of southernmost Florida. These scattered islands once harbored the greatest variety of tropical species in the continental United States. The NWRs of the Florida Keys offer glimpses of that past biodiversity, smack in the midst of intense commercial development. National Key Deer Refuge, on Big Pine Key, is our focus here; other refuge units on the Keys are noted at the end.

HISTORY

Believe it or not, southern Florida and the Keys were once home to mammoths and mastodons, condors, lions, camels, and saber-toothed tigers. The sea level was lower then, and most of the Keys were part of the mainland. Things have changed a bit since the Pleistocene era: Ocean levels rose, limestone bedrock eroded, and new coral reefs formed. Amerindians, freed slaves, pirates, and seamen lived here before the 20th century brought a trickle of settlers, some of whom hunted birds for their plumes to fashion stylish hats.

Enter the developers and then the conservationists. In 1904, Henry Flagler built a railroad from Miami to Key West. A hurricane in the 1930s destroyed the railroad, but the state built a road in its place. Fortunately, fragile areas received protection by the NWR System, The Nature Conservancy, state parks, and other organizations. As a result of this conservation, the Florida Keys today has four NWRs: Key West NWR (1908), Great White Heron NWR (1938), National Key Deer (1957), and Crocodile Lake (1980). The combined refuges cover 25,000 acres of land and an astonishing 391,000 acres of open water. Because boats, personal watercraft, low-flying airplanes, and inappropriate beach use can damage fragile habitats, some islands and open water are posted to restrict entry.

GETTING THERE

The Florida Keys refuges are mostly northwest of US 1. From Marathon Key, drive south on US 1 to Big Pine Key. Turn north (right) at the only traffic light onto FL 940 (Key Deer Blvd.) and follow NWR signs for one-quarter mi. The refuge headquarters is in the shopping center on the right (opposite Winn Dixie), 0.25 mi. past the junction of US 1 and Key Deer Blvd.

■ **SEASON:** Open year-round.

■ **HOURS:** Refuge: Opens a half-hour before sunrise and closes a half-hour after sunset. Office: Open Mon.–Fri., 8 a.m.–5 p.m.

■ **FEES:** None.

■ **ADDRESS:** P.O. Box 430510, Big Pine Key, FL 33043-0510

■ **TELEPHONE:** 305/872-2239

TOURING THE FLORIDA KEYS NWRS

■ **BY AUTOMOBILE:** Key Deer Blvd. and Watson Blvd. can be driven. Early morning and evening driving may provide wildlife sightings.

■ **BY FOOT:** The Watson and Mannillo trails are short, easy trails with an information kiosk and interpretive signs. A refuge volunteer is often there to answer questions.

WHAT TO SEE

■ **LANDSCAPE AND CLIMATE** The keys are low-lying islands containing pine rocklands, wetlands, mangrove borders, and mudflats. The "higher" areas (elevation 10 feet) support hardwood hammocks and scarce supplies of fresh water. Coral reefs flourish in the shallow sea between the keys. The refuges protect many species of plants and animals that are disappearing from the West Indies.

■ **PLANT LIFE** Red, black, and white mangroves shield the Keys from ocean waves. Inland from the mangroves live pines, palm trees, poisonwood (which can cause a skin rash), and gumbo-limbo or "tourist tree" (whose peeling bark makes it look as if it has a rash or a sunburn). Tropical swamps are an orchid hothouse, and the wetlands of the Keys contain several species of these lovely, fragile plants, as well as other epiphytic air plants.

■ **ANIMAL LIFE**

Birds Migratory and overwintering birds from the north share habitats with tropical birds on the Keys. Great white herons, ibises, egrets, and roseate spoonbills feed on the mudflats. Look for indigo and painted buntings in the woodlands. The occasional coot or blue-winged teal can be seen swimming in the freshwater at Blue Hole. Peregrine falcons, kites, green herons, great blue herons, and great white herons may appear, and birdwatchers will be pleased to find many other birds for their life lists, such as the mangrove cuckoo.

Mammals Key deer, much like Key limes, are much smaller than their mainland counterparts, standing just over 2 feet tall at the shoulder, as if proportioned to match the size of their island habitat. Newborns weigh 2 to 4 pounds. Hunting and development reduced the population to fewer than 50 deer in the 1940s, but a national campaign succeeded in saving them. Today, about 600 deer live on Big Pine Key and in a few other areas. Their existence here is still precarious; many are killed by cars and dogs.

Other mammals—Key Largo woodrats, Key Largo cotton mice, Lower Keys marsh rabbits and silver rice rats—live only in the Keys.

Reptiles and amphibians Alligators and turtles sunbathe in Blue Hole quarry. Many species of tropical and subtropical lizards and snakes thrive on the refuge.

Invertebrates Threatened tree snails climb trees, shrubs, grasses, and the walls of buildings. Their strong, brightly marked shells protect them when they fall. Disturbing or collecting the snails is prohibited.

HUNTING AND FISHING Both fishing and lobstering are allowed at the Key West and Great White Heron refuges. You're likely to find saltwater species such as **bonefish, tarpon, permit,** and **snapper,** as well as **Florida lobster**.

ACTIVITIES

■ **WILDLIFE OBSERVATION AND PHOTOGRAPHY:** Roadside viewing and walking the two short trails listed below provide the best opportunities in cool parts of the day. Snorkeling will take you underwater to view a colorful array of fish and coral reefs.

■ **HIKES AND WALKS:** Two trails on the refuge start from Key Deer Blvd. and are well signed. Blue Hole Trail leads to a freshwater quarry and is wheelchair-accessible. Watson Trail starts 0.25 mile beyond the Blue Hole parking lot and forms a 0.7-mile loop. Mannillo Trail also starts 0.25 mile beyond the Blue Hole, and is a 700-foot-long wheelchair-accessible interpretive trail.

SATELLITE REFUGES

■ **Crocodile Lake NWR** This refuge protects one of the few nesting areas of the endangered American crocodile in the United States. The Schaus' swallowtail butterfly, Key Largo woodrat, Key Largo cotton mouse, and other rare species—as well as tropical hardwood forests containing lignumvitae, gumbo-limbo, mahogany, and paradise trees—find refuge here. This refuge is presently closed to the public, but there are plans to build an observation platform, a boardwalk, and a butterfly observation area. Similar habitats and species can be seen on the adjoining Key Largo Hammocks State Botanical Site nature trail.

■ **Great White Heron NWR** Accessible only by boat, Great White Heron NWR contains a designated wilderness area. Visitors should closely follow any restrictions posted (no kayaking, for example, through the mangroves)—the ecosystem here supports such threatened species as sea turtles, which nest on the sandy beaches. Mangrove communities, sand flats, and sea-grass meadows provide habitat for many rare birds. Raccoons are not present on most of these remote islands to prey on more fragile wildlife. Public use is permitted on a few island beaches.

■ **Key West NWR** Partly a designated wilderness area, Key West NWR is accessible by boat only and is raccoon-free. Coral reef snorkeling and beach use are allowed on most of the refuge islands unless posted. Commercial outfitters provide rental boats and trips.

J. N. "Ding" Darling NWR

Sanibel, Florida

Auto-tour loop and wildlife, J.N. "Ding" Darling NWR

J. N. "Ding" Darling National Wildlife Refuge is as unusual as its name. The refuge forms a different kind of island: an island surrounded on one side by water and on the other by a crowded, bustling tourist community. Midway up the west coast of Florida, near Fort Myers, the refuge is truly a sanctuary—and one that was saved just in time, although the residents of Sanibel Island continue to work hard to maintain natural areas in a realm of high real estate prices and burgeoning development. The refuge has high visitation, but it offers quiet places and some of the best wildlife-watching opportunities in Florida. A new Visitor Center, a series of education programs, and careful management make this refuge a showcase of environmental protection.

HISTORY

The illustrator Jay Norwood "Ding" Darling (1876–1962) won two Pulitzer prizes in a field that he practically (re)invented: political cartooning. Because of the strong emphasis on environmental preservation in his cartoons, President Franklin Roosevelt in 1934 appointed Ding chief of the U.S. Biological Survey (later to become the U.S. Fish & Wildlife Service). Darling started an innovative program of land protection and restoration to increase dwindling populations of game birds and other wildlife species. One of Darling's cartoons offers advice to a politician spouting conservation promises: "Don't say it—sign it!" He also garnered public support with statements such as "Ducks can't lay eggs on a picket fence" that helped to raise funds even during the Great Depression. Darling's legacy also includes the annual Duck Stamp program (he drew the first one), which provides substantial wildlife preservation funds to this day. The NWR blue goose symbol that we see on every refuge sign is Darling's. He sought personal refuge from his hectic life and controversial work on nearby Captiva Island. Darling predicted the growth of tourism on the islands and worked to establish a refuge on Sanibel (accomplished by 1945). In 1978, the Sanibel Island NWR was renamed for him.

GETTING THERE

Make your way from Fort Meyers or Cape Coral to the toll causeway for Sanibel Island. Just after the causeway, bear right on Periwinkle Way. Turn right on Tarpon Bay Rd. and then left on Sanibel-Captiva Rd. After 2 mi., turn right at refuge sign onto entrance road. The Wildlife Drive starts on the left side of the parking lot.

Bailey Tract: From the end of Periwinkle Way, turn left and look for refuge sign on right in 0.2 mi.

■ **SEASON:** All year; Wildlife Drive and Visitor Center closed on Fri.

■ **HOURS:** Visitor Center: 9 a.m.–5 p.m. daily except Fri. from Nov. to April; 9 a.m.–4 p.m. May through Oct. Wildlife Drive: daylight hours; closed on Fri. Trails: daylight hours every day.

■ **FEES:** Visitor Center: free; Wildlife Drive: $5/car; $1/bicycle.

■ **ADDRESS:** 1 Wildlife Drive, Sanibel, FL 33957

■ **TELEPHONE:** 941/472-1100

TOURING J. N. "DING" DARLING

■ **BY AUTOMOBILE:** The 5-mile Wildlife Drive ($5) is open each day except Friday.

■ **BY FOOT:** Hiking trails include Indigo Trail (2 miles), Cross Dike Trail (0.25 mile), Red Mangrove Overlook (0.1 mile), and Shell Mound Trail (0.3 mile). The nearby Bailey Tract has 1.75 miles of trail winding along dikes and around a pond. Walking trails are open on Friday, though the Visitor Center and Wildlife Drive are closed.

■ **BY BICYCLE:** The 5-mile wildlife drive is open to bicycles for a fee of $1 every day except Friday. Bikes can be rented at Tarpon Bay and other island businesses.

Osprey in flight

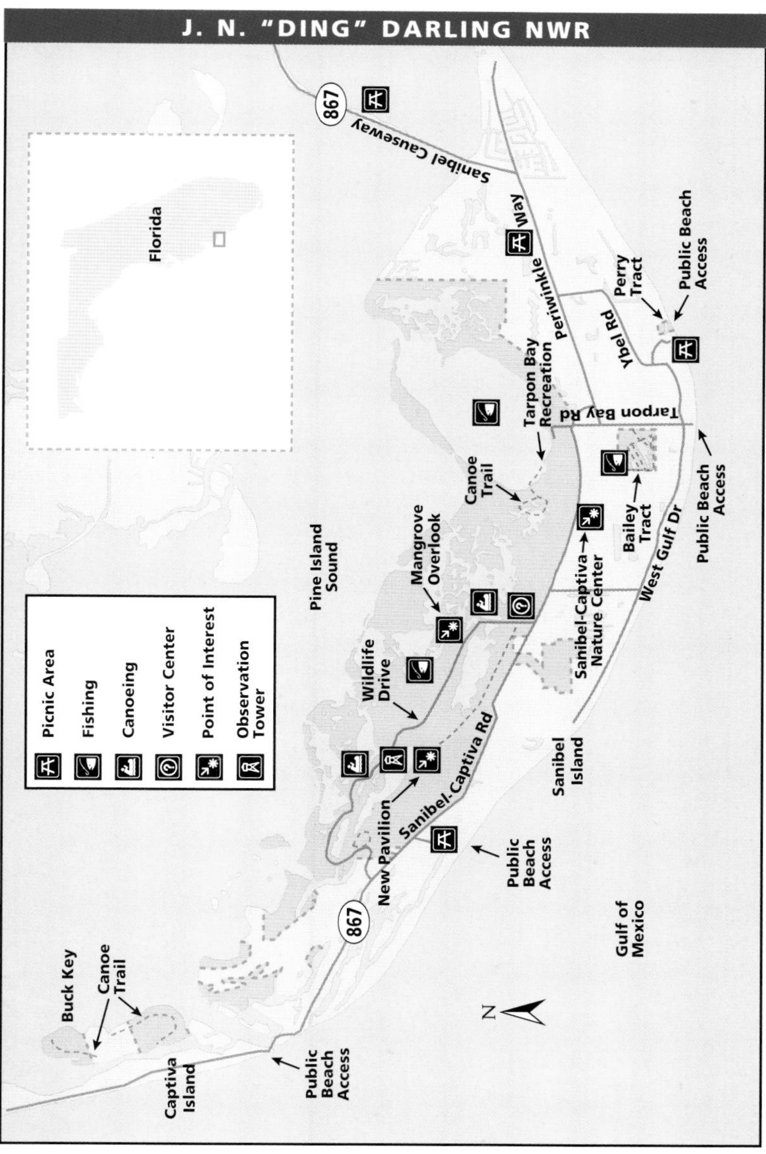

■ **BY CANOE, KAYAK, OR BOAT:** Canoes can be rented in nearby Tarpon Bay. Two canoe trails (Commodore Creek, 2 miles) and Buck Key (4 miles) go through mangrove forests and open water along marshes. Buck Key Canoe Trail is the only visitor access to a mangrove island near Captiva Island.

WHAT TO SEE

■ **LANDSCAPE AND CLIMATE** J. N. "Ding" Darling refuge is on the northern side of Sanibel Island, tucked inside its east-west curve. Protected here from surf on the southern edge of the island, the refuge has no beach but plenty of marsh, mudflats, and forests of mangroves, trees with sturdy roots that help to build up new land. Most of the wetlands are only a few feet above sea level and are ruled by tidal changes affecting the activities of wildlife, especially birds. Expect hot days almost any time of year, so plan your outing as the wildlife does: Come out in the cool hours of morning and evening. Wildlife-attracting wetlands include salt and freshwater marshes, open water, and tree-lined canals.

■ PLANT LIFE Open water, mangrove islands, sloughs and mudflats, marshes, and hardwood hammocks characterize this refuge, and many of its plant species have tropical origins. Red mangroves dominate the edges of the refuge and build land by holding moist soils in place with their roots. Red mangroves "walk" by sending ropelike roots out from the branches (rather than the trunk), reaching down through the briny water. Their seeds germinate on the tree and drop off to bob in the water until they come to a wet shallow place to sprout roots and leaves. Red mangroves build soil, allowing black mangroves and other species to seed and grow. The roots of these trees send up air tubes, which look like black drinking straws, through which the trees "breathe." Other kinds of mangroves live farther inland. Not only do mangroves make land and stabilize soil, they also hang out over the water and drop leaves that decay to feed aquatic larvae and other small animals. Periodic hurricanes or fires destroy or rearrange mangroves, and then they can start "walking" again.

Other tropical plants here include gumbo-limbo (called the "tourist tree," with its peeling, red bark), sea grape, and the invasive Brazilian pepper, which crowds out native plants.

On the short boardwalk behind the Visitor Center, look for labeled plants, including shoestring fern, Christmasberry, and Florida mayten ("gutta percha"), whose sap is a base for chewing gum and temporary dental fillings.

Snowy egret

Marsh grasses, shrubbery, hammocks, and mangrove clumps vary the view along the Wildlife Drive and provide dense cover and abundant food for wildlife.

■ ANIMAL LIFE Development came recently to Sanibel Island. The causeway opened in 1973, long after the refuge was established. Wildlife populations suffered from farming and logging early in this century, but tangles of mangroves and expanses of mudflats preserved the best habitats. Management strategies and protection now increase many animal populations.

Birds Darling is one of the best places to observe large wading birds: wood storks, herons, ibises, and egrets. Roseate spoonbills stand in shallow water and swing their heads back and forth while opening their bills to catch fish and crustaceans that get stirred up. Cormorants and anhingas use the deeper water channels to dive for fish, and the smaller types of herons (yellow-crowned night, green, and little blue) stand on mangrove roots or along marsh edges. Grebes, moorhens, and mergansers swim in channels along with more kinds of ducks than can be listed here (pick up a birding guide at the Visitor Center). Ospreys nest from December to March, high on tree snags or platforms. Sandpipers, willets, dowitchers, and other types of shorebirds also seen on beaches probe the mudflats for prey. Pelicans, which do their fishing in more open water, may fly by.

On your second tour of the Wildlife Drive (it's worth several visits), look for smaller birds: migrating warblers and vireos. Palm warblers, prairie warblers, and kingfishers nest here. Small ground doves are plentiful, but the uncommon mangrove cuckoo will be hard to spot. Bring your bird book and your checklist: Nearly 250 species of birds have been recorded at Darling.

Mammals Opossums, bobcats, and raccoons may leave tracks in soft soil or be seen crossing the road. River otters dive for fish. Dolphins and manatees may be sighted from the canoe trails or through the mangroves. Interestingly, Darling is one of the few refuges in the southeast—in the country, even—with no deer.

Reptiles and amphibians American Alligators frequent the refuge, building their composting nests and caring for their babies. On Indigo Trail, look for alligator tracks crossing the dike from one ditch to the other. At the time of this writing, one crocodile, a female, lives on the refuge near the end of the Wildlife Drive. Frogs and toads live in freshwater to the left of the Wildlife Drive and in the pond of the Bailey Tract.

Fish Freshwater, saltwater, and brackish water fish inhabit the refuge, and many get their start in the shelter of estuary grasses or mangroves roots. Top-feeding killifish eat mosquito larvae. Seahorses can be found under the mangroves, and snook, redfish, mangrove snapper, and small tarpon are among the many game fish that feed in the open waters.

Gopher tortoise

Invertebrates Dragonflies eat many of the mosquitoes that escape the killifish, and butterflies get nectar from refuge flowers, including mangrove blossoms. Horseshoe crabs come ashore to spawn. Fiddler crabs dig burrows in the fertile mudflats and are a favorite food of spoonbills and shorebirds. On the mangrove overlook, search the branches for mangrove tree crabs.

In the 1960s, the cross dike was built to control mosquitoes; raising and lowering water levels interrupted breeding cycles. However, this also upset the balance of nutrients needed for diversity of food chains. Refuge managers added culverts that can be closed by sliding boards into slots. Look for them along the Wildlife Drive.

ACTIVITIES

■ **CAMPING AND SWIMMING:** Although there is no camping or swimming on the refuge, you'll find several fine public beaches on the other side of Sanibel and Captiva islands.

■ **WILDLIFE OBSERVATION:** In summer, a few birds nest and feed in the refuge, but fall, winter, and early spring are prime time for viewing. Along the Wildlife Drive, it may be best to stay in your car because the animals are accustomed to traffic. But if you are biking or walking, move slowly and keep a respectful distance. On Cross Dike Trail on the Drive there is an observation tower overlooking the marsh. Low tides bring out more birds because more food is available, and in low water, birds will be clustered in large groups. During early-morning low tides, hundreds of roseate spoonbills congregate. Ask at the Visitor Center about tide tables. The tides in the estuaries here are more than an hour later than the Gulf tides because the water moves slowly through marshes and mudflats.

■ **PHOTOGRAPHY:** The Wildlife Drive and the observation tower provide fine photography opportunities, but you may meet large flocks of photography buffs with more equipment than they can carry. Toward the end of the Wildlife Drive, alligators, gopher tortoises, and the crocodile pose in the sunlight. Use a zoom lens for close-ups and keep your distance.

■ **HIKES AND WALKS:** The Indigo Trail starts to the left of the Visitor Center on a short boardwalk through a swamp dominated by black mangroves. Trees, shrubs, ferns, and flowers are labeled. The trail then crosses the Wildlife Drive and runs parallel to it along a dike. It's an easy walk between two canals lined with thick bushes; you will get only glimpses or moorhens, ducks, and herons, but you should have a better chance of seeing small birds. A good morning or evening walk is the 2-mile Indigo Trail and a return by Wildlife Drive if traffic isn't heavy.

A GREAT LEAP FORWARD In 1934 J.N. "Ding" Darling had a problem: too much money. It was his own fault. As Chief of the U.S. Biological Survey (later Fish & Wildlife Service), he drew government funds from many sources to buy and improve land for wildlife. (Or, as he put it, he used a "straw to suck funds from the other fellow's barrel.")

He couldn't, however, spend it all in one place. In fact, as a political cartoonist, he didn't have the biological expertise to know where to spend it. And he had only one fiscal year.

So much money, so little time, and so many swamps, lakes, prairies, barrier islands, and deserts. Darling hired J. Clark Salyer II, a biologist who shared his obsession for wildlife. Salyer drove thousands of miles to visit habitats and talk with wildlife experts. He recorded habitats full of nesting animals as well as eroded gullies with potential.

Salyer and Darling justified each acquisition with—of course—paperwork. In a dramatic finale, Salyer rushed through the last papers (refuges in the Dakotas) just before the deadline, only to find that the secretary of agriculture had gone home for the weekend.

In desperation, Salyer signed and dated the papers himself and presented them on Monday morning. The secretary approved the purchases. With the heroic and inventive efforts of Darling, Salyer, and many other conservationists, the National Wildlife Refuge System fully doubled in acreage in the 1930s.

Endangered brown pelicans

Bailey Tract Trail on Tarpon Bay Road winds through 100 acres of tall cordgrass. Many small birds, lizards, and perhaps a black racer (snake) can be seen. Leather ferns and other large ferns grow along a canal, and alligators are common here.

■ **SEASONAL EVENTS:** The refuge celebrates National Wildlife Refuge Week in October with special events. "Ding" Darling Days in October (part of NWR Week) is a community event with exhibits, free tram rides, volunteer-led walks, and a visit by the winning artist of the annual Federal Duck Stamp Contest. Winners of annual photography contests (anyone can enter) and children's cartoon and duck stamp contests are announced.

International Migratory Bird Day comes in May, and National Fishing Week occurs in July.

A quarterly newsletter describing refuge events is available in the Visitor Center, and there are weekly naturalist programs.

■ **PUBLICATIONS:** Bird lists, guides, newsletters, tide charts, maps, and more are available at the volunteer desk in the Visitor Center. A well-stocked bookstore sells guides, children's books, and calendars.

SATELLITE REFUGES

■ **Island Bay NWR (1908), Matlacha Pass NWR (1908), Pine Island NWR (1908), and Caloosahatchee NWR (1924)** These lands all became satellite refuges. They are mangrove islands with boat access only, and areas around them are popular for fishing. Vigorous mosquito populations help to protect the wildlife of the islands.

Lake Woodruff NWR

De Leon Springs, Florida

Lake Woodruff NWR wetlands

West of the whizzing traffic between Daytona Beach and Orlando lies Lake Woodruff NWR, a peaceful, sunny lake surrounded by marshes, swamps, and pine forests-a welcome respite from urban encroachment on the landscape.

Alligators, black bears, river otters, and most of Florida's species of birds live here, and a public—use area provides good wildlife-viewing opportunities. Don't let certain place names on the refuge keep you away from this rich environment: Norris Dead River, Ziegler Dead River, St. Francis Dead River (all probably called "dead" because of slow-moving swamp water); Tick Island and Mud Lake look better than they sound; and Spring Garden Creek provides canoe access to various sites, but, alas, no pot of gold.

HISTORY

Timucuan Indians and their ancestors lived hereabouts since 8000 B.C., as shown by burial mounds and shell middens. Nearby Ponce De Leon Spring pumps millions of gallons of fresh warm water into the St. Johns River watershed.

The botanist William Bartram slogged through the area in the 1760s, taking note of massive live oaks and magnolias while camping on the St. Johns River: "Our repose however was incomplete, from the stings of musquetoes [sic], the roaring of crocodiles, and the continual noise and restlessness of the sea fowl... all promiscuously lodging together, and in such incredible numbers, that the trees were entirely covered."

Major Joseph Woodruff bought the springs in 1823 to power his grist and sugar mills. Nine years later, John James Audubon, who surely knew Bartram's work, painted birds on a visit to De Leon Springs.

GETTING THERE

From DeLand, go north on US 17 to De Leon Springs. Turn west (left) on Retta

St. for one block; turn left on Grand Ave. (CR 4053) and continue 1 mi. to refuge headquarters. The public use area and parking are 1 mi. west of the headquarters on Mud Lake Rd.

■ **SEASON:** Refuge open year-round.

■ **HOURS:** Daylight hours.

■ **FEES:** None.

■ **ADDRESS:** 4490 Grand Ave., P.O. Box 488, De Leon Springs, FL 32130

■ **TELEPHONE:** 904/985-4673

TOURING LAKE WOODRUFF NWR

■ **BY AUTOMOBILE:** There is no auto route through this refuge.

■ **BY FOOT:** Two nature trails pass through pinewoods and cross the tops of several miles of grassy dikes that traverse the three refuge impoundments.

■ **BY BICYCLE:** Refuge roads and trails are open to bicycles.

■ **BY CANOE OR BOAT:** The St. Johns River, Lake Woodruff, and swamps and canals are best explored by boat. Canoes and small boats my be rented and launched at nearby De Leon Springs State Park or Hontoon State Park.

WHAT TO SEE

■ **LANDSCAPE AND CLIMATE** Fall, winter, and early spring are the best times to observe birds. Many migratory birds stop here, attracted by the wetlands, the large natural areas of the refuge, and the adjacent Ocala National Forest. Summer is hot, with mosquitoes, ticks, and other pests discouraging visitation. Controlled fires occur during winter months as part of the habitat management plan.

■ **PLANT LIFE** Open water, freshwater marshes with tall cordgrass and saw grass, cypress swamps, pine uplands, and many streams make up the habitats of the refuge's 19,000 acres. High up in the host cypress trees, look for Spanish moss, air plants, orchids, and ferns. These epiphytes, some of which are related to pineapples, do not harm host trees.

In the swamps you may find blooming at various times pickerelweed, alligator flag, and irises. Follow the trails upland to see longleaf pine, with its white buds and impressive needles, some up to 18 inches long.

■ **ANIMAL LIFE**

Birds Lake Woodruff rewards the attentive birder. The variety of wetland habitats attracts a large number of bird species, including endangered wood storks and snail kites. Bald eagles nest here, and 21 duck species typically stop by in winter. Herons, egrets, ibises (including the glossy ibis) stay all year.

Limpkins, unusually abundant here, inhabit the swamps and marshes. Nocturnal and reclusive, these crow-sized birds, related to cranes and rails, make eerie calls, echoing through the swamps. With their down-curved bills, limpkins eat mostly apple snails but also catch frogs and insects. In another water habitat, the lakes and ponds, you may spot ospreys nesting and fishing. Along footpaths in the pine woods, wild turkey nest and feed. Moorhens, rails, and wood ducks are common at Lake Woodruff in summer.

Mammals Black bears live in Lake Woodruff's woodlands. The endangered Florida panthers lived here once and may have returned. Bobcats leave tracks in mud or show themselves briefly. These mammals are rather seldom seen, but deer, raccoons, and smaller mammals are common. The manatee, an aquatic mammal, lives in the refuge waters the majority of the year except the coldest months, when they retreat to Blue Springs State Park to bask in the warmer waters. River otters, bats, weasels, opossums, striped skunks, round-tailed muskrats are all also good bets for wildlife observation here.

Reptiles and amphibians Such a watery world as Lake Woodruff is bound to favor certain reptiles over amphibians. Alligators drape themselves on the banks of lake and dikes, and turtles bask on logs in the sun. The mating calls of frogs make the wetlands a noisy place, while other quieter amphibians stay hidden. Nonvenomous water snakes pose as venomous cottonmouth moccasins, and both may sun on the same logs. Lake Woodruff's other venomous snakes are coral snake, diamondback rattlesnake, and ground rattlesnake. Gopher tortoises (sometimes sharing a burrow) thrive here.

Invertebrates Apple snails, food for limpkins and snail kites, can be seen crawling up trees in the swamps.

ACTIVITIES

■ **CAMPING:** Blue Spring State Park, in Orange City (14 miles from the refuge), offers both camping and primitive camping facilities and six family vacation cabins. Call for reservations (904/775-3663).

■ **WILDLIFE OBSERVATION AND PHOTOGRAPHY:** Three water impoundments and an award-winning tower with a fixed telescope at the public-use area provide good opportunities for waterfowl and wading-bird observation and photos. The West Volusia Audubon Society was presented a "Rachel Carson Award" for the design and construction of Lake Woodruff's observation tower. Quiet canoe rides are the best way to explore this refuge, giving paddlers frequent glimpses of swamp flowers and animals. The chances of seeing limpkins are good.

■ **HIKES AND WALKS:** Follow the footpaths on the dikes around impoundments for walking in the open—about 6 miles of hiking with good views, and you can improvise your route. Two short, established nature trails through woods (good shade on hot days) start from the public-use area. Ask for maps at refuge headquarters.

■ **SEASONAL EVENTS:** The refuge celebrates National Wildlife Refuge Week in October with special events.

■ **PUBLICATIONS:** Amphibian and reptile list; bird list; Young People's Checklist.

HUNTING AND FISHING You may hunt **deer** and **wild hog** from Sept. through Nov., in accordance with local hunting regulations. Contact the refuge for further details.

Fishing is allowed year-round, on the banks or in boats. You will most commonly find **bass, crappie, bream, catfish,** and **striper**.

Lower Suwannee NWR

Chiefland, Florida

River otter

Stephen Foster never actually saw the Suwannee River, but his popular love song "The Old Folks at Home" captured the romance of these lush wetlands. The Suwannee is one of the few major rivers in the United States with no dams or big riverside cities. It has Okefenokee NWR as its source and Lower Suwannee NWR as its mouth on the Gulf of Mexico, near the southern end of Florida's Big Bend Region. Look southwest from Gainesville in the Florida midlands to find the Lower Suwannee National Wildlife Refuge out on the Gulf Coast.

HISTORY

Lower Suwanee NWR, established in 1979, contains a variety of undisturbed wetlands: river, estuary, cypress swamp, salt marsh, tidal flat, and delta. Several canoe trails follow the riverbank and wind through narrow creeks in the majestic cypress swamp. With an impressive area of 52,000 acres, the refuge protects 20 miles of the river and 26 miles of coast.

The refuge even boasts the largest Indian shell midden in Florida, located on a short trail in the southern part of this refuge. A boardwalk leads to an outstanding view of the placid lower Suwannee River.

GETTING THERE

The refuge office is off County 347, 13 mi. from Chiefland. From Chiefland follow US 19/98 south for 5 mi. Turn west (right off US 19 onto County 347) and drive 16 mi. to refuge office on right. The Wildlife Drive, the Shell Mound, and Dennis Creek Trails are well marked, farther down on County 347.

■ **SEASON:** Refuge open all year.

■ **HOURS:** Refuge: open daylight hours; roads and fishing areas also open at night. Office: 7:30 a.m.–4 p.m., weekdays.

■ **FEES:** No fees.

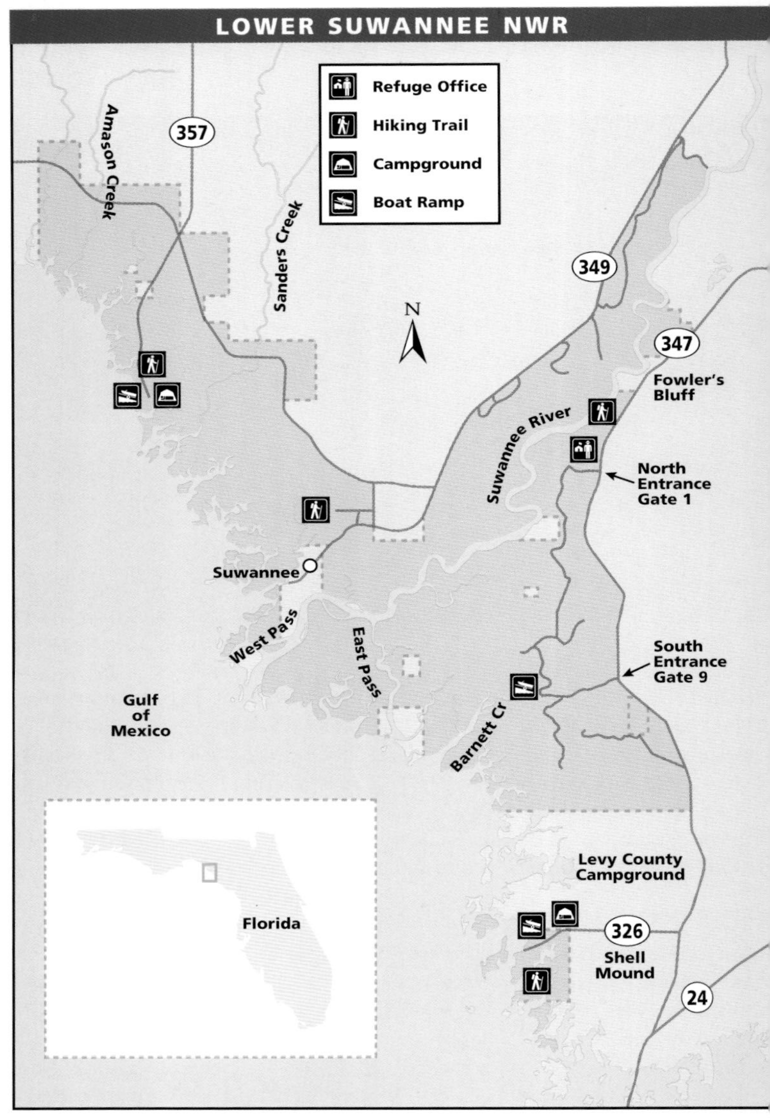

■ **ADDRESS:** 16450 NW 31st Place, Chiefland, FL 32626
■ **TELEPHONE:** 352/493-0238

TOURING LOWER SUWANNEE

■ **BY AUTOMOBILE:** There are 50 miles of paved and gravel roads open to cars, including the Wildlife Drive that starts just past the refuge office on FL 347.
■ **BY FOOT:** Three trails, River Trail (0.6 mile), Shell Mound Trail (0.3 mile), and Dennis Creek Trail (1-mile loop), take visitors to representative habitats in the refuge. Many miles of gated, old logging roads are open to hiking and bicycles.
■ **BY BICYCLE:** Gravel and paved roads, as well as gated secondary roads on the refuge, are open to bicycles.

■ BY CANOE, KAYAK, OR BOAT: There are three marked river and swamp creek canoe trails. Canoes can be rented and launched in the town of Suwannee.

WHAT TO SEE

■ LANDSCAPE AND CLIMATE Suwannee's undeveloped wetlands and coastal forests perform many functions—one being the protection of a large number of plant and animal species. Estuary waters provide nutrients to larval invertebrates and newly hatched ocean fish as river silt blends with salt water to form brackish environments. Swamps and marshes filter water and release it slowly into the river—natural, nondestructive flood control. Bottomland hardwoods (which in Florida means land just a few feet above sea level) border the broad river floodplain and delta. Slightly higher land features dry scrub pinelands, habitat for threatened scrub jays and many woodpeckers. Small coastal islands provide safety for rookeries. Summers are, predictably, hot and humid here, but late fall, winter, and early spring are good times to hike, canoe, fish, and observe wildlife.

■ PLANT LIFE The Suwannee River region was explored by a team of naturalists a century before Stephen Foster wrote his famous song. Although the river uplands have been converted to pine plantations, the bottomlands hardwood terrain has changed little in 200 years. Bottomland hardwoods include tupelo, hickory, and maple. Tupelo, a swamp tree related to the black gum of eastern forests, grows in swamps that have standing water all year. Beekeepers value it for honey, as seen in the Peter Fonda movie *Ulee's Gold,* and loggers cut it for use in boxes, pulpwood, fishing floats, excelsior (fine wood shavings), and corks. The hickories shower the ground with abundant nuts, providing plenty of food for wildlife.

Yellow-crowned night-heron

Scrub uplands are dominated by slash- and longleaf pines, with an understory of oaks, shrubs, grasses, palmettos, and (three-leafed) poison ivy.

Living closer to the river are cypress swamps. These conifers have narrow needles, round cones, and buttressed bases. They send up knobby knees for reasons known only to themselves. Cypresses were also logged because of their rot-resistant wood—anything that lives in swamp water has to be tough. Epiphytes cling to all the trees, and flowers such as the showy white swamp lily float in the water.

Water weeds and grasses sway in the warm estuary waters and feed the manatees (see Crystal River NWR). *Spartina* grass of the salt marshes produces vast amounts of organic matter, which nourishes coastal environments.

■ **ANIMAL LIFE** Because it attracts migratory birds and contains undisturbed habitats for the original resident wildlife of Florida, Suwannee NWR supports a rich collection of birds and animals.

Birds Birders, get out your checklists: Anhingas, various herons, brown pelicans, cormorants, five kinds of woodpeckers, wood ducks, ospreys, four kinds of owls, and several warblers and sparrows are just a few of the species that nest on Lower Suwannee Refuge. Kingfishers fly along the wide river, chattering and diving for small fish. You will see them from the swamp boardwalk and the canoe trails. Many long-legged waterbirds, such as ibis and herons, feed on the salt marshes and mudflats. Binoculars will allow you to see these birds up close. Dennis Creek Trail leads across a muddy place, where you can practice identifying bird tracks and discarded feathers. Migratory birds include tundra swans, snow geese, 15 species of ducks, and nearly 200 species of other birds.

Ibis in flight

Mammals Manatees and river otters feed in deep water in the river, and dolphins can be seen from the fishing pier and other venues overlooking the Gulf of Mexico. Florida black bears hide in the swamps (you may see claw marks on tree trunks), and white-tailed deer graze in the drier woodlands. Armadillos keep to the dry land and cross the roads at night. Squirrels, raccoons, and feral hogs are hunted during designated seasons. Bobcats forage for crabs and other prey. In all, 42 species of mammals, almost enough for Noah's Ark, live on the refuge.

Reptiles and amphibians Alligators rule among reptiles, of course, but 72 other species live here, including turtles, lizards, and several species of woodland and wetland snakes. Threatened loggerhead turtles and endangered Kemp's Ripley sea turtles nest along the Gulf coast. Frogs and toads, in subtle variety, comprise most of the 39 species of amphibians on the refuge.

Fish If game fishing is your thing, you can try here for largemouth bass, Suwannee bass, channel catfish, and other freshwater and saltwater varieties. The threatened Gulf sturgeon uses the clean, deep Suwannee waterway to spawn as it once did in many Florida rivers. Many fish start their lives in safe backwaters and go out to sea when they are big enough to defend themselves.

Fiddler crabs at low tide in mudflats

Invertebrates The salt marshes are nurseries for larval shrimp, clams, oysters, and other shellfish. Fiddler crabs mine the tidal flats for bits of organic matter and form piles of round sand balls. Look in the shallow water near the fishing pier to see blue crabs scooting about.

ACTIVITIES

■ **CAMPING:** There is no camping on the refuge, but two county campgrounds, one on County 357 and one on County 326 near the Shell Mound Trail, are adjacent to Lower Suwannee. One of the best Florida state parks, Manatee Springs, lies six miles west of Chiefland on County 320, just upriver from the refuge. There you can camp, swim, dive, ride inner tubes, hike, and watch manatees in a clear 80,000-gallon-per-minute spring that flows into the Suwannee River above the refuge. Reservations suggested.

■ **SWIMMING:** There is no swimming on the refuge, but, as mentioned above, there are swimming areas at Manatee Springs State Park, some roped off and safe for children.

■ **WILDLIFE OBSERVATION AND PHOTOGRAPHY:** Photographers find the open vistas on the coast, birds in the salt marshes, and the wide Suwannee River from the boardwalk, with reflections of bald cypress trees, prime subjects for photographs. The Wildlife Drive passes through woodlands and cleared areas where deer, wild turkey, migratory warblers, and other animals may be observed.

■ **HIKES AND WALKS:** Shell Mound Trail is a special treat on this refuge. Just 0.3 mile long, it leads over the top of a 5-acre shell mound—a 28-foot-tall pile of shells that the ancestors of Timucuan Indians built. The tribe ate oysters and tossed the shells on the mound for 2,500 years. They must have lived upwind from the mound when it was in use, but now it is a solid mass of crushed shells with a growth of trees and bushes. It is the largest shell midden in Florida. The Timucuans who built it disappeared around A.D. 1000.

Suwannee River Boardwalk Trail (0.6 mile) meanders through a shaded, peaceful cypress swamp to a wooden deck overlooking the river, nearly 0.5-mile wide at this point.

Dennis Creek Trail (a 1-mile loop) leaves from the same parking lot as the Shell Mound Trail. It passes through piney woods with palmetto and tall grass (watch for ticks) and then curves around to mudflats with a boardwalk. Look for fiddler crabs, crab-eating birds, and in moist soils try to spot some bird and bobcat tracks.

■ **BOATING:** The three canoe trails take one, two, or three hours at a fast paddle speed, but visitors will want to spend more time than that exploring the creeks and watching alligators and ospreys. Rental canoes are available in the town of Suwannee and at Manatee Springs State Park.

■ **SEASONAL EVENTS:** The refuge observes National Wildlife Week in October and has many environmental education programs. As a relatively new refuge, Lower Suwannee is developing more programs and visitor services.

■ **PUBLICATIONS:** Bird lists, brochures, a canoe trail guide, hunting regulations, and maps—all in the refuge office.

HUNTING AND FISHING If game fishing is your thing, you can try here for **largemouth bass, Suwannee bass, channel catfish, bluegill, redear sunfish** and other freshwater and saltwater varieties. Fishing is allowed year-round. Popular fishing spots include Fishbone and Barnett Creeks (small boat launching and bank), Salt Creek (handicapped-accessible fishing pier), Shired Island (boat launch; handicapped-accessible fishing pier at Shell Mound), and in the towns of Suwannee, Cedar Key, and Fowler's Bluff (public boat launches). From Sept. through Nov., you may hunt **deer** and **wild hog**. **Waterfowl** are in season from Nov. through Jan. You may hunt **small game** in Jan., **raccoons** in Feb., and **wild turkey** in April. Permits are required for all hunting; contact refuge for details.

SATELLITE REFUGE

■ **Cedar Keys NWR** Adjacent to Suwannee on the south coastal corner, Cedar Keys NWR is administered by Lower Suwannee NWR. Established in 1929, this 800-acre cluster of 13 islands protects several rookeries that are closed to the public when the birds are nesting. Large populations of cottonmouth snakes inhabit the islands.

Seahorse Key (at Cedar Keys) has an 1851 lighthouse and is used by the University of Florida as a research station. Usually closed to the public, Seahorse occasionally hosts an open house and environmental education programs for schools. Access to the Cedar Keys NWR is by boat only, but once out there you may roam the beaches except for a 300-yard buffer around Seahorse Key. Atsena Otie Key, closest to the refuge boat launch, has a hiking trail through the interior.

Merritt Island NWR

Titusville, Florida

Merritt Island NWR

The occasional blastoff from nearby NASA launch pads doesn't seem to bother the vast array of wild animals that inhabit this barrier island refuge off the Atlantic coast of Florida. More endangered or threatened species live here than in any other American refuge. These include manatees, bald eagles, scrub jays, five species of sea turtles, and even a beach mouse. The refuge shares Merritt Island with the John F. Kennedy Space Center and Canaveral National Seashore. Although Merritt Island NWR serves as a buffer around two NASA launch complexes, it remains a placid haven for wildlife. It's a refuge as well for visitors, who can canoe in quiet lagoons, hike on one of four trails, cruise a wildlife drive with close-up views of birds, or swim on one of the most beautiful beaches on the Atlantic.

HISTORY

Humans have inhabited these shifting barrier islands for at least 7,000 years, and the ancients have left shell middens and burial mounds as evidence. In 1513, Juan Ponce de Leon landed near Cape Canaveral and met the Timucuan Indians—the first recorded contact between Europeans and native Americans. Ponce de Leon named the islands *Canaveral* for the canes growing there and named the area *Florida* for its abundant flowers. After the English and then the Americans took over Florida, settlers farmed citrus, set up small villages, and subsisted on fish. But the marshes (and their mosquitoes) discouraged settlement, and by the 20th century few people lived on the islands.

In October 1957, the Russians launched Sputnik, sending American scientists into a frenzy of cold war activity to develop a competitive space program. NASA, established as an independent government organization in 1959, bought land here to provide military security for missile-launching sites. Administration of a buffer of salt marshes, oak hammocks, and lagoons was turned over to the U.S. Fish & Wildlife Service for use as a wildlife refuge in 1963. In 1975 the National

Park Service designated Canaveral National Seashore, protecting miles of undeveloped beach in the area.

GETTING THERE

Leave I-95 at Titusville (Exit 80) and drive 3 mi. into Titusville. The refuge Visitor Center is 5 mi. east of town on FL 402. After a bridge over the Intracoastal Waterway, look for an information board about the refuge and the seashore. Then follow signs to the Visitor Center.

■ **SEASON:** Refuge is open all year.

■ **HOURS:** Refuge and National Seashore: daylight hours. Visitor Center: 8 a.m.–4:30 p.m. Mon.–Fri. and 9 a.m.–5 p.m. weekends, closed on federal holidays. April through October: closed on Sundays.

■ **FEES:** Refuge: no fees. Cape Canaveral National Seashore: $5 per car and $1 per pedestrian.

■ **ADDRESS:** Refuge: P.O. Box 6504, Titusville, FL 32782; National Seashore: 308 Julia St., Titusville, FL 32796-3521

■ **TELEPHONE:** Refuge: 407/861-0667; National Seashore: 407/267-1110

TOURING MERRITT ISLAND NWR

■ **BY AUTOMOBILE:** The 7-mile, one-way Black Point Wildlife Drive starts on FL 406 about 1 mile from its intersection with FL 402. There is a leaflet at the Visitor Center describing 11 stops along the drive.

■ **BY FOOT:** There are four trails: a 0.25-mile boardwalk behind the Visitor Center, Cruikshank Trail (5 miles) at Stop 8 on the Wildlife Drive, and Oak Hammock (0.5 mile) and Palm Hammock trails (2.0 miles). The latter two trails start from the same parking lot on FL 402, 1 mile east of the Visitor Center.

■ **BY BICYCLE:** The Wildlife Drive and other roads in the refuge are open to bicycles.

■ **BY CANOE, KAYAK, OR BOAT:** Canoes and small motorboats are allowed on Mosquito Lagoon, the Intracoastal Waterway, and Indian River. Three boat launches on the refuge and two on the National Seashore provide water access. Motorboats may be limited in manatee-protection areas; watch for signs or check at the Visitor Center. NASA security areas are, predictably, closed.

WHAT TO SEE

■ **LANDSCAPE AND CLIMATE** Merritt Island and Cape Canaveral form an elbow-shaped barrier island on the broad, shallow continental shelf of North America. Several such elbows (capes Cod, Hatteras, Lookout, Fear, and Romain) lie north of Cape Canaveral and share geological origins. A combination of ocean currents, westerly winds, and an endless supply of sand causes these capes and barrier islands to develop offshore. The Gulf Stream moves northeastward from the tropics, spawning countercurrents that deposit sand ridges and capes. Barrier islands constantly shift, which is fine for wildlife but not so good for lighthouses and homes. Attempts to stabilize barrier islands with breakwaters, dredging, and renourishment (moving sand to receding beaches) never work; the ocean always wins.

Though fragile, barrier islands protect the mainland; fortunately, our National Seashore, some state parks, and some NWRs preserve many of these islands. The beaches and dunes of Canaveral National Seashore stand guard against the ocean for the lagoons and salt marshes of Merritt Island NWR as well as the NASA launch pads.

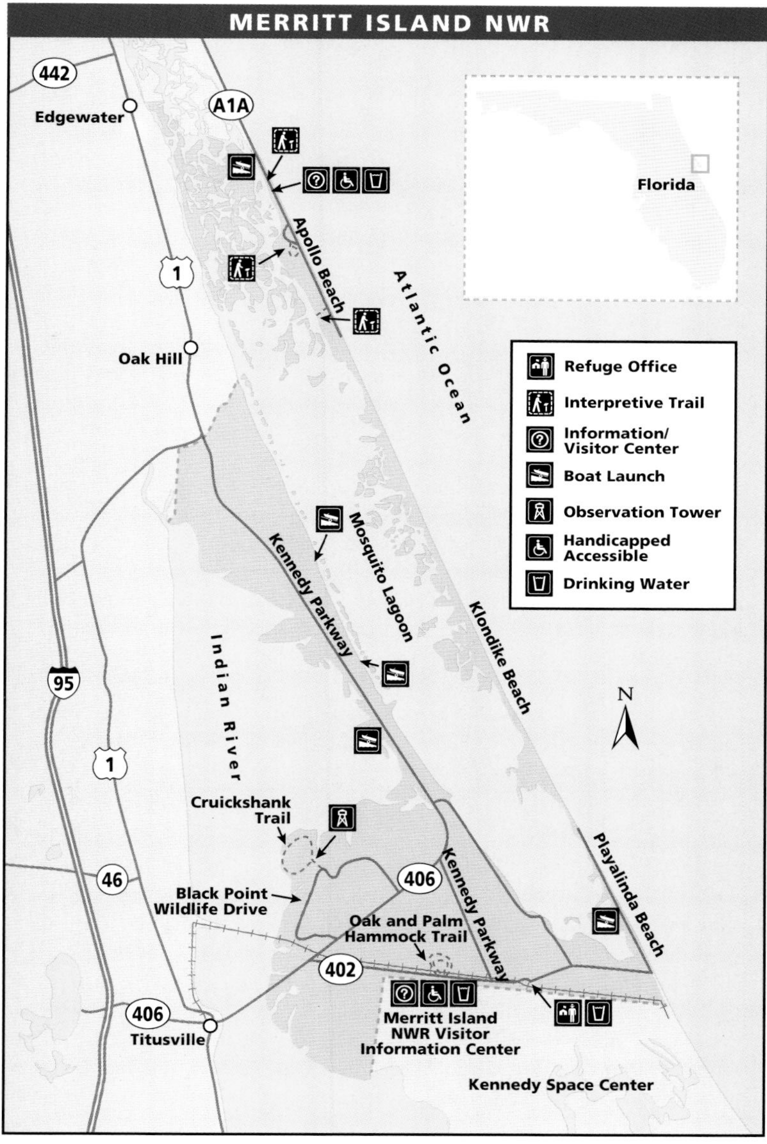

The central Florida coast has hot summers mitigated by ocean breezes. Winters may have cool periods, but some winter days may be warm enough for swimming, and cold-blooded animals may be active here all year.

■ **PLANT LIFE** Almost all the habitats on Merritt NWR are linked, in one way or another, to the proximity of water: salt marsh, lagoons, estuaries, impoundments, beaches, and coastal dunes. A little farther inland, behind the dunes, you will find palm and oak hammocks, pine flatwoods, scrub, and mangrove borders. Manatee and turtle grasses, favorite foods of manatees, grow in the lagoons. Tall and short grasses cluster in and around the impoundments, providing food and

CATCHING IT Let's see.... The ibis is the one with the curved beak and orange legs; the wood stork has a naked head and black legs; and great egrets have yellow beaks and black legs. How do all these knobby-kneed, long-necked birds live in the same place and not compete with each other for food?

Some, such as herons and egrets, stand statue-still with spring-loaded necks. When a fish or frog comes into range, they spear it with sharp bills. Small fish may be grabbed and swallowed. Larger fish (some looking impossible to swallow) must be removed from the spear; the heron may toss it and then grab it or may walk to solid ground, drop it, and then grab it head first.

Spoonbills are feel-feeders. Their spoons have nerves that can detect the slightest movement. They stick their long beaks into the soft mud and shake their heads back and forth while opening and closing their beaks. Whatever wiggles gets eaten. They feed mostly at low tide and often at night.

Wood storks stick their naked heads (the better to shake off water when they come up for air) and stand on one leg. They kick back and forth with the other leg, scaring up fish and invertebrates, and grab them. Wood storks need deep pools with concentrations of prey to succeed at this strange technique; wetland draining may have hurt them more than other species, but alligator holes in swamps work well for them. Ibises, by contrast, prefer crayfish and can feel into crayfish hiding places with their long, curved beaks.

On Merritt Island's Wildlife Drive, patient observation of these feeding strategies and others, as well as of the birds' feedling timetables, will reveal to you how all can survive in the same busy habitat.

shelter for many animals. Still another variety, cordgrass (Spartina), grows to a good height in the salt marshes and contributes to the organic matter in the mud. Nonnative bulrushes, however, have moved in to compete with the grasses in fresh water, requiring periodic saltwater flushing to keep the invader in check.

Red mangroves root on the edges of wetlands and build land that supports black mangroves and other trees needing drier soil. Oaks, pines, cabbage palms, and vines occupy hammocks and pine forests.

The fragile dunes are stabilized by sea oats, sea grapes, saw palmetto, prickly pear (food for gopher tortoises in spite of its wicked spines), and Spanish bayonet. Walking on dunes at Merritt is prohibited for good reason: A person can undo nature's patient, effective work to keep sand in place with just a few errant footsteps. Use the long boardwalks through the dunes for access to the beaches.

Local farmers lease citrus groves on the northern part of the refuge, where they produce the famous Indian River grapefruits and oranges. The lease agreements prohibit farming practices (such as spraying with pesticides) that harm wildlife, which allows local beekeepers to bring their hives into the groves.

Scrub—a dry, sandy habitat similar to desert, well behind the dunes—grows small oaks, wax myrtle, greenbrier, and palmettoes.

Exotic plants create management problems because they displace native plants. The most invasive, the Brazilian pepper tree, was imported to the area by landscapers for use as an ornamental plant. The tree's bright red berries are eaten by birds, who then scatter them far and wide. Another invasive exotic, the Australian pine, was brought over from Australia by citrus growers and planted as windbreaks around the fruit groves.

■ ANIMAL LIFE

Birds Merritt holds the record among NWRs for greatest number of bird species on one property: At least 300 types of birds live here or migrate through. Many big wading birds—wood storks, roseate spoonbills, ibises, great blue and tricolored herons, and egrets—can be seen along the Black Point Wildlife Drive and elsewhere in the marshes. Impoundments and scattered deep pools near the road make close observation especially easy.

Bald eagles, looking fierce and powerful, nest on the tops of pine trees or on high platforms. At Stop 8 of the Wildlife Drive, look for eagle nests and for eagles flying. More than 100 eaglets have fledged from this area since 1970, a large number for this species. Ospreys nest here also.

Gallinule feeding in duckweed

Ducks, grebes, and gallinules (aka moorhens) swim in the impoundments along the drive. Black skimmers fly close to the water and slice through it with their lower mandible (about one-third longer than its upper one), catching unwary surface fish. Big flights of beach birds, such as sandpipers, willets, dowitchers, and plovers, probe the mudflats when they are not dodging the waves on the beach. Most birdwatchers call all these birds "peeps" because they are hard to tell apart.

Endangered Florida scrub jays—which have blue heads, wings, and tails—breed on the refuge. It takes a colony to raise a scrub jay: Several birds, especially older siblings, pitch in. These handsome colonial nesters need large territories. Much of their original habitat is now citrus groves or residences. Along the brushy banks of canals, flocks of robins, Carolina wrens, cedar waxwings, and other small migratory birds alight. There is also one dark story here in birdland: Merritt Island salt marshes were once the home of the dusky seaside sparrow, a bird declared extinct when the last one, a male, died in captivity in December 1990.

Mammals The largest mammal here (West Indian manatee) and the smallest (southeastern beach mouse) are both endangered because of loss of habitat. Manatees swim and feed in the sanctuary area of the Banana River and in no-motor zones. Most Florida manatees have motorboat scars on their backs, and many die of the wounds. Since motorboats were banned in certain locations on the refuge in 1990, the refuge manatee population has risen dramatically, along with fish and invertebrate populations. There is a manatee-observation platform with interpretive signs at Haulover Canal on Kennedy Parkway. Dolphins also visit the lagoons and estuaries.

Bobcats, deer, river otters, marsh rabbits (with cinnamon-brown fur and rounded ears), squirrels, and raccoons wander the refuge. Feral hogs, who are uninvited guests, compete with native animals for food.

Reptiles and amphibians Between May and August, the beaches of Merritt NWR and Canaveral National Seashore provide safe nesting spots for loggerhead, leatherback, and green sea turtles, whose hatchlings emerge about 60 days later. Rangers and volunteers protect the nests with wire mesh to keep hungry raccoons out. They also record hatching success to find out which management strategies work best. The area is closed at night except for special nature programs.

Soft-shelled and slider turtles live in freshwater impoundments. Gopher tortoises do as much as refuge managers to support some threatened species. These tortoises dig deep, roomy burrows (wide enough for a tortoise to turn around in and up to 35 feet long) where many nondiggers—indigo snakes, rattlesnakes, gopher frogs, burrowing owls, mice, lizards, and insects—find shelter.

Look for alligators basking in the sun on embankments and along roadsides behind the Visitor Center. Anolis lizards, common frogs and toads, and various other small reptiles and amphibians live on the refuge.

The threatened eastern indigo snake, a shiny blue-black, can reach 7 or 8 feet in length (the longest snake in Florida!) and has a healthy population here. The indigo eats mammals, birds, frogs, cottonmouths, and rattlesnakes (many of which share its habit of retreating to gopher tortoise burrows). You might hear the nonvenomous indigo rattling its tail when disturbed in a convincing imitation of venomous snakes.

Fish Fishing from canoes and small motorboats is popular in the brackish waters of the lagoons and wide rivers of the refuge—but not in protected manatee areas. Fish commonly caught on the refuge include sea trout and redfish.

Gopher tortoise

Invertebrates As you would expect in such a watery world, many species of crab, shrimp, oyster, and clam live and breed on the refuge. Zebra longwings, butterflies whose wings are longer than they are wide, feed on flowering shrubs along with other moths and butterflies.

Zebra longwing butterfly

And here's an irony to be thankful for: At least 23 species of mosquitoes breed and thrive in salt- and freshwater habitats. Salt-marsh mosquitoes, with nasty biting habits, help to reduce spreading suburban development. However, impoundments and water control, favoring other wildlife, now interrupt their life cycle. Beach breezes deter the mosquitoes, but the sheltered areas behind the dunes have robust populations. If you're exploring those areas, whether you're canoeing or hiking, use insect repellent.

ACTIVITIES

■ **CAMPING:** Camping is not allowed on the refuge. Camping at the National Seashore is by permit only in the backcountry or offered on a first-come, first-served basis in designated campsites. Brevard County has campgrounds, including Jetty Park in the town of Cape Canaveral, south of the Kennedy Space Center.

■ **SWIMMING:** Visitors can swim, beachcomb, or surf on the National Seashore. There are restrooms and parking at Playalinda and Apollo Beaches; access to Klondike Beach is by foot. Beach access may be closed when parking lots are full or when NASA has scheduled rocket launches.

■ **WILDLIFE OBSERVATION AND PHOTOGRAPHY:** Black Point Wildlife Drive affords close views of many birds with various backgrounds. Bald eagles and ospreys are easy to observe as they nest in spring. Staying in your car or using it as a blind works well.

Canoeing in the lagoon and estuaries provides a different opportunity to approach wildlife quietly. But if your activities disturb manatees or resting birds, move away. Stay at least 15 to 20 feet away from alligators; they will remind you of the wisdom of this advice by opening their sawtooth jaws or by snorting. Gopher tortoises and marsh rabbits will continue to graze nearby if you move slowly. Despite their stumpy legs, the tortoises can lumber off at a surprising speed.

■ **HIKES AND WALKS:** For a stroll through a wetland and an oak hammock, try the short (0.25 mile) boardwalk behind the Visitor Center. It is wheelchair- and stroller-accessible and may provide a look at alligators and migratory birds. Anolis lizards may appear on the palmettoes; sometimes they scamper to the other side of a frond, but you can still spy their silhouette.

Oak Hammock Trail (0.5 mile) and Palm Hammock Trail (2 miles) share a parking lot located 1 mile beyond the Visitor Center. Mostly boardwalk, these trails wind through shady woods with black gum, black mangrove, and cabbage palms. Look for the little air tubes sticking up from the ground; these tubes are called pneumatophors, through which the water-soaked mangrove roots "breathe." There are interpretive signs along the way. Open areas overlook salt marsh, where crabs and wading birds may be seen. The shade is welcome on a hot day, but, alas, the mosquitoes like it too.

Cruikshank Trail (5 miles) starts and ends at Stop 8 of the Black Point Wildlife Drive, making a loop on dikes past marshes, canals, and brushy borders. Birds seen from afar on the wildlife drive can sometimes be seen here, up close, if you proceed quietly. The trail is exposed to full sunshine except for a few trees, so morning or evening may be best. Brazilian pepper grows along the dikes; leather fern and prickly pear are common, and gopher tortoises may be out to eat it. Fire ants are just waiting for an unwary someone to step on their gray, sandy mounds. An observation tower near the Cruikshank trailhead overlooks the marsh and a canal; from here, look for anhingas, marsh rabbits, and some of the smaller herons.

HUNTING AND FISHING Fishing from canoes and small motorboats is popular in the brackish waters of the lagoons and wide rivers of the refuge—but not in protected manatee areas. Fishing is allowed year-round, and species commonly caught on the refuge include **sea trout** and **redfish**.

You may hunt **ducks** and **coots** in accordance with state regulations, in Jan. only. There are separate seasons for the two waterfowl; contact the refuge for exact dates.

■ **SEASONAL EVENTS:** May: International Migratory Bird Celebration, beach cleanup; June and July: Ranger-led sea-turtle watches; October: National Wildlife Refuge celebration; summer and fall: scheduled waterfowl hunting and fishing events.

■ **PUBLICATIONS:** Manatee Observation Area pamphlet; bird checklist; Black Point (Wildlife) Drive guide. *Merritt Island NWR,* an attractive book with outstanding photographs, the third in a series of NWR books from the Public Lands Interpretive Association; ask for it at the Visitor Center.

SATELLITE REFUGES

■ **Pelican Island NWR** On March 14, 1903, President Teddy Roosevelt launched the National Wildlife Refuge System by protecting the tiny, 5.5-acre Pelican Island. Before the refuge designation, plume hunters shot pelicans, egrets, roseate spoonbills, and herons in rookeries here, which are usually exposed on the tops of trees. Pelican Island struck conservationists as important also because sea turtles nest on the refuge, and manatees graze in the warm waters.

But the new concept of a nature preserve did not register with everyone immediately in 1903. Early conservationists hired Paul Kroegel as warden for $7 a month. When plume hunters approached the island, he rushed out and shot over their bows. Now, that's wildlife management! Many rookeries had already been destroyed, but a few brown pelicans remained, and, with continued protection, the other birds came back.

Today, Pelican Island NWR has additional honors: National Historic Landmark, National Wilderness Area, and Wetland of International Importance. The refuge has also expanded to encompass 5,000 acres of wetlands and open water. Though Pelican is accessible only by boat, the refuge is adding more visitor services, such as a viewing tower, an information display, restrooms, and trails. Inquire in Sebastian for boat trips to Pelican Island.

■ Archie Carr NWR Twenty miles long and only 108 acres, this slender refuge is nonetheless wide enough to provide nesting habitat for 20,000 loggerhead and green sea turtles a year—one-fourth of all the sea turtles nesting in the United States. Archie Carr is 5 miles south of Melbourne Beach on FL A1A.

Named for a biologist who devoted his life to sea-turtle research and protection, the refuge was established in 1990. There are no visitor services, but the beach is open to hiking and swimming. Refuge managers control night use of the beach to protect turtles from predators and present interpretive programs and turtle watches.

■ St. Johns NWR Just west of Titusville, St. Johns NWR is open to visitors by permit only, but it plans more public access in the future.

Brown pelican

■ Lake Wales Ridge NWR With four tracts of scrubland on ridges and sand dunes, Lake Wales Ridge NWR was the first refuge established (1990) for the protection of endangered plants and wildlife and scrub communities. More land acquisition and visitor facilities are planned, but currently there is no public use except for a birding festival in March and a Scrub Appreciation Day (perhaps the only such event in the world) in October. If you visit, look for the unusual sand skink—a small, streamlined lizard with one toe on each front foot, two toes on each back foot, and a window in his eyelids. Sand skinks "swim" through the sand and eat termites.

St. Marks NWR

St. Marks, Florida

Queen butterfly, monarch family

Hiking, birds, and monarch butterflies—three excellent reasons to visit St. Marks NWR. But there's more: canoeing, wildlife observation, environmental education, and a lighthouse with ospreys sitting on top. Curving for 35 miles along the Florida Panhandle coast, this 70,000-acre refuge includes 43 miles of the Florida Trail, seven rivers, and wonderful place names like Sopchoppy, Panacea, Ochlockonee (the third "o" is silent), and Purifying Creek. Many species of birds nest here, and migratory birds refuel going to or from Mexico and points south. The size and diversity of habitats at St. Marks provide living space for many other species of plants and animals.

HISTORY

Florida's panhandle has been inhabited for more than 10,000 years (an archaeologist's dream), as evident from sites such as shell mounds and ancient dwellings. Spanish explorers found the Apalache Indians here in the 1500s, and this gave rise to the name "Appalachia" for the lands and mountains to the north. The Spaniards built Fort San Marcos on the St. Marks River but weren't able to defend it, losing all of Florida eventually. By 1839 American sea commerce demanded a St. Marks Lighthouse, and the tower still warns ships in the Gulf today. During the Civil War, the Confederates needed salt to preserve food during the army's long marches; they excused coastal farmers and fishermen from the draft to produce the salt by distilling sea water. Resistance by coastal residents (possibly the salt workers) prevented the Union from reaching Tallahassee, the only southern capital east of the Mississippi not taken by the North.

After the war, the panhandle was logged and farmed for several generations. President Herbert Hoover established St. Marks refuge in 1931. Other units were added in 1937 and 1938, and part of the refuge was designated as Wilderness in 1975. Refuge staff would like to expand the refuge today by purchase from willing landowners to provide more habitat for wildlife, create better corridors for wildlife movement, and prevent disturbance and construction near critical habitats.

GETTING THERE

St. Marks NWR is about 20 mi. south of Tallahassee. Take FL 363 south to Wakulla Station. Turn left on FL 267 and drive about 4 mi. to US 98 at Newport. Look for refuge signs on Lighthouse Rd. (CR 59) and drive 3 mi. to the Visitor Center. From the east or west, take US 98 to Newport and turn south on Lighthouse Rd. as above.

■ **SEASON:** Refuge open all year.

■ **HOURS:** Daylight hours for refuge; Visitor Center open 8:15 a.m.–4 p.m., Mon.–Fri.; 10 a.m.–5 p.m., weekends. Closed on federal holidays.

■ **FEES:** Federal entrance fee passes, annual passes, or daily admission.

■ **ADDRESS:** P.O. Box 68, St. Marks, FL 32355

■ **TELEPHONE:** 850/925-6121

TOURING ST. MARKS

■ **BY AUTOMOBILE:** A refuge wildlife drive (7 miles) is a paved road through impoundments and wilderness salt marsh down to Apalachee Bay. Restrooms and picnic areas are available near the lighthouse.

■ **BY FOOT:** Eight day hikes wind or loop through the three parts of the refuge. These and 43 miles of the Florida Trail add up to 75 miles of hiking. Other walks include a short hike and boardwalk behind the Visitor Center, marked trails along Lighthouse Rd., and open paths along the many dikes and levees. Signs may indicate that some areas are closed between October 15 and March 15 to protect wintering or nesting birds.

■ **BY BICYCLE:** The 7-mile drive from the Visitor Center to the lighthouse can be used by bicycles, with many places to stop and view waterfowl and other wildlife. Other paved and unpaved roads on the refuge are also open for biking.

■ **BY CANOE, KAYAK, OR BOAT:** Canoes and other boats can be launched at the lighthouse, at Panacea, at Aucilla River, and at the end of the Wakulla Beach Rd. Canoes and kayaks can be used on any of the rivers, and sea kayaking is possible, but some areas may be restricted. Canoes can be rented from outfitters near St. Marks Refuge.

WHAT TO SEE

■ **LANDSCAPE AND CLIMATE** St. Marks NWR extends 2 to 4 miles inland from the Gulf coast and includes a large variety of typical coastal habitats: bay, dune, brackish estuary, saltwater and freshwater marsh, cypress swamp, pine forest, hardwood hammocks, longleaf pine sandhills, and springs and rivers. Dikes and levees create impoundments attracting both migrating and nesting waterfowl. Cooler than the more southern parts of Florida, this refuge still gets very hot in summer, and the extensive wetlands breed plenty of mosquitoes (whose main role in the ecosystem is, of course, not to bite people but to feed larvae, bats, and small fish). Gulf breezes cool the beach areas. Fall, winter, and spring are the best times to view wildlife, because most animals also have the good sense to avoid hot sun. However, summer morning and evening hikes or bike rides may reveal basking snakes and alligators and feeding birds.

■ **PLANT LIFE** Diversity of habitats leads to a great diversity of plants. Underwater grasses wave in the water of the bay, and highly productive saw grass and sedges live in the marshes. Islands scattered throughout the marshes harbor slash pines and patches of cabbage palms. Cypress swamps, a little higher than the open marshes, hold water and grow cypress trees along with maple and black gum. Clinging to crevices in the tree bark are epiphytic orchids, Spanish moss, and spiny-leaved bromeliads (tropical or subtropical plants related to pineapples); they collect water and nutrients from their own root masses. In the swamps and other wet areas, you can hunt for blooming duck potatoes, water lilies, pitcher plants, bladderworts, and sundews.

Forests here are equally diverse. Longleaf pines, a species more common before European settlement, live in flatlands and sandhills. Prescribed burns help these trees to compete with invading oaks, and fire helps to stimulate pine seed germination. To identify saw palmetto, walk in the flatlands and look for stiff, sharp spines along the tree's stalks. Live oaks with resurrection ferns on horizontal branches root on hammocks along with other hardwoods.

Along the dikes (good for walking), lantana, yucca, and prickly pear cactus bloom. As a special treat for visitors from northern states, spring wildflowers start blooming in February.

■ ANIMAL LIFE

Birds Serious and casual birders make pilgrimages to St. Marks, toting cameras, life lists, and spotting scopes to see many of the nearly 300 species of birds reported on the refuge. Some migratory birds from the northern United States and Canada spend the winter here, while others stop to feed for energy to cross the Gulf of Mexico.

Bitterns and rails nest in the marshes, but it takes patience and persistence to see them because they successfully pretend to be grasses. Great blue, tricolored, and little blue herons and ibises wait singly to spear fish, while grebes and gallinules swim alone or in small groups. Anhingas, or snake birds, dive to catch fish and then hang themselves up to dry on branches.

Red-headed woodpecker

Ducks keep birders busy, too. Eight or 10 species form large, noisy rafts that you can either enjoy looking at or try desperately to identify. Wood ducks nest on the refuge and don't seem as likely to associate with the other ducks that are just passing through.

Turn your binoculars to the tops of tall, isolated trees to search for bald eagles nesting on complex piles of sticks; these birds don't mind being watched. Thirteen nests produced 13 fledglings of this threatened bird in 1995. In wooded areas, look for smaller birds: cardinals, brown thrashers, Carolina wrens, catbirds, and towhees.

Many migratory warblers and other songbirds pass through the refuge in mid-April. Pileated, red-headed, and red-bellied woodpeckers nest in the pine

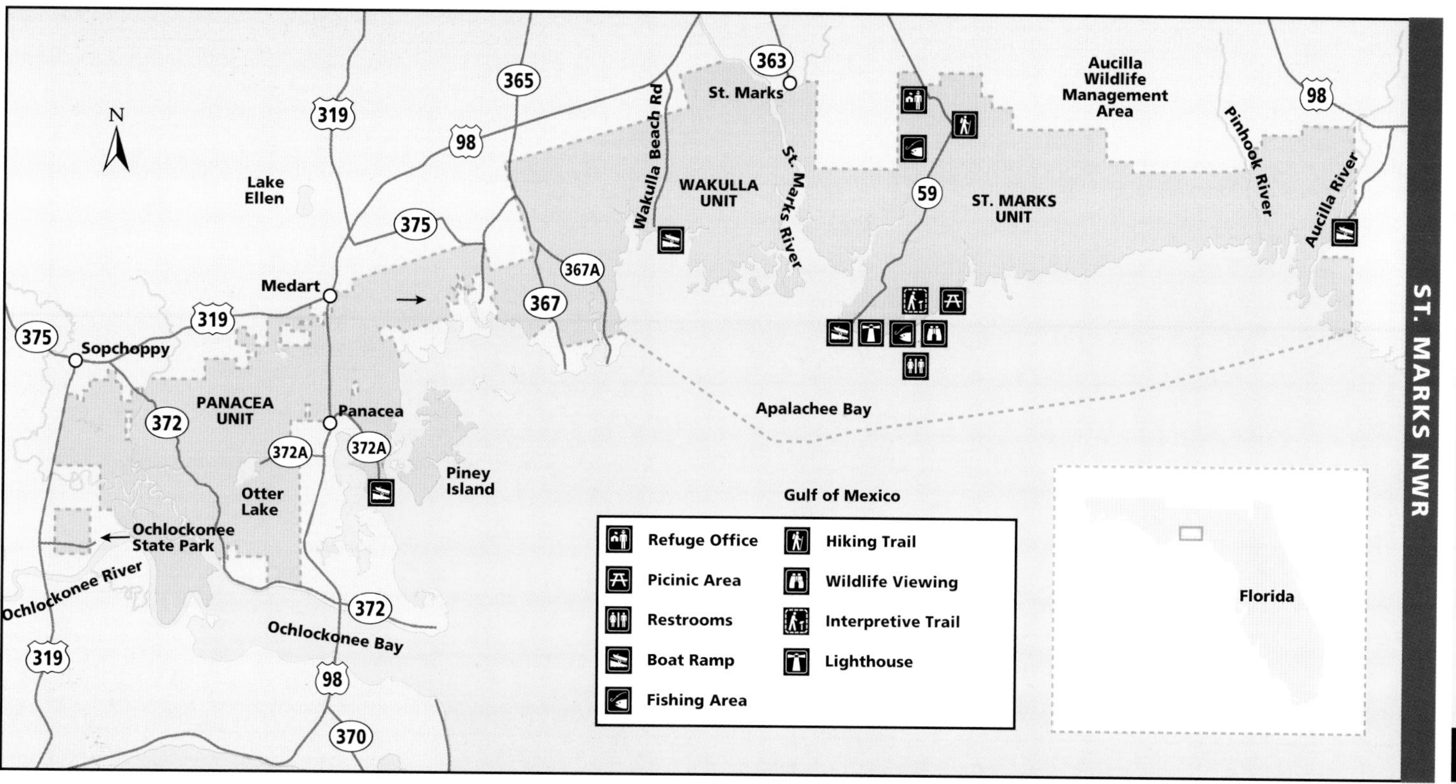
ST. MARKS NWR
N
Lake Ellen
Medart
Sopchoppy
PANACEA UNIT
Panacea
Otter Lake
Piney Island
Ochlockonee State Park
Ochlockonee River
Ochlockonee Bay
Wakulla Beach Rd
WAKULLA UNIT
St. Marks
St. Marks River
ST. MARKS UNIT
Aucilla Wildlife Management Area
Pinhook River
Aucilla River
Apalachee Bay
Gulf of Mexico
Florida
319
98
365
363
375
367A
367
59
372
372A
370
Refuge Office
Picinic Area
Restrooms
Boat Ramp
Fishing Area
Hiking Trail
Wildlife Viewing
Interpretive Trail
Lighthouse

woods, as well as the endangered red-cockaded woodpecker and a few other small species. Pelicans and several species of gulls can be seen near the bay, and ospreys frequent the lighthouse. Occasionally the refuge staff offers night walks to see—or hear—owls, nightjars, whip-poor-wills, and nighthawks.

Needless to say, St. Marks is a haven for birds and birders. Simply pick up a bird list at the Visitor Center, and soon you'll be tracking a young osprey's flying lessons or watching a wood duck performing a mating dance.

Mammals Mammals do not take a backseat to birds at St. Marks. Deer, bear, raccoon, opossum, bat, fox, and squirrel are among the 52 species recorded here. Visit the pond behind the Visitor Center or any of the impoundments for a chance to see otters fishing. Bobcats venture out into open areas to catch crabs; look for their tracks on mudflats. West Indian manatees may be seen in warm waters from the lighthouse area in summer, but they usually don't come close to shore.

There are interlopers, too: Nonnative feral hogs, jaguarundis (a Mexican wildcat), and the recently arrived armadillo occupy wooded areas, although the armadillos also seem to like crossing roads.

Reptiles and amphibians The most visible amphibians are American alligators. In marshes and open water, their corrugated backs look like old tire retreads. Gopher tortoises live in burrows but are sometimes seen eating vegetation. Because they dig deep, homey burrows, other less-talented reptiles often slither down there with them. Twenty-one species of frogs and toads present a good challenge for people who want to recognize amphibian songs and calls. About the same number of salamanders are present, but, except for the occasional newt, they remain hidden most of the time. Anolis lizards, racerunners, fence lizards, and skinks can be seen sunning on the boardwalks.

Among snakes, more than 30 species hide or bask in the refuge, including the threatened indigo snake and water, rat, garter, corn, pine, king, hognose, and ring-

Carnivorous sundew, feeding on bluet damselfly

neck snakes. Venomous snakes here include coral snakes, cottonmouths, pygmy rattlesnakes, and diamondback rattlesnakes.

There are many turtle species, too, including four types of sea turtles that sea kayakers and people on shore with binoculars may spot out in the bay. All told, about 100 species of reptiles and amphibians call St. Marks home, and populations are relatively stable.

Invertebrates The migration of monarch butterflies are a special attraction at St. Marks in fall. These 1-gram wonders gather here to collect nectar from lantana, goldenrod, and clover to fuel up for the last big leg of their migration to Mexico; some fly along the coast and others fly across the Gulf. Though they don't volunteer, some of them also collect a tiny identification tag on a wing so biologists can monitor their populations and their fantastic journey. Other butterflies include fritillaries, sulfurs, and swallowtails.

On the shoreline, blue crabs are popular with human and avian crabbers. You will see fiddler crabs dash into burrows on mud flats at the slightest disturbance. Salt marshes and sea grasses shelter the larvae of shrimp, oysters, and many other invertebrates that are important to the economy and to the marine food chain.

ACTIVITIES

■ **CAMPING:** Camping in the refuge is allowed only for long-distance hikers on the Florida National Scenic Trail; permits are required for the six campsites. However, there are many camping areas nearby outside the refuge (ask headquarters for a list).

■ **WILDLIFE OBSERVATION:** Mornings and evenings are excellent times to look for wildlife, but in this refuge, with its abundance of species and its open viewing areas, there is plenty to see at any time. Start with a drive along Lighthouse Rd.; then choose among the many short or long hikes. An observation

CARNIVOROUS PLANTS Plants absorb minerals from the soil and make their own food. At least that's how it's supposed to work. Some plants, however, digest meat (fly meat, gnat meat, and so on) to get minerals. The carnivorous plants on southeastern refuges live in acidic wetlands where minerals are scarce, except on the wing. Their leaves catch flying or crawling mineral packages. Pitcher plant leaves form rain-filled tubes with nectar glands and bright colors. Victims land and slide into a digestive enzyme bath. Bristles around the mouth of the tube point downward and prevent escape.

Carnivorous bladderworts open their sesame-seed-sized sacs when worms or mosquito larvae happen by, sucking them inside.

Sundews, common in roadside ditches and on sphagnum moss, secrete globs of glue and enzymes on the ends of stiff hairs. When an unsuspecting insect, attracted by red color and delicious scents, touches a glob, the other globs turn toward it, Tar Baby–style, digesting as they go.

The Venus's-flytrap also attracts prey with color and scent. Red bristled leaves close like a clam shell when an insect touches trigger hairs on the inside. After enzymes do their work, the shell opens and dumps the shriveled remains.

Sounds charming, right? Remember, many humans are carnivores, too. Have a nice swamp walk, and be sure to smell the flowers.

tower near the lighthouse affords long-distance views, but the lighthouse itself is currently closed except for special programs.

■ **PHOTOGRAPHY:** The deck behind the Visitor Center, the open areas along Lighthouse Rd. and at the lighthouse, and the walks along the dikes provide easy-access photography spots. Animals are accustomed to slowly moving or stopped cars, so you may have plenty of time to take pictures through an open car window before the subject flaps or slithers away.

■ **HIKES AND WALKS:** St. Marks is the only NWR with a segment of the Florida National Scenic Trail (FNST), which crosses the refuge east to west. FNST winds through all three units of the refuge, taking hikers through areas unavailable to car-bound visitors. Parking areas allow hikers to do day hikes on portions of the Trail. Some FNST campsites are closed during hunting seasons.

Raccoon, fishing

Eight other loop or connecting trails—well marked, quiet, and usually private—link all the habitats. A hiking guide with maps and regulations is a must; buy one at the Visitor Center. Shorter trails have self-guiding pamphlets.

■ **SEASONAL EVENTS:** Among other special events (call for details) there are these highlights. April: Welcome Back Songbirds Festival and Spring Wildflower Days; May: Welcome Back Manatee Festival and Lighthouse Open House; October: National Wildlife Refuge Week, Monarch Butterfly Weekend; November to January: Winter Duck Tours.

■ **PUBLICATIONS:** Brochures; species lists (birds, mammals, reptiles, amphibians, flowers, and more); trail guide (about $1.00); guide to the wildlife drive (small charge). The bookstore provides a good selection of guidebooks and other relevant publications. St. Marks has an active environmental education program, and information booklets for teachers are available on request as well as booklets and a fact sheet written for elementary-school children containing wildlife details, descriptions, and games.

SATELLITE REFUGE

■ **St. Vincent NWR** Located on a Gulf coast barrier island, the refuge lies southwest of the town of Apalachicola on US 98. The Visitor Center is in Apalachicola, but access to the refuge is by boat. There are 14 miles of beaches and 80 miles of roads and trails for day use only. Endangered sea turtles nest on the beaches, and many of the same species of birds found at St. Marks breed or migrate here. A population of endangered red wolves has been established, and it supplies wolves for introduction elsewhere. Previous owners transplanted a herd of Asian sambar deer to the island.

Okefenokee NWR

Folkston, Georgia

Wetland prairie, Okefenokee NWR

Okefenokee Swamp does an outstanding job of protecting its denizens while providing wonderful opportunities for visitors to glimpse animals and experience a feel of ancient wilderness. This 438,000-acre wetlands, whose Indian name means "Land of Trembling Earth," lies in the southeastern corner of Georgia, 40 miles inland from the Atlantic Ocean. The 396,000-acre Okefenokee NWR includes most of the swamp in south Georgia, extending also a short way into Florida. American alligators, black bears, sandhill cranes, migrating ducks and myriad other birds, and a wide variety of other animals have free range in Okefenokee Swamp. Humans, though, must stay within certain limits. Visitors can view wildlife from canoes, small motorboats, boardwalks, perimeter trails, and short walks on sandy islands. Designated paddling trails, just wider than a canoe, wind through shady cypress forests. The boardwalks give access to great open prairies (tallgrass areas on watery peat beds) where cranes and egrets walk easily, but a person would sink into the mud. This trembling earth and mysterious black water once harbored Indians, escaped slaves, and settlers but now receives several hundred thousand visitors each year who come to observe and marvel.

HISTORY

Okefenokee Swamp formed about 250,000 years ago as the Atlantic Ocean shifted eastward. Most of the newly exposed land became sloping coastal plain, but 100-mile Trail Ridge, a north-south former barrier island, created a large saucer-shaped depression just north of the present border between Georgia and Florida. Fresh water collected in the shallow depression, and six to eight thousand years ago sphagnum moss and other small plants formed peat, a mass of decaying organic matter that eventually supported a wide variety of plant life. Peat holds water from seasonal rainfall like a sponge, so that the swamp remains wet all year.

The first human settlers were probably the Deptford Indians of 2,500 years

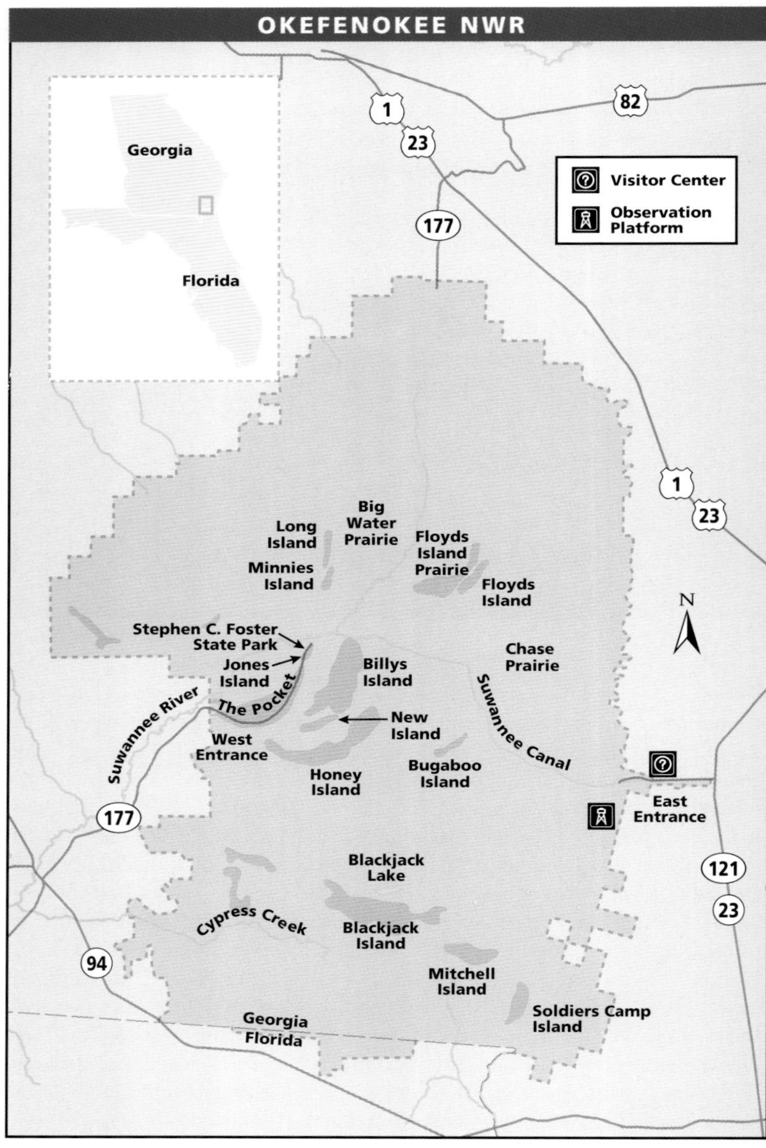

ago. Sometime around 1500, the Seminoles, a branch of the Creek Indians, moved into the swamp; they were the swamp's occupants when European settlers arrived. The usual conflicts arose, and in 1850, General Charles Floyd led soldiers into the swamp to remove the Indians to Oklahoma or points west. The Indians, of course, knew the swamp well and were determined not be captured. Government troops floundered in the mud while the Seminoles, led by Chief Billy Bowlegs, escaped south out of Okefenokee and resettled in the swamps of south Florida.

A few farmers and trappers moved into Okefenokee Swamp, and a drainage canal was attempted in the 1890s. Five years of digging resulted in about 11 miles of man-made canal. But the project was abandoned after the company went bankrupt. The next assault on the swamp was by logging companies, who would lay railroad track on pilings driven through the peat to the firm sand below. They cut the massive cypresses and other trees. Cypress wood was especially valuable because of its strength and resistance to rot. By the 1930s, most of the swamp had been overlogged, but, luckily, a few patches of remote old-growth forest remained as a refuge for plants and animals that could someday repopulate the swamp. In 1937, the property was purchased from the Hebard Lumber Company by the U.S. government for inclusion in the National Wildlife Refuge system. State parks, state forests, and private efforts have protected areas surrounding the wildlife refuge. In 1974 the refuge was designated as a Wilderness Area, increasing its protection. A current threat to the refuge is a strip mining proposal by DuPont to dredge for titanium on the eastern edge of Trail Ridge. Ecologists fear that, even with good reclamation efforts, this project will upset the delicate water balance of the swamp. The mining is currently on hold, but DuPont owns the mineral rights, and the issue may crop up again.

GETTING THERE

The NWR office and Visitor Center are on the east side of the refuge. From Folkston, GA, take Rte. 121/23 south for 8 mi. to the entrance sign and then 3 mi. to the Visitor Center. For information about guided tours, boat rental, and open hours for the trails and boardwalks, call the refuge office.

There are two other entrances to Okefenokee, one on private land and one at a state park. Canoe trips from both lead into NWR areas. The north entrance is at Okefenokee Swamp Park, a nonprofit organization. From Waycross, GA, take Rte. 1 for 10 mi. south. Address: Okefenokee Swamp Park, Waycross, GA, 31501; 912-283-0583. There is an entrance fee.

Swamp scene, Okefenokee NWR

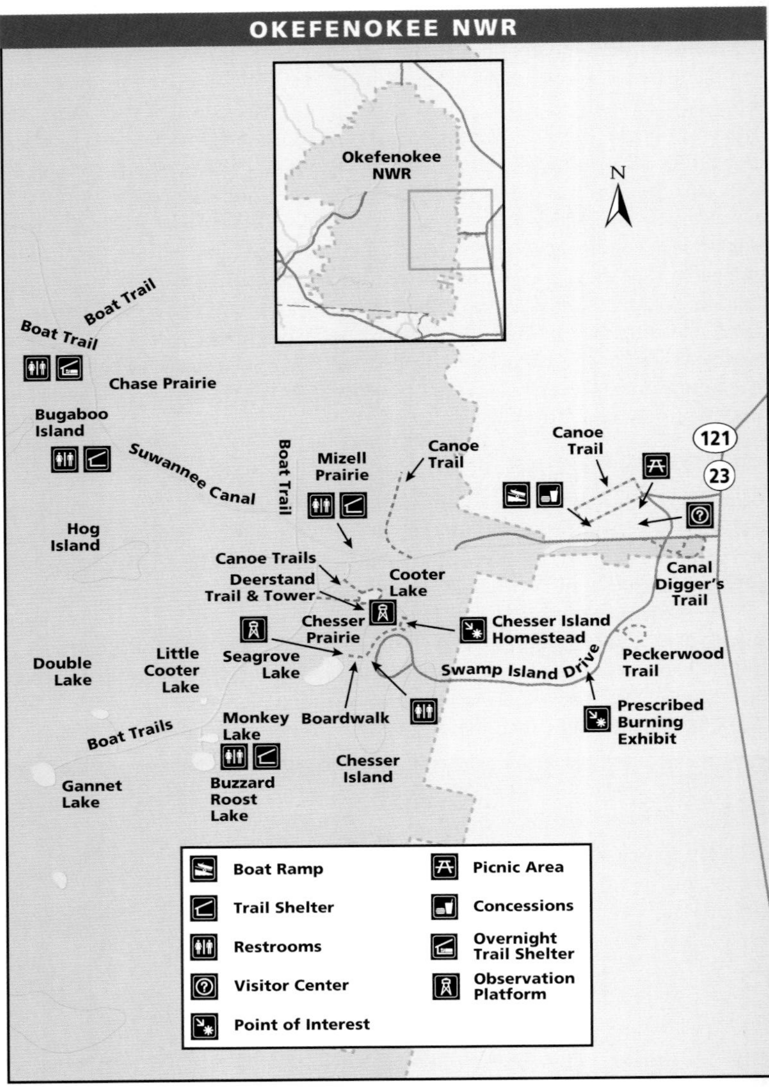

The west entrance lies near Fargo, GA, and houses Stephen Foster State Park. Take Rte. 94 south from Fargo to Spur Rd. 177 and turn left. Address: Stephen Foster State Park, Fargo, GA, 31631; 912-637-5274. There are entrance fees, rental cabins, a campground, and boat rentals. The state park office administers overnight wilderness canoe camping on the refuge by advanced reservation and permit.

■ **SEASON:** Refuge is open year-round except Christmas Day.

■ **HOURS:** The refuge office is open from 7 a.m.–3:30 p.m. on weekdays, and the Visitor Center is open 9 a.m.–5 p.m. every day except Christmas.

■ **FEES:** $5 per vehicle at the east entrance.

■ **ADDRESS:** Okefenokee National Wildlife Refuge, Rte. 2, Box 3330, Folkston, GA 31537; 912/496-7836

UP CLOSE AND PERSONAL *Hundreds of Alligators are to be seen, floating like logs. Huge flocks, seemingly of the large Wood Ibis [wood stork], muddy the waters as they wade about and strike the fishes with their bills. Here are the blue herons, the hoarsely crying sandhill cranes, the anhingas, or snakebirds, perched on dead branches, and the fishing cormorants. Buzzards wait patiently, like a mourning train, for the banks to dry and leave food for them. Against the horizon a Bald Eagle overtakes a Wood Duck, singled out from clouds of them that had been bred in the district. Then it is that you hear the Alligator at his work, in a deep spot which the hunter calls the Alligators' Hole, where they lie close together, stir about, splash, and, on missing a catch, throw the fish up into the air by a lash of their tails. So truly gentle are they at this season that I have waded through such lakes with no more than a stick in one hand to drive them off if they attempted to attack. The first time I tried moving along up to my waist in this way I felt, I admit, great uneasiness in the midst of, sometimes, hundreds of these animals. But the companion and experienced hunter who led the way banished my fears. After a few days I thought nothing of it. There is no danger, if one goes toward the head of the Alligator which, before it will attack the fearless man, swims instead after a dog, Deer, or horse.*

—John James Audubon, *Journal* (1826)

TOURING OKEFENOKEE

■ **BY AUTOMOBILE:** The 9-mile round-trip Swamp Island Wildlife Observation Drive starts near the NWR Visitor Center.

■ **BY FOOT:** Walking trails keep to the edge of the swamp or follow paths on sandy islands. Near the Refuge Visitor Center is a 0.75-mile boardwalk with an observation tower, and there's a short walk to the Chesser Island Homestead. The Chessers lived in the swamp from 1828 until the 1920s, growing sugarcane and collecting turpentine for sale while subsisting on hunting, other farming, and gathering honey. The restored homestead displays tools such as fans and brooms made of native materials like saw palmetto.

■ **BY BICYCLE:** Rental bikes are not available, but bikes can be used along the entrance roads, on the 9-mile Swamp Island Drive and around the Stephen Foster State Park campground. Watch for the mounds of fire ants in the roadside grass and alligators in the drainage ditches.

■ **BY CANOE:** Canoe trails cross the lakes and wind through the cypress stands. It is possible to paddle from the east entrance, by permit only. Reservations are required to camp along the way. Rental canoes are available at the east entrance and Stephen Foster State Park. Guided boat tours are given at all three entrances; call for schedules and reservations. Okefenokee Pastimes Campground is right outside of the east entrance.

WHAT TO SEE

■ **LANDSCAPE AND CLIMATE** Okefenokee Swamp has four types of habitat: open-water lakes, sandy permanent islands, cypress "houses," and open wet grassy prairies. Except for the sandy islands, a thick layer of peat lies under each habitat. Because it holds huge amounts of water, the layer of peat gives the swamp stability, but it also fosters continual changes in land form, creating the "trembling earth" that gave Okefenokee its name. Anaerobic decay deep in the peat causes methane gas to push parts of the layer upward, and plants flourish on the resultant mounds. Some of these mounds subside into the muck again, while others support cypresses and other trees that can anchor their roots to the sandy swamp bottom. Periodic floods, droughts, hurricanes, and fires keep the swamp in a state of flux, with thickets and waterways appearing and disappearing. The shifting swamp saved wildlife from trappers and settlers, and even the determined loggers couldn't get to all the cypress houses. These remote pockets preserved plants and wildlife that have since repopulated the entire swamp.

Okefenokee Swamp is unusual in that it lies slightly higher than the surrounding area rather than lower, and it gives birth to two rivers—Suwannee and St. Marys—instead of receiving water from the outside. The mass of peat makes this possible because it can hold so much water. In 1960 an earthen sill was built on the western side to retain water in the swamp to help reduce the chance of catastrophic wildfires. Fire, however, is essential to the long-term health of the swamp, and the sill is minimally effective.

■ **PLANT LIFE** Pond cypress and bald cypress grow on "houses" (tangled clumps of plants on peat mounds that tremble or shift underfoot because of the water content). The understory includes bamboo vines, cassena trees, titi shrubs, and other flowering woody plants. Spanish moss, a flowering epiphyte related to pineapples, hangs in great clumps from almost every branch. Marsh and water plants abound, including water lilies, milkwort, sphagnum and other ferns, and mosses. Pitcher plants, bladderworts, sundews, golden clubs, and butterworts show special adaptations for living in acidic swamp water. Pines, maples, black gums, and scrub oaks grow on the islands. In fall, the maples and gums become bright red, while the cypress needles turn a rich bronze.

Tricolored heron

■ ANIMAL LIFE

Birds Sandhill cranes, ospreys, red-tailed hawks, prothonotary warblers, red-cockaded woodpeckers, and many other birds nest in Okefenokee in spring, and many species of ducks, warblers, and other birds overwinter or migrate through the swamp. From the boardwalk on the prairies, visitors have a good chance of seeing cranes, as well as herons, egrets, ibises, and wood storks nesting in the swamp.

Mammals More elusive than birds but definitely present on the refuge are black bears, river otters, foxes, deer, bats, and bobcats. And, of course, the opossums, models for Walt Kelly's Pogo, skulk about at night. Raccoons are also common in the swamp, and armadillos are recent arrivals.

Opposum

Reptiles and amphibians Reptiles are the stars of this wetland environment, probably getting more notice than even the birds. Alligators, turtles, lizards, and snakes bask unabashedly in the sun in full view of quiet paddlers. Frogs and toads perform mating choruses in spring.

Invertebrates Before bemoaning the mosquitoes' unlimited habitat here, remember that they feed fish, bats, and many other creatures. They also pollinate flowering plants. Dragonflies of many colors flit around and dip down to the water's surface to lay eggs. Fire ants, more recent immigrants, build sandy mounds in open, grassy areas. Beware of ticks in open areas.

ACTIVITIES

■ **CAMPING:** Camping is available only at Stephen Foster State Park, on the western side, where you'll find a large campground, camp store, and a few rental cabins. Seven backcountry campsites on canoe trails are available but are in heavy demand. They must be reserved three months before a trip; call the park for details. Campgrounds and other accommodations are available in Fargo, Waycross, and Folkston.

■ **WILDLIFE OBSERVATION:** The best times to visit the swamp are spring and fall. Migrating ducks, warblers, and other birds rest in the swamp; in spring, native birds court and nest here. Sandhill cranes perform courtship dances in March and can often be seen from the boardwalks. Alligators mate in April, and many species of frogs and toads sing, romantically, in spring. The best month for fall color is November, when the cypresses turn golden brown and black gums and maples provide bright shades of red. Summer may be hot, dry (dry enough, in fact, for brush and forest fires), and buggy, with occasional thunderstorms that can be dangerous because the swamp is so flat. Alas, mosquitoes, ticks, and fire ants are active most of the year. In 1990, 1998, and 1999, fires forced the west entrance to the swamp to close; check before your visit.

■ **PHOTOGRAPHY:** From the boardwalk and observation areas at the east entrance, there are excellent opportunities for photography. In a canoe or kayak, you can quietly approach basking alligators and water snakes to within 15 to 20 feet. Water lilies and other flowers reflected in the dark swamp water can make dramatic settings for photographers.

■ **HIKES AND WALKS:** Each of the three refuge entrances has a short nature trail with interpretive signs. Canoe trails in the swamp are marked for nature study, and, to preserve wilderness quality, access is limited. For reservations, call two months before your visit. Along the canoe trails are platforms where you can dock your canoe while you stretch your legs on a sandy island. The largest of these is Billy's Island (named for Seminole Chief Billy Bowlegs, mentioned earlier), which can be accessed from the west entrance. The island is where subsistence farmers lived until the logging company set up a 600-person town there, complete with schools, stores, and a movie house. You can follow a marked trail through pine woods and see rusted sawmill machinery and household materials. For overnight canoe trips across the swamp, reservations are required and a shuttle service is available to get you back to your car.

■ **SEASONAL EVENTS:** The refuge celebrates National Wildlife Refuge Week in October with special events. Folkston Okefenokee Festival is held in the second week of October: It includes tours of the swamp and the restored Chesser Island Homestead; programs about human history and self-sufficient living in the swamp. Call the refuge office for information.

Annual Pogo Festival in Waycross, October; call Okefenokee Swamp State Park for information.

The Okefenokee Swamp State Park also has information about "Lydia, Queen of the Swamp," a woman who became wealthy raising cattle and timber on the northern edge of the swamp before the refuge was formed.

Other events: The Swamp Birding Festival, February; NWR and Earthday celebrations, April; and International Migratory Bird Day, May.

HUNTING AND FISHING Fishing for **warmouth bass, flier,** and **chain pickerel** is permitted in the lakes of the swamp; limited hunting is allowed throughout the refuge; call the Visitor Center for permit information.

■ **PUBLICATIONS:** At each entrance (in Visitor Center and store): Okefenokee NWR brochures, booklets, and checklists. A series of books called *Exploring the Okefenokee* covers natural and cultural history.

Piedmont NWR

Round Oak, Georgia

Old-growth pine forest, Piedmont NWR

Piedmont National Wildlife Refuge is a land-reclamation success story. Decades of tree planting and habitat protection are returning these mountain foothills to their original form—the kind of mature forest European settlers would have encountered on arrival in the New World. Hiking trails, a wildlife drive, and a population of the endangered red-cockaded woodpecker make Piedmont NWR a pleasant break for travelers. Situated between Round Oak and Juliette, the refuge is 25 miles north of Macon and only 10 miles from I-75 at Forsyth.

HISTORY

The soil of these mountain foothills was depleted over the years by overfarming, erosion, and infestations of cotton boll weevils, which left the land too damaged to support crops. To reclaim the land, Piedmont NWR was established in 1939. Today the refuge provides diverse and secure habitats for plant and animal species. Management by controlled fires, impoundments, clearings, and plantings has also increased wildlife populations.

GETTING THERE

From Macon, take US 23 (Exit 55 from I-75) north 17 mi. to Juliette Rd. Turn right, go through Juliette, cross over the Ocmulgee River, and continue on the paved road for 8 mi. Turn left on the entrance road to the Visitor Center (you will see signs along the way directing you to the Visitor Center). The Visitor Center parking lot gate is closed when the center is closed, but trails can be reached by going 0.5 mi. to the Allison Lake parking area. From the north, take Exit 61 off I-75, and head east 18 mi. on Juliette Road; follow refuge signs as above. From Round Oak, take GA 11 north for 0.5 mi. and follow refuge signs on left.

■ **SEASON:** Refuge open year-round.

■ HOURS: Refuge: daylight hours. Visitor Center: Mon-Fri., 8 a.m.–4:30 p.m.; weekends, 9 a.m.–5 p.m.; closed on federal holidays.
■ FEES: None.
■ ADDRESS: Piedmont NWR, 718 Round Oak/Juliette Rd., Round Oak, GA 31038
■ TELEPHONE: 912/986-5441

TOURING PIEDMONT

■ BY AUTOMOBILE: Little Rock Wildlife Drive, about 2.5 miles west of the Visitor Center, is a 6-mile gravel road.
■ BY FOOT: Trails start at or are within walking distance of the Visitor Center. Pine Trail (0.5 mile) and Creek Trail (0.8 mile) form a loop. Allison Lake Trail (0.9-mile loop) starts either from the end of the Creek Trail or from a parking area just beyond the Visitor Center. Red-cockaded Woodpecker Trail (2.9-mile loop) starts from the same parking area. All trails are closed to hunting.
■ BY BICYCLE: There are many gravel roads on the refuge for mountain biking. Check with the refuge office about hunting seasons.
■ BY CANOE, KAYAK, OR BOAT: A small boat ramp and pier on Allison Lake can be used for a canoe or kayak, May 1–September 30.

WHAT TO SEE

■ LANDSCAPE AND CLIMATE The southern Piedmont plateau rises between the Atlantic coastal plain and the Appalachian Mountains. Most piedmont land was heavily farmed and settled; the refuge and the adjacent Oconee National Forest foster regrowth of the original landscape between Atlanta and Macon.

Spring is the best time to visit. Migratory birds pass through, wildflowers bloom, and in May woodpeckers start nesting. Fall and winter provide good hiking under pleasant conditions, but summer may be hot except for early morning and evening. Bring insect repellent and check yourself frequently for chiggers and ticks (especially in summer and early fall).

■ PLANT LIFE The uplands consist mostly of pine forest (loblolly and shortleaf pines) in different stages of maturity. Creek valleys and coves produce oaks, shagbark hickories, black gums, and maples. Dogwoods and azaleas provide a riot of blooming flowers in spring. Game clearings are covered with native grasses and summer flowers. Trails from the Visitor Center have mayapples, trilliums, and other spring wildflowers. Behind the center, a "Backyard Wildlife Habitat Demonstration" shows what you can attract at home. Out on the Wildlife Drive, enjoy the carefully maintained "green tree reservoir" of oaks and other nut-producing trees, favorites of wood ducks, migratory waterfowl, and other wildlife. On the eastern side of the refuge, farmers grow grain crops that help to feed species such as migratory geese.

■ ANIMAL LIFE Most piedmont animals managed to survive the onslaught of civilization by clustering in pockets of undisturbed land; these animals have nowadays recolonized protected places.
Birds Attentive birders have recorded nearly 200 species of birds at Piedmont. Woodpeckers thrive here, including 36 colonies of endangered red-cockaded woodpeckers. This small woodpecker requires mature pines, which almost disap-

peared during the times of heavy logging but are now preserved by wildlife managers. Young red-cockaded woodpeckers stay with the parents for a few years, forming colonies to raise nestlings.

By contrast, red-headed woodpeckers live in less mature pines; hairy woodpeckers favor sheltered hardwood coves; and downy woodpeckers like creek bottoms. Pileated woodpeckers, the largest species, nest in all habitats on the refuge. A serious birder can have fun looking for each variety here.

Other birds at Piedmont include flickers, cardinals, migrating warblers and waterfowl, yellow-billed cuckoos, and vultures. Wood ducks nest near pond edges; look for wood duck boxes on posts with metal guards to repel predators. Wild turkeys display their fanlike tail feathers in clearings, along the Wildlife Drive, and in open woods.

Mammals Deer, raccoon, opossum, river otter, mink, swamp rabbit, beaver, and muskrat are among the 40 species of mammals found at Piedmont.

Reptiles and amphibians Reptile admirers, take note: Open areas and young pine woodlands provide habitat for garter snakes, scarlet king snakes, hognose snakes, and snake food: toads, mice, salamanders, frogs, and earthworms. More mature habitats support secretive corn snakes, crowned snakes, and glass lizards, as well as box turtles and skinks. Soft-shelled turtles, watersnakes, and spotted salamanders frequent ponds and bottomlands, while several species of frogs breed in the ponds. Fence lizards and skinks sun themselves in openings and thin woods. Venomous copperheads, water moccasins, and rattlesnakes also enjoy the varied habitats here but are rarely seen.

Invertebrates Ticks, chiggers, and mosquitoes—important in the food chain, though not friendly to people—are most common and may be present all year. Look for butterflies, dragonflies, colorful wasps, and other helpful invertebrate pollinators in the demonstration garden.

ACTIVITIES

■ **CAMPING:** Camping and open fires are permitted only in conjunction with refuge big-game hunts in the designated campground.

■ **WILDLIFE OBSERVATION:** Open spots on the Wildlife Drive provide good chances to view birds and mammals, and the Red-cockaded Woodpecker Trail is superb for observing this endangered bird, especially during the April-to-June nesting period. A small dock on Allison Lake (handicapped-accessible) can be used for observation and fishing.

■ **PHOTOGRAPHY:** Recommendation: the photography and observation blind on Allison Lake Trail.

■ **SEASONAL EVENTS:** The refuge celebrates National Wildlife Refuge Week in October with special events. National Wildlife Week and Earthday are held in April, and International Migratory Bird Week is held in May.

■ **PUBLICATIONS:** At the Visitor Center, look for trail and wildlife guides, bird lists, and maps. The guides are good entertainment for children during a visit to Piedmont NWR.

Savannah Coastal NWRs

Savannah, Georgia

Savannah NWR

Squadrons of pelicans patrol the barrier islands that once hid Blackbeard's ships. The Golden Isles of Georgia, rich in beautiful beaches, fresh- and salt-water marshes, and live oak forests, run the length of the coastline. Scattered between large estuaries and busy vacation spots are seven units of the National Wildlife Refuge coastal refuge complex.

The area's natural resources attract a rich variety of birds. Look to see endangered wood storks feeding their hatchlings in freshwater ponds; spot great blue herons spearfishing in the marshes. Inland from the islands lie wide salt marshes, swamps, bottomland forests, and upland forests on bluffs and sandhills.

Here we will focus on Savannah NWR, with details of the other Georgia refuges administered from the Savannah refuge office. Pinckney Island NWR, part of the same complex, merits its own narrative and so is described separately.

HISTORY

Savannah NWR, established in 1927, comprises 26,349 acres, about half in Georgia and half in South Carolina. Upstream from the city of Savannah, it consists of wetlands and impoundments in the low country along the Savannah River. Though the refuge is one of the oldest in the system, it started small (2,352 acres), and parcels have been added by purchase or donation—from 34 acres in 1967 to 12,472 acres in 1978.

Humans have lived, hunted, and harvested oysters along the Georgia coast for a very long time; indeed archaeological sites show signs of habitation from as far back as 4,500 years ago. When European settlers arrived, they found Creek Indians living inland and Guale Indians on the barrier islands.

In 1733 General James Oglethorpe, a British philanthropist and member of Parliament, established Savannah as the first British colony in Georgia. After bringing poor and destitute settlers to the new land (many of them straight from debtors' prisons), he fought off Spaniards trying to expand their New World holdings northward from Florida, experimented with peaches and cotton, and made plans for other Georgia settlements before returning to Parliament. The colony prospered on the backs of slaves and tenant farmers, growing rice and sea island cotton on vast plantations. All that changed when another general, William Tecumseh Sherman, arrived toward the end of the Civil War.

The Georgia coast barrier islands and salt marshes remained relatively undisturbed by early Georgian settlement, a few wars, Sherman's March to the Sea, and Savannah's subsequent recovery as the South's busiest port. Beachfront development now threatens some of these rich habitats, making the Savannah Coastal Refuges and other protected lands critical for preserving wildlife.

GETTING THERE

From Port Wentworth, drive 3 mi. north on GA 25 to the refuge sign on right of the refuge field office. The entrance to Laurel Hill Wildlife Drive is a few miles north of Savannah on SC 170.

■ **SEASON:** Refuge open year-round.

■ **HOURS:** Daylight hours. The Savannah Coastal Refuges office is open 8 a.m.–4:30 p.m., weekdays.

■ **FEES:** None.

■ **ADDRESS:** Savannah Coastal Refuges, Parkway Business Ctr., Suite 10, 1000 Business Center Dr., Savannah, GA 31405

■ **TELEPHONE:** 912/652-4415

TOURING SAVANNAH NWR

■ **BY AUTOMOBILE:** Laurel Hill Wildlife Drive, a 4-mile loop, starts on SC 170 a few miles north of Savannah.

■ **BY FOOT:** Cistern Trail (50 yards, handicapped-accessible) starts about 1 mile in on the Laurel Hill Wildlife Drive. The dikes around the impoundments are

JOHN MUIR, EXPLORING THE SOUTHEAST ON FOOT In 1867 John Muir walked from Jefferson, Indiana (near Louisville, Kentucky), to Cedar Key, Florida, which today is a National Wildlife Refuge. Although he averaged more than 20 miles a day and spent a lot of time socializing, Muir considered this a botanical expedition, and he noted plants new to him as he traversed different habitats. Approaching Savannah, Muir marveled at the cypress swamp tree, which botanists call bald cypress (*Taxodium distichum*). It can reach skyward up to 170 feet on a massive trunk. With crooked roots ("knees") partially above water, the cypress was popular with boat builders who cut curved members for their crafts from its durable wood.

Here, too, I found an impenetrable cypress swamp. This remarkable tree, called cypress, is a taxodium, grows large and high, and is remarkable for its flat crown. The whole forest seems almost level on the top, as if each tree had grown up against a ceiling, or had been rolled while growing. This taxodium is the only level-topped tree that I have seen. The branches, though spreading, are careful not to pass each other, and stop suddenly on reaching the general level.

—John Muir, *A Thousand-Mile Walk to the Gulf* (1867)

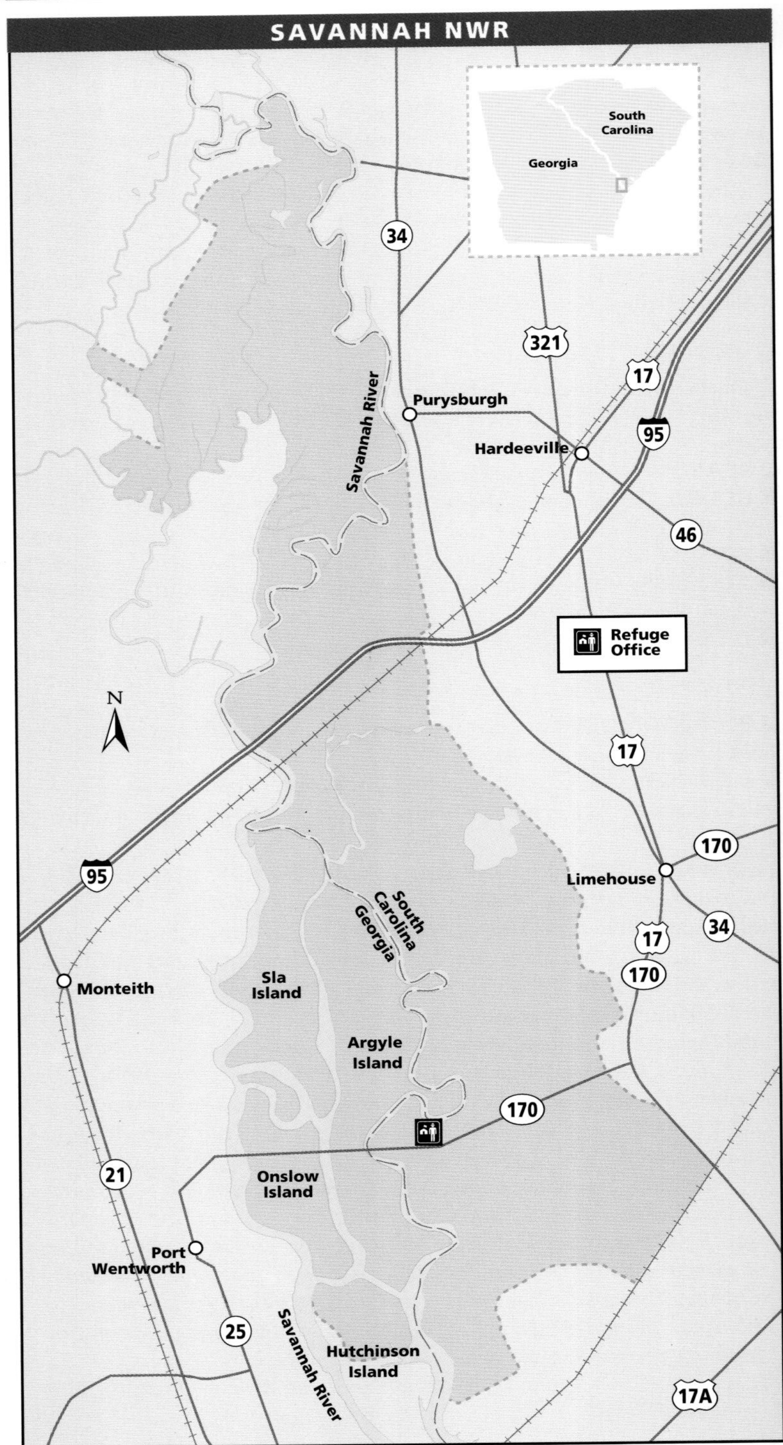
SAVANNAH NWR
South Carolina
Georgia
34
321
17
Purysburgh
95
Hardeeville
Savannah River
46
Refuge Office
N
17
170
Limehouse
95
South Carolina
Georgia
34
17
170
Monteith
Sla Island
Argyle Island
170
21
Onslow Island
Port Wentworth
25
Savannah River
Hutchinson Island
17A

open and provide about 36 miles of walking in an area 2 miles north of Port Wentworth, GA, and 6 miles south of Hardeeville, SC. The dikes and impoundments north of SC 170 are closed between December 1 and February 28 to reduce disturbance of waterfowl. Tupelo Swamp Trail (1 mile) goes through a cypress/tupelo swamp.

■ BY BICYCLE: Bicycles are allowed on Laurel Hill Wildlife Drive and on other refuge roads.

■ BY CANOE OR BOAT: The Savannah River and many creeks and swampy areas are available for boating. Ask refuge staff about tides and currents on the river. There are several boat landings.

WHAT TO SEE

■ LANDSCAPE AND CLIMATE Savannah NWR extends for 20 river miles up the Savannah River, starting about 20 miles north of the city of Savannah. The botanist William Bartram described the area in the 1790s: "Nearly one-third of this vast plain is what the inhabitants call swamps, which are the sources of numerous small rivers and their branches; these they call salt rivers because the tides flow near to their sources, and generally carry a good depth and breadth of water for small craft, twenty or thirty miles upward from the sea, when they branch and spread abroad like an open hand." Bartram also mentions being "a little incommoded by the heats of the season." It is indeed hot and humid in summer; the cooler months are better times to visit and view wildlife.

Most of the area is flat and wet (which historically has made it almost impossible to drain for agriculture and discourages extensive logging) and interspersed with sand ridges and bluffs. Because of the inward curve of Georgia's coast, tides are high and carry salt water many miles inland on the estuaries and river system. The string of barrier islands acts to buffer the mainland against storm surges caused by hurricanes and surge tides, which occur on a frequent basis in this part of the country.

■ PLANT LIFE The lower part of the refuge is mostly swamp, bottomland hardwoods, marshes, and tidal creeks. Cypress trees and tupelos grow in the swamps, along with water oak, swamp white oak, willow-leaved oak, and other trees that can live among standing water and periodic flooding. Fringe trees bloom along the edge of the swamp in May. The delicate fragrant flower clusters hang down and look like white lace from a distance. Spanish moss hangs from cypress and live oak branches.

Ruby-throated hummingbird

The freshwater marshes and remnants of former rice plantations attract waterfowl, and hardwood hammocks of oak and maple provide a varied landscape for other migratory birds. Upland hardwood forests grow on the bluffs around the northeastern edge of the refuge, a distinct contrast to the wetlands.

Massive live oaks, with narrow, leathery leaves, thrive near the start of Laurel Hill Drive, planted here by former owners of Laurel Hill rice plantation. Their horizontal branches support thick rows of resurrection fern, so-called because it curls up enough to be almost invisible in dry weather and then pops up to full size in rainy weather.

Tall grasses, rushes, and sedges grow in the marshes, where abundant organic matter (otherwise known as mud) and efficient photosynthesis support a highly fertile area supporting large populations of vertebrate and invertebrate wildlife.

Wild azaleas, cabbage and saw palmetto, and southern magnolia, with waxy, tough leaves and scented, creamy-white flowers, are found on high ground. Here are greenbrier, muscadine grapes, and yaupon holly (cassena bush).

Millet and other crops are planted by the U.S. Fish & Wildlife Service for waterfowl food.

■ ANIMAL LIFE

Birds Endangered and threatened species, including wood storks, bald eagles, and peregrine falcons, find refuge on the Savannah coastal complex. White and glossy ibis nest here. Both have down-curved bills and fly with their necks straight, unlike herons, which curve their necks into a tight S when in flight. The glossy ibis looks almost black from a distance, but up close it reveals greenish wings and a dark red-to-purple back. Bring binoculars for a better view of these stunning birds.

Who says you can't walk on water? Common and purple gallinules, ducklike birds that live on the banks of rivers, swamps, and lakes, use their big feet to walk on lily pads.

Wood ducks form large flocks in the impoundments and nest in boxes or tree cavities at heights up to 50 feet. These ducks also sometimes court in trees, dancing precariously on horizontal branches. The handsome males are bedecked with green heads and backs, red beaks, white chins, iridescent feathers, and swept-back green and white crests. Wood ducklings don't initially fly from the nest; they use

Young American alligator basking in the sun

their sharp claws to scramble out of the nest and tumble down to where their mother calls them. After a bouncy landing, the ducklings follow her to the water, where snapping turtles pose a threat.

Many species of ducks winter on the refuge, as well as a variety of sparrows and warblers. Herons, egrets, bitterns, anhingas, and ruby-throated hummingbirds also stop in. Fish crows stand on tree branches and call out "*Uh oh, uh oh!*"

Mammals Visitors to the refuge will likely see any number of animals in action. They may see river otters popping their heads up in the impoundments, and marsh rabbits swimming furiously in swamp waters to escape predators. As elsewhere in eastern wildlands, white-tailed deer, raccoons, opossums, marsh rats, and other small mammals live in this refuge's varied habitats.

Reptiles and amphibians Alligators inhabit most southern swamps and reside very comfortably at the top of the food chain. Under ideal habitat conditions, with almost no predators, the alligators at Savannah refuge grow 10 to 12 feet long indeed—and should be treated with respect from a distance of 20 feet or more. They have been known to outrun humans for a short duration.

Water moccasins (poisonous) and harmless water snakes laze about on swamp logs; fence lizards, skinks, and anolis lizards scurry up tree trunks. Snapping, stinkpot, cooter, and soft-shelled turtles live in freshwater but must lay their eggs on dry land, leaving the eggs vulnerable to such predators as raccoons and alligators. The stinkpot is so named because its musk glands exude a foul-smelling liquid, while the softshell's shell is actually more leathery than soft. Freshwater marshes and open water support frogs and toads, as well as amphiumas—ill-tempered, slippery-skinned fellows that can grow up to 40 inches long, live as long as 27 years, and have a nasty bite. Sirens, salamanders that closely resemble eels, live here as well.

ACTIVITIES

■ **CAMPING:** There are no campsites on Savannah refuge. Skidaway Island State Park, about 15 miles south of Savannah, however, has 88 developed campsites and primitive camping areas (800/864-7275).

■ **WILDLIFE OBSERVATION:** Laurel Hill Wildlife Drive links several hardwood hammocks in a marsh. Stop several times along the way as the habitats change. Large wading birds can be seen in the marsh or on open water. When you reach the hammocks, you will find good places to see colorful migrants, such as black-throated blue warblers, chestnut-sided warblers, black-and-white warblers, American redstarts, and ruby-crowned kinglet.

■ **HIKES AND WALKS:** The 50-yard cistern trail starts at the foundation of a plantation cistern on the Wildlife Drive. It is handicapped-accessible and goes through a hardwood hammock.

Tupelo Trail (1 mile) borders a freshwater creek with cypress and tupelo trees. Iris bloom in spring, and summer flowers include lizard's tail (long heart-shaped leaves and a spike of white flowers) and

HUNTING AND FISHING Fishing is allowed in the refuge waters year-round. Bank fishing is available from the wildlife drives on the South Carolina side, and you may fish from boats in the tidal creeks. You'll find a variety of freshwater species, including **largemouth bass** and **crappies**. You may hunt for **deer** and **feral hog** in Oct. and Nov., and **small game** in Oct. only. **Turkey** is in season in April only. Contact the refuge for further details.

golden club (long pointed leaves and a tight cluster of yellow flowers on a fleshy stalk). Prothonotary warblers nest along this trail.

■ **SEASONAL EVENTS:** October: National Wildlife Refuge Week.

■ **PUBLICATIONS:** Bird list, maps and brochures, Guide to Laurel Hill Wildlife Drive.

SATELLITE REFUGES

■ **Blackbeard Island** This island refuge (5,619 acres) has been in government ownership since 1800 and was used first for live oak timber harvest (in the shipbuilding trade) and then as a quarantine station for yellow fever. In 1924 it became a biological preserve, and it entered the NWR system in 1940. Legend has it that Blackbeard the Pirate (Edward Teach) used the island as a savings bank, but no one has found his buried treasure yet—or if they have, they haven't mentioned it.

The island, about 50 miles south of Savannah, is accessible only by boat; the Savannah NWR has a list of boat services and charters to and from Blackbeard Island. A public landing on the western side of the refuge gives access to several trails past freshwater ponds, impoundments, live oak forest, salt marsh, dunes, and beach.

The southern half of the refuge was designated as Wilderness in 1975. Loggerhead sea turtles and wood storks nest on the islands, and alligators, wading birds, waterfowl, and neotropical migrants abound. Piping plovers visit in winter.

■ **Harris Neck NWR** Just northwest of Blackbeard Island, Harris Neck NWR (2,762 acres) can be reached by car. From Exit 12 on I-95, drive south 1 mile on US 17. Turn east (left) onto GA 131 and proceed 7 miles to the refuge.

Before the Civil War this island produced many harvests of sea island cotton. By raising only one crop, the soil was eventually exhausted. Harris Neck has an unusual hiking and auto-tour feature: a triangular airbase with a network of old runways that were once part of a World War II army airfield. But even after all that, waterfowl and wading birds are willing to try it again, and wood storks have

Egrets and ibises, roosting

established a rookery. Salt marsh, freshwater impoundments, mudflats, and swamps attract birds and other wildlife. Visitor activities include hiking, biking, and environmental education programs. There is a visitor information station and a boat ramp providing easy access to tidal creeks and nearby Blackbeard Island NWR, which is approximately a 30-minute motorboat ride away. Call the Savannah NWR for information about Harris Neck.

■ **Tybee NWR** Established in 1938, Tybee started as a 1-acre island and acquired land not by purchase but by receiving dredging soil from the Savannah River shipping channel. Now 400 acres, it provides habitat for shorebirds, gulls, terns, and a variety of neotropical migratory songbirds. It is not open for public use.

■ **Wassaw NWR** Wassaw was established in 1969 after a Nature Conservancy purchase. It is accessible by boat only. Skidaway Narrows on Skidaway Island has a boat ramp, and tidal creeks lead to an information kiosk on Wassaw Island.

This low-lying 10,070-acre barrier island consists mostly of salt marsh with a smaller area of dunes, forest, and freshwater ponds. A network of roads and trails on the ocean side provides good hiking and biking and access to the beach. Endangered piping plovers, alligators, loggerhead sea turtles, bald eagles, and peregrine falcons use the island, and manatees, dolphins, right whales, and other species of sea turtles may be seen offshore.

■ **Wolf Island NWR** Another barrier island, Wolf Island was established in 1930 and is a 5,126-acre National Wilderness Area. Public use of the island is not allowed, but the waters around the refuge are open to wildlife observation, fishing, and boating.

Noxubee NWR

Brooksville, Mississippi

Great egrets

Noxubee NWR provides a window into the past. Old-growth forests of pine trees and wetland forests of oak, cypress, and tupelo gum offer views of eastern Mississippi as it was long ago.

This is a great refuge for hiking. Well-maintained trails wind through river bottom forests, past red-cockaded woodpecker habitat and along Bluff and Loakfoma lakes and the wide Noxubee River.

HISTORY

Native Americans gave the local waters and landforms their names. Hernando De Soto entered Mississippi near the present-day Noxubee NWR in 1540. He traded with Choctaw and Chickasaw Indians but found no gold and lost interest. More than a century later, French explorers claimed the territory and held it until 1763. British and, later, American settlers farmed the red clay hills of central Mississippi. The soil was fertile but not very stable.

Some refuges exist to preserve beautiful land and its wildlife; others work to restore an area to its former beauty. Noxubee is one of the latter—even before the 1930s, farming, logging, overgrazing, and draining had devastated this land. The 48,000-acre refuge was established in 1940 to protect the remaining patches of bottomland hardwoods and other wetlands. Careful management has resulted in the repopulation of trees and other plants and allowed animals to recover in sustainable numbers.

GETTING THERE

From MS 12 in Starkville, take Spring St. (MS 25) south for 1.5 mi., turn right on Oktoc Rd., go 13 mi., and turn right on Skinner Rd. Follow refuge signs. After crossing the Noxubee River, turn right at refuge sign; go 2 mi., turn left onto gravel road, and follow signs to refuge office.

From Louisville, take MS 25 for 18 mi. north, turn right at refuge sign, and follow directions as above.

■ **SEASON:** Refuge open year-round.

■ **HOURS:** Refuge: daylight hours; office: 8 a.m.–4:30 p.m.

■ **FEES:** None.

■ **ADDRESS:** Rte. #1, Box 142, Noxubee, MS 39739

■ **TELEPHONE:** 662/323-5548

TOURING NOXUBEE

■ **BY AUTOMOBILE:** Ungated refuge roads are open to cars. Some roads are gated from October 1 through May 1.

■ **BY FOOT:** There are six hiking trails, open all year: Woodpecker Trail (0.25-mile loop) begins near the refuge office and is handicapped-accessible; Beaver Dam Trail (2-mile round-trip), near the Bluff Lake spillway; Bluff Lake Boardwalk; Trail of the Big Trees (4-mile round-trip), on River Rd.; Wilderness Trail (4-mile round-trip); Scattertown Trail (1.75 miles round-trip), in the uplands. Short trails and boardwalks off these major trails lead to overlooks and observation platforms

■ **BY BICYCLE:** All trails and ungated refuge roads are open to bicycles.

■ **BY CANOE, KAYAK, OR BOAT:** Bluff Lake, Loakfoma Lake, and creeks are available for boating, but the lakes are closed from November 1 to February 29 to protect wintering waterfowl.

WHAT TO SEE

■ **LANDSCAPE AND CLIMATE** The river rises in the Tombigbee National Forest and flows west, forming a wide floodplain that gathers up the waters of Oktoc, Loakfoma, and Cinchahoma creeks. Pine ridges, bottomland forests, swamps, and a tangled network of creeks make up the natural habitats of Noxubee refuge; fields and impoundments have been added. The Noxubee River floodplain protected the land from logging and agriculture—it's so flat that there was no place to drain the water—and trees have been allowed to grow big here.

■ **PLANT LIFE** The bottomland stars here are oak trees—several species, large specimens—that can withstand periodic flooding. Water oaks predominate and have bluish-green leaves that are wider toward the ends. Their small, dark acorns feed ducks, turkeys, and squirrels—and at one time fed passenger pigeons, now extinct.

Along the rivers and creeks, cypress and oak trees that survived early settlement are now huge, with massive buttressed trunks. Many pines on the red clay ridges are old enough to attract endangered red-cockaded woodpeckers, which prefer to nest in trees with a disease called red heart—and only old trees have this disease. Woodpeckers also favor larger trees containing several cavities.

Trilliums, mayapples, phlox, and several kinds of violets bloom here in spring. Maypops (passionflowers) blossom in June and produce sweet, edible fruit in August. Pawpaws, muscadine grapes, persimmons, and wild plums also provide sweet, sticky fruits for animals. Summer flowers at Noxubee include black-eyed Susans and ironweed.

The refuge grows some crops for wildlife and manages several greentree reservoirs to provide mast (nuts and other high-protein food). Greentree reservoirs contain water-tolerant oaks and hickories. These are flooded in fall before the mast falls; when waterfowl arrive later in late fall, food is waiting for them.

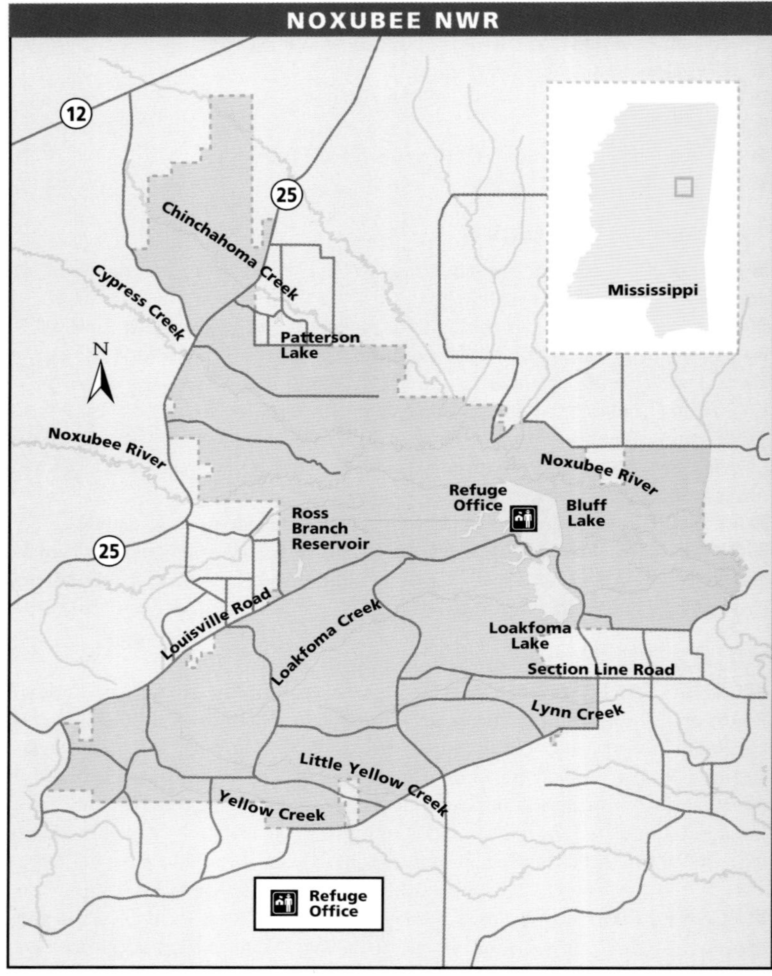

■ ANIMAL LIFE

Birds Red-cockaded woodpeckers nest on large pine trees with red heart disease. They excavate deep nests and peck holes in the sap wood surrounding the holes so that pine pitch seeps out. Somehow they manage to land at these holes without getting their feet stuck, but snakes and other predators cannot get past the sticky barrier. These woodpeckers are endangered because logging has removed the biggest trees, their favorite haunts. Chicken-sized pileated woodpeckers, with bright red crests like Woody Woodpecker, also nest here and cackle as they fly. They can shred a dead log into splinters looking for beetle larvae and usually leave roughly oblong holes. More woodpeckers—such as flickers, red-headed, red-bellied (which have a barely visible red patch on their bellies), and downy—also excavate dead wood at Noxubee. Prothonotary warblers, with orange heads, yellow bellies, and long curved beaks, nest in swamps and use old woodpecker holes. Barred owls call out eerily—something like *"who cooks for you-all"*—in the woods. They also nest in old woodpecker holes.

Some Canada geese nest here and lead their goslings past observation spots,

Pileated woodpecker

as if on parade. Other waterfowl and bald eagles spend the winter here, whereas colorful small migrants, including warblers, tanagers, and thrushes, migrate through the refuge to summer homes in the tropics and then back to northern woodlands.

Great blue herons, cattle egrets, and white ibises build messy stick nests on the tops of cypress trees. Elusive glossy ibises may also be seen. All of the taller birds are likely to be seen waterside, fishing.

Mammals Visitors who roam the woods and swamps of Noxubee will have beavers, foxes, deer, raccoon, opossums, gray and fox squirrels, muskrats, and rabbits roaming these spaces with them. Nutria, a large South American rodent, armadillos, and coyotes have moved into the refuge in the last 15 to 20 years, causing major problems for native species.

Reptiles and amphibians Alligators live on the refuge but are near the edge of their northern range at this latitude. The snake world is busy at Noxubee. Venomous snakes include cottonmouths, pygmy rattlesnakes, southern copperheads, and timber rattlesnakes. Several kinds of rat snakes, king snakes, and other constrictors prefer warm-blooded prey, such as birds and rodents, while water snakes, and garter snakes eat fish, frogs, salamanders, worms, and other cold-blooded prey. Hognose snakes specialize in eating toads. The mud snake burrows in swamp mud; it's pretty, with iridescent scales and red spots, but rarely seen. The mud snake has the unusual habit of piercing its prey (salamanders and fish) with its sharp tail to subdue and straighten out for easier swallowing.

ACTIVITIES

■ **CAMPING AND SWIMMING:** There is no camping or swimming at Noxubee refuge, but the nearby Tombigbee National Forest offers campgrounds and a swimming lake (877/444-6777).

■ **WILDLIFE OBSERVATION AND PHOTOGRAPHY:** Two observation towers provide good views and photography opportunities. A 60-foot tower overlooks Bluff Lake, where Canada geese and other waterfowl feed in winter. The tower also overlooks farm fields shared by waterfowl and deer. A short boardwalk leads to the tower and is handicapped-accessible.

Morgan Hill Overlook's wide vista at Loakfoma Lake serves up views of waterfowl, wading birds, and wintering bald eagles. The short trail to the tower goes through the Alabama Black Belt Prairie Restoration Area and is handicapped-accessible. Prairie grasses and flowers grow there.

Canoe trips add swamp and open lake experiences.

■ **HIKES AND WALKS:** Noxubee refuge provides a variety of trails for walkers and hikers.

NOXUBEE HUNTING AND FISHING SEASONS

Hunting (Seasons may vary)	Jan	Feb	Mar	Apr	May	Jun	Jul	Aug	Sep	Oct	Nov	Dec
white-tailed deer	□	□	□	□	□	□	□	□	□	■	■	■
wild turkey	□	□	■	■	■	□	□	□	□	□	□	□
small game	■	■	□	□	□	□	□	□	□	■	■	■
Fishing	□	□	■	■	■	■	■	■	■	■	□	□

For information on current fishing regulations, license requirements, seasons, and bag limits, consult refuge office.

Woodpecker Trail (0.5 mile) near the refuge office leads through a forest of loblolly pine, favored by red-cockaded woodpeckers. A colony nests here, and visitors can see the parents and their helpers entering and leaving the nests. Management strategies to increase the population of these woodpeckers include clearing underbrush with fire, rehabilitating injured birds, and installing artificial nest cavities. Sweetgum, dogwood, and oak trees also grow along the trail, which has resting benches at various points providing views of Bluff Lake. The trail is handicapped-accessible.

Beaver Dam Trail (2-mile round-trip) starts at the Bluff Lake Levee and meanders through bottomland hardwoods toward a greentree reservoir beyond the end of the trail. It passes through a cypress swamp and has a side trail to Oktoc Creek.

Bluff Lake Boardwalk crosses a cypress swamp to end at the overview of Bluff Lake and a large cattle egret rookery.

Trail of the Big Trees (4-mile round-trip) runs along the Noxubee River to a giant, but now fallen, Shumard (red) Oak, distinguishable by its deep-lobed, sharp-pointed leaves. At one time the refuge had two National Champion trees; all the record-breaking trees, however, have been lost to storms or other natural causes. Other oaks are growing to take their place in the wet bottomlands.

Wilderness Trail starts on a footbridge across the Noxubee River and goes 2 miles through an undisturbed bottomland forest that is managed as Wilderness area—which means no burning, cutting, or human-made structures except the trail.

Scattertown Trail (1.75-mile loop) is an upland trail over red clay hills through shortleaf pine, hickory, and native bamboo (cane).

Remember, this is a wet place: Some of the bottomland trails may be flooded and impassable. Other hikes can be designed using refuge roads and levees, but to avoid getting lost in the maze, get a map and directions first.

■ **SEASONAL EVENTS:** May: International Migratory Bird Day bird counts; August and September: "Owl Prowls" and alligator counts; October: National Wildlife Refuge Week; December: Annual Christmas bird count.

■ **PUBLICATIONS:** Refuge brochure; interpretive pamphlets; a trail guide; hunting and fishing regulations.

Yazoo NWR

Hollandale, Mississippi

Yazoo NWR

Stretched out along the floodplains of the Mississippi River, this refuge attracts vast numbers of birds using the Mississippi Flyway. Mallards, Canada geese, snow geese, and small migratory birds land here on their seasonal journeys. Visitors will find plenty of wood ducks, herons, egrets, and ibises nesting around ponds and lakes. Sunning alligators crowd lakes, sloughs, and the pond named in their honor, Alligator Pond.

HISTORY

Choctaw Indians lived and fished in what was once a paradise of oxbow lakes and river delta. During the Civil War, the dense and impenetrable swamps, bayous, and marshes of the Yazoo River Basin prevented Union troops from reaching Vicksburg and controlling the Mississippi. The story is darker today, with pesticides and agricultural fertilizer runoff making fish unsafe to eat; siltation and flooding are problems, as well. The good news is that the steadily improving habitats of the Yazoo Refuge Complex are attracting more wildlife. Understaffed, the refuges has few visitor facilities, but the hope is to provide more in the future.

This 12,941-acre Yazoo refuge, which consists of five wetland refuges along the eastern bank of the Mississippi, started out in 1936 with just 2,166 acres. Since then, the refuge has acquired bits of land, some of it eroded or overfarmed. Refuge managers have been able to restore forests and other wildlife habitats on these areas.

GETTING THERE

From Greenville, MS, drive 26 mi. on MS 1 south to refuge entrance sign on left. Turn northeast and drive 2.5 mi. to headquarters.

■ **SEASON:** Refuge open year-round.

■ **HOURS:** Refuge: daylight hours; office: 7:30 a.m.–4 p.m., weekdays.

■ **FEES:** None.
■ **ADDRESS:** 728 Yazoo Refuge Rd., Rte. 1, Box 286, Hollandale, MS, 38748
■ **TELEPHONE:** 601/839-2638

TOURING YAZOO NWR

■ **BY AUTOMOBILE:** Several paved and gravel refuge roads are open to cars, and the 2.5-mile Yazoo Refuge Road provides wildlife-viewing opportunities.
■ **BY FOOT:** Refuge roads and levees at Yazoo are open to hiking.
■ **BY BICYCLE:** Bicycles may be used on refuge roads (remember, most are unpaved).
■ **BY CANOE, KAYAK, OR BOAT:** Small canoes or boats ply the waters of Swan Lake and other lakes, bayous, and creeks, as well as in deeper parts of the swamps. Be sure to carry a map.

WHAT TO SEE

■ **LANDSCAPE AND CLIMATE** The flat Mississippi Delta floodplain has year-round water underfoot in many places, and some of its forests are seasonally flooded. Bluffs or ridges of loess support pine and hardwood stands on several refuge units. Cypress swamps and the dense underbrush around them form thickets called brakes. These contrast sharply with the refuge's cleared fields, some of which continue to be cultivated as cropland; others are now being reverted to forest.

■ **PLANT LIFE** The resplendent plant mix at Yazoo resonates in deep greens and bright hues. Spanish moss and resurrection ferns (see the Savannah Coastal Refuge) grow on cypress branches, while water hyacinths, white water lilies, and yellow lotus bloom below on black swamp water, their pastels highlighted by the dark background.

Local farmers work with refuge managers by planting soybeans, corn, milo, wheat, and rice on fields where ducks and geese can feed. The fields offer clear views of these birds during seasonal migrations.

Wild water hyacinth

■ **ANIMAL LIFE**

Birds It takes some work to tell one duck from another, but a way to start is to divide them into large groups-and then deal with the small details. The two groups seen on most refuges are:
Puddle ducks (or dabblers) such as wood ducks, teal, and mallards. These ducks upend themselves to graze on vegetation and so prefer shallow water. Dabblers also leap straight out of the water, helicopter style, when they take off in flight.
Divers, such as redhead, scaup, goldeneye, and bufflehead. Often larger than the dabblers, these ducks dive completely underwater for food and run across the top of the water, as though it were a tarmac, to take off.

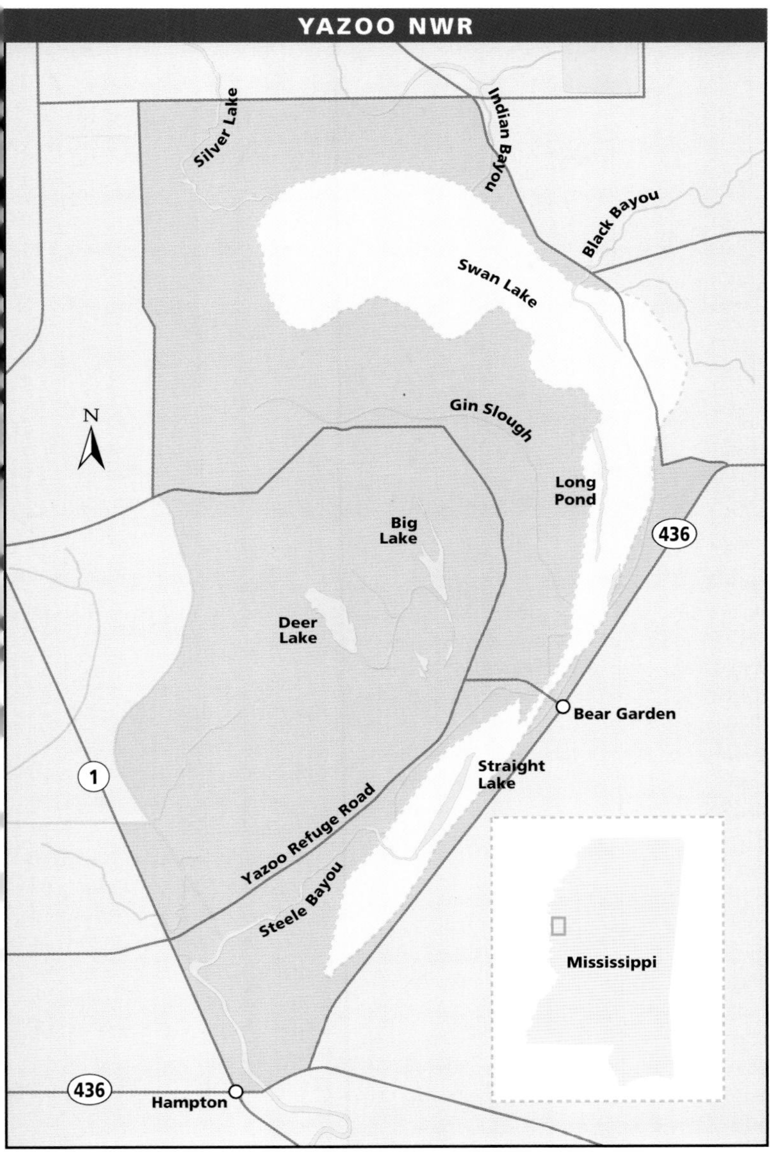

Yazoo's bird list is a long one. Canada, snow, and white-fronted geese spend the winter here before flying up the Mississippi Valley to summer in Canada.

Egrets, herons, anhingas, turkeys, and songbirds like indigo and painted buntings find good nesting habitat. Cormorants and white pelicans, birds typically associated with the ocean, migrate through the refuge.

Mammals Mammals found at Yazoo are generally those you will find throughout the southeastern refuges, including the nearly ubiquitous white-tailed deer, squirrels, beavers, raccoons, opossums, and rabbits, rats, chipmunks, and mice. Nutria are invasive rodents that eat water vegetation; the need to control their numbers is critical to the survival of native species. This group may be preyed

Blue-winged teal

upon here and elsewhere by members of other species, also widely distributed throughout the region: foxes, mink, weasels, or bobcats. Striped and spotted skunks and armadillos probably have less to worry about.

Reptiles and amphibians In a wet landscape like Yazoo, amphibians and reptiles enjoy a heyday. Alligators nest in the swamps, wallow in the ponds, haul themselves over the levees to sit in the abundant sun, and eat whatever they can catch. Although fascinating to watch, they must not be approached closely.

Alligator snapping, stinkpot, spiny softshell, painted, map, and mud turtles live in the water, while three-toed box turtles (tan with a red neck and face) occasionally roam on land. Toads, peepers, tree frogs, and small-mouthed salamander are some of Yazoo's many examples of amphibian diversity. Snakes and lizards carry out their jobs as predators.

HUNTING AND FISHING From Oct. through Dec., you may hunt **deer, feral hog,** and **small game**; small game are also in season in the month of Feb. **Turkey** may be hunted in April and May. **Waterfowl** are in season according to the state season, which fluctuates from year to year—contact the refuge for details. No fishing is allowed in the refuge waters.

ACTIVITIES:

■ **CAMPING:** There is no camping at Yazoo, but LeRoy Percy State Park, 8 miles north of the refuge, has a campground (601-827-5436).

■ **WILDLIFE OBSERVATION AND PHOTOGRAPHY:** The best observation areas are along the entrance road, around the lakes and ponds, and on nature trails.

■ **SEASONAL EVENTS:** The refuge celebrates National Wildlife Refuge Week in October with special events.

SATELLITE REFUGES

Contact Yazoo NWR for directions and current access conditions before visiting these satellite refuges.

■ **Hillside NWR** Established in 1975, Hillside NWR is a 15,572-acre swampy part of the Mississippi floodplain, located 13 miles north of Yazoo City on US 49E. Bottomland hardwoods, cypress swamps, recovering forests, croplands, and ponds and streams make up its varied habitats. The U.S. Army Corps of Engineers built levees here to trap silt for flood control but later turned the area over to the U.S. Fish & Wildlife Service. The flow of silt damages bottomland habitats, and managers are counteracting the process by reforesting parts of the refuge. Access to some sections of Hillside is often difficult because strips of private land run through the refuge, but there are hiking trails near the refuge office. Waterfowl and other migratory birds spend the winter or pass through here.

Alligator Slough Nature Trail (0.5 mile) starts with a boardwalk through a cypress swamp and then crosses levees to return. Roads and levees are open to hiking but may be flooded during rainy parts of the year.

■ **Panther Swamp NWR** Established in 1978, Panther Swamp is a 12,022-acre wetland located between Yazoo City and Holly Bluff. Large flocks of wintering ducks use the ponds and feed on farmed fields. Trails are being developed, and refuge roads are open to hiking.

■ **Mathews Brake NWR and Morgan Brake NWR** Mathews Brake established in 1980 and Morgan Brake established in 1977, lie south of Greenwood, MS, on US 49E. These small refuges (2,418 acres and 7,318 acres, respectively) are forested islands set down in wide expanses of cotton fields. They provide wetland habitats for many birds and other animals. A brake is a thick, tangled swampy area; in this case, it's a cypress and tupelo swamp. Mathews Brake surrounds an oxbow lake (good for canoeing) that was left behind when the mighty Mississippi made one of its many course changes. The shallow lake is sometimes choked with water lilies, and beavers perform some of the refuge management by controlling water levels and thinning the bordering trees.

Morgan Brake refuge has gated roads open to hiking, accessible from US 49E, and a reception area where maps are available.

Alligator River NWR and Pea Island NWR

Manteo, North Carolina

Alligator River NWR

In a 1969 Apollo 9 photograph, North Carolina's Outer Banks appear as a long, slender thread stretched at its midpoint way out into the deep blue depths of the Atlantic. A vast green expanse of wetlands and shallow bay separates the fragile barrier island from the mainland. Migrating birds drop in by the thousands to spend winters in this watery paradise.

Tundra swans, snow geese, flocks of ducks, and hundreds of other bird species stay at Alligator River and Pea Island NWRs, while some just pass through. But the birds are not alone on these refuges. Red wolves and black bears, for instance, roam the extensive swamps.

Nor are the animals the only creatures enjoying the eastern edge of the continent. Pea Island refuge, with its beautiful 12-mile ocean beach, gets an estimated annual visitation of 2 million people—more than any other southeastern NWR. Equally fascinating, however, is the Alligator River Refuge, which offers boardwalks crisscrossing peat-rich swamps, excellent canoe trails, and wolf-howling programs. Alligator River NWR and Pea Island NWR differ in landscape, climate, and wildlife. However, since they are administered by the same office and close enough together to combine them on a visit, they are both described in this narrative.

Tundra swans, snow geese, flocks of ducks, and hundreds of other bird species stay at both refuges or pass through. Red wolves and black bears roam the swamps of Alligator River, which provides many opportunities to develop a greater appreciation for swamps.

HISTORY

Ocean currents bearing sand constantly reshape this narrow barrier island system. The Gulf Stream flows northeast, spinning off small currents, or gyres, that pick up and drop sand as they curve toward the Atlantic coast and lose speed. The shifting sand islands protect inland wetlands and forests from storm tides. This part of North Carolina extends farther east than the rest of the southern coastline and has a wider band of the flat bottomland swamps that stubbornly resisted development by early European settlers. Today, however, the effects of modern agriculture, draining, logging, and resort development have degraded these rich wildlife habitats.

The 152,195-acre Alligator River NWR (opened in 1984) administers the smaller, 5,915-acre Pea Island refuge (1938). Pea Island was originally established to protect the dwindling population of snow geese; it has succeeded, along with other refuges, in increasing their numbers. Waterfowl are also safe from hunting in 26,000 acres of adjacent waters of Pamlico Sound, thanks to a Presidential Proclamation.

Red-winged blackbird

Much of the Alligator River Refuge was donated by the Prudential Life Insurance Company after their plans to mine the peat fields and drain the wetlands were dropped. Other parcels of swampland and fields have been added to improve waterfowl management; one parcel of a few acres was even turned over to the refuge by the Drug Enforcement Administration (DEA) after a backcountry drug bust. The possibility of future land acquisition—preferably by the traditional means—and the proximity of Pocosin and Mattamuskeet NWRs, make this large region an ideal habitat for wildlife (like wolves and bears) that need long distances to move about safely.

And there is this anomaly: War planes practicing over the Dare County Bombing Range, which is surrounded by the southern part of Alligator River NWR, often fly above Sawyer Lake and other parts of the refuge. This doesn't seem to bother the birds, and refuge staff have even installed an overlook plaque of silhouettes: "Know Your Jets."

GETTING THERE

Alligator River NWR: US 64/264 runs through the northern part of the refuge for about 5 mi. east of the bridge over the Intracoastal Waterway. Signs mark trails and boardwalks along US 64. The refuge administrative office is on US 64 in Manteo.

Pea Island NWR: From Manteo, take US 64/264 east. Cross over Roanoke Sound on a causeway and turn south (right) on NC 12. At 9 mi., cross Oregon Inlet on another causeway, leading to the refuge. The Visitor Center is 3 mi. farther on NC 12.

■ **SEASON:** The refuges are open all year.

■ **HOURS:** Refuges: open in daylight hours; Pea Island Visitor Center, 9 a.m.–4 p.m. daily April through Nov. and 9 a.m.–4 p.m. weekends rest of year.

■ **FEES:** None.
■ **ADDRESS:** P.O. Box 1969, 708 N. Hwy. 64, Manteo, NC 27954
■ **TELEPHONE:** 252/473-1131

TOURING PEA ISLAND AND ALLIGATOR RIVER

■ **BY AUTOMOBILE:** Alligator River NWR: US 64 crosses the northern part of Alligator River refuge; Buffalo City Rd. and Milltail Rd. turn south from it. A Wildlife Drive and other gravel roads in the refuge are open to cars.

Pea Island: The two-lane NC 12 runs the length of the Pea Island NWR with several parking pullouts; vehicles are not allowed on the beach here as they are on many other parts of the Outer Banks. Summer traffic along this stretch of road at Pea Island may be heavy .

■ **BY FOOT:** Alligator River NWR trails and boardwalks: Creef Cut Trail (0.5 mile), handicapped-accessible, leads past a fishing dock and to a 250-foot swamp boardwalk. A second boardwalk curves through a swampy open area with many dead trees used by cavity nesters.

Sandy Ridge Trail starts at the end of 2-mile Buffalo City Road off US 64 is handicapped accessible. It has a shady swamp boardwalk, and runs 0.5 mile to a creek culvert.

Pea Island Trails: North Pond Wildlife Trail (0.5 mile) leads from the Pea Island Visitor Center and provides overlooks and two observation towers with spotting scopes for viewing wildlife. A 4-mile service road continues around North Pond and is open to hikers. The beach is 12.2 miles long and has several access points with parking lots.

■ **BY BICYCLE:** Biking is allowed on the beach at Pea Island and on open refuge roads (but not on trails). US 64 through Alligator River and NC 12 through Pea Island are not safe bike routes because of fast traffic.

Sandbags in reconstructed dune, Pea Island NWR

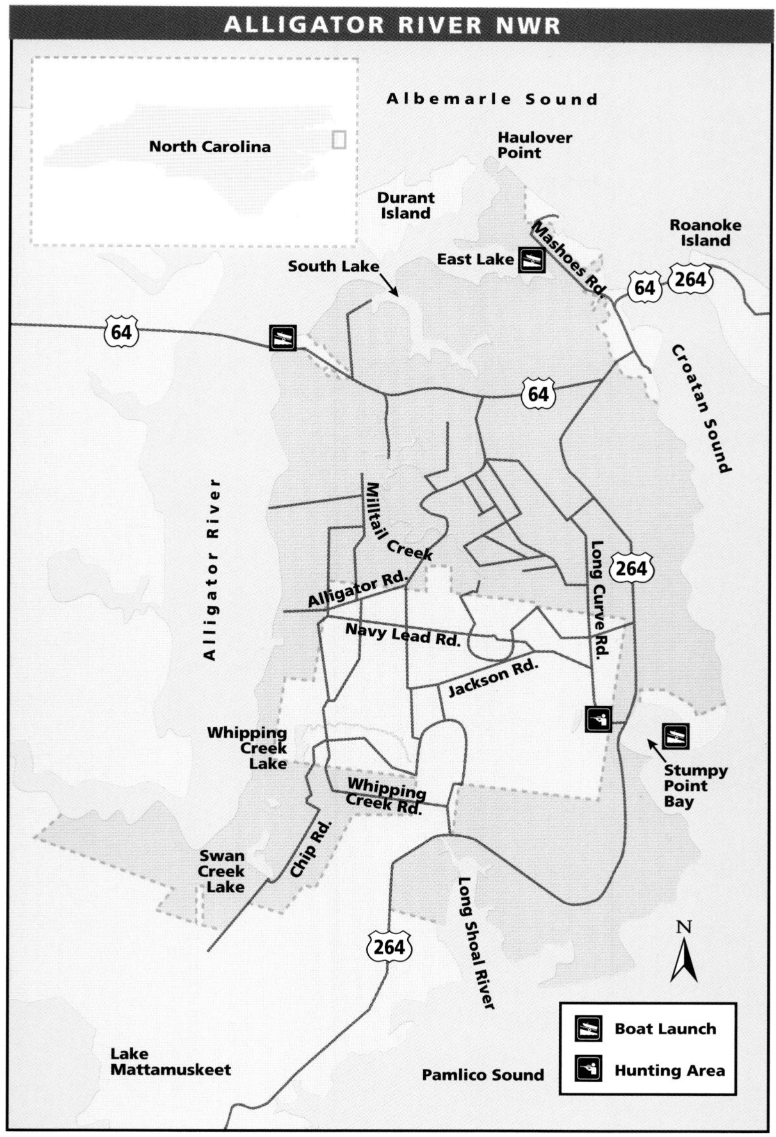

■ BY CANOE OR BOAT: Alligator River: There are 15 miles of marked canoe trails along Milltail Creek and Sawyer Lake. Maps are available at office, and the trails are included in the Albemarle Region Canoe and Small Boat Trails System, a 10-county cooperative.

Pea Island: Small boats and canoes can be launched at New Inlet about 2 miles south of the Visitor Center.

WHAT TO SEE

■ LANDSCAPE AND CLIMATE Winter is the best birdwatching time on the barrier islands, but all seasons are good for beach walking and swamp canoeing.

PEA ISLAND NWR

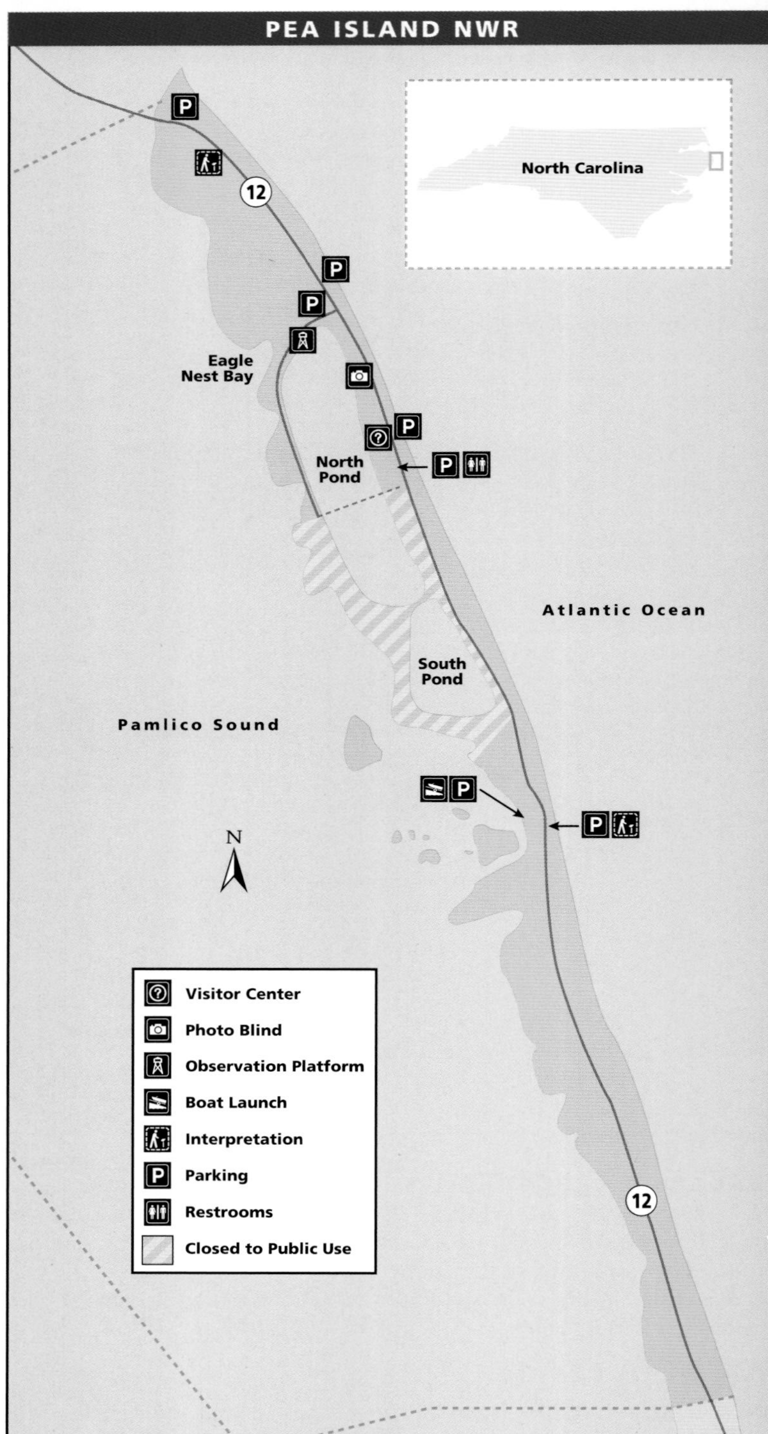

PEA ISLAND'S LIFESAVING HEROES Mariners called the Outer Banks the "Graveyard of the Atlantic" because winds, currents, and heavy shoaling drove so many ships aground. In 1871 the U.S. Lifesaving Service (later to become the Coast Guard) established crews of surfmen to rescue shipwreck victims.

Many crews were "checkerboard"—black and white men serving together; however, when the service appointed a black man, Richard Etheridge, as keeper of the Pea Island crew, the white members left. An all-black crew of surfmen served from 1880 to 1947, saving more than 600 lives and gaining a reputation as the bravest, most dedicated crew on the Outer Banks. They received no formal recognition until 1995, when the Coast Guard awarded them a gold medal posthumously. An exhibit at Pea Island refuge commemorates their efforts.

Beach, dunes, marsh, tidal creeks, and impoundments make up the Pea Island habitats, and from the top of the dunes you can see both the Atlantic Ocean and Pamlico Sound. Ocean waves fueled by nor'easters occasionally dump deep sand on NC 12, closing the road until bulldozers arrive. The road has been relocated more than once because of dune shifting; surprisingly, the present dunes, in this naturally sandy realm, are human-made.

Alligator River NWR consists of swamps, creeks, river, small lakes, forested sand ridges, canals, and cultivated fields. You may have the swamp all to yourself in fall and spring, when the weather is pleasant; biting insects are abundant in summer—best leave the swamp to them! For canoeing or walking, early mornings are cool enough. If crowds are not your thing, remember that the Pea Island beach, main road, and parking lots see heavy use in summer.

■ **PLANT LIFE** Dunes support (and are stabilized by) sea oats, dune grass, evergreen shrubs like wax myrtle, and dune peas, small plants in the legume (bean) family whose beans are favored by snow and Canada geese. Sea pennies (pennywort) grow their scalloped round leaves flat on the sand.

The west side of NC 12 is lined with evergreen shrubs, such as low-growing live oaks and red cedars. A live oak arbor forms the entrance to the dike walk around the impoundments near the Pea Island Visitor Center. Yaupon holly, a shrub whose leaves contain caffeine, grows here. Also called cassena or Christmasberry, yaupon was valued by American Indians for its medicinal qualities—it induces vomiting—and for its use in brewing a special ceremonial drink. Rose mallow and seaside goldenrod bloom around the impoundments.

The dominant swamp trees of Alligator River are cypress and tupelo, with maple, oak, and sweet gum mixed in. Sweetbay magnolia evergreens line canals and creeks—the leaves give off a spicy smell when crumpled. Loblolly pines inhabit sandy ridges, and pond pines grow on pocosins. Yellow swamp iris and water lilies add vibrant colors to watery places, and mats of sphagnum moss hold water like sponges. Insectivorous pitcher plants and sundews help out with pest control.

■ **ANIMAL LIFE**

Birds Anywhere and everywhere at Pea Island you will see birds, and many can be easily spotted from the Visitor Center. Snow geese, tundra swans (also called

Red wolf, Alligator River NWR

whistling swans), and 25 species of ducks swim and feed in the Pea Island impoundments and marshes. Herons and avocets (long-legged, with bills curving up at the ends) feed in the marshes and mudflats. On the beach right at waterline, sanderlings, sandpipers, dunlins, and godwits follow the waves in and out, and some frequent the dunes, as well. Terns and seagulls stand facing the wind, while brown pelicans fly in formation.

Near the Pea Island Visitor Center, look about for boat-tailed grackles, red-winged blackbirds, and meadowlarks perching on tall grass. Indigo and painted buntings (blue head, red breast, and green back) may be spotted here.

Peregrine falcons (a threatened species) find a safe home here, as do black-necked stilts. In swamp trees you are bound to see holes pecked out by pileated woodpeckers and flickers. What you probably won't see, you may well hear: barred owls calling at night or on cloudy afternoons. The best places to see colorful neotropical migrants in April are along the swamp boardwalks.

Mammals Red wolves and big black bears, the stars of Alligator River, roam freely in the swamps. Like owls, wolves are more likely to be heard than seen, but bears may venture out to open fields. Wolves once again inhabit the area thanks to an intense recovery project over the last two decades (see sidebar), but the bears survived the old-fashioned way: hiding out until the land around them became a wildlife refuge. The introduced wolves didn't know about the dangers of traffic, but new generations born on these refuges are more street-smart.

Raccoons, mink, otter, and nutria (a destructive alien rodent from South America about the size of a muskrat) live on the refuges, too. Rice rats at Pea Island dig tunnels under marsh wrack (piles of grass stems and other organic debris). The tunnels run between the marsh and the roots of wax myrtle trees, where the rats can find safety during hurricanes.

Reptiles and amphibians Nonvenomous snakes here include black racers, green snakes, water snakes, and king snakes. The Carolina salt-marsh snake, a type of water snake, can live and catch food in salt or brackish water. Venomous water moccasins prefer freshwater marshes, while canebrake rattle-

THE RETURN OF THE RED WOLF Red wolves once ranged throughout the southeast but were almost extirpated during the colonization by European settlers.

The few wolves remaining in the swamps of Louisiana and Texas (just one more good thing about swamps) had crossbred with dogs and coyotes. Between 1974 and 1980, the U.S. Fish & Wildlife Service captured many of these animals and with DNA testing and bone measurements selected the wolves most like the original inhabitants. Only 14 wolves passed the tests to enter into a breeding program in a Tacoma, Washington, zoo.

As the captive red wolf population increased, other zoos took on breeding programs. By 1987 there were enough red wolves to release into the wild. Alligator River NWR received the first of the new wolves, and similar reintroductions have succeeded on coastal refuges in South Carolina, Florida, and Mississippi. Reintroductions in the Great Smoky Mountains National Park and Land Between the Lakes (in Tennessee) have been abandoned, but wolf populations thrive in larger areas.

Red wolves are cinnamon in color, weigh 40 to 60 pounds, and have long, spindly legs. They maintain family packs of six to ten wolves and prey on white-tailed deer, raccoon, nutria, and small rodents. Although sightings of these shy animals are still very rare, Alligator River NWR schedules regular wolf-howling programs. Visitors meet at designated sites, where a refuge biologist provides an update on the status of the wolves. After that, everyone caravans into the middle of the refuge where the biologist starts to howl, followed soon by the visitors. Astonishingly, refuge wolves have howled back every time but twice in the past two years. The howlings are more than just a thrilling experience for refuge visitors—they provide communication between humans beings and an animal that almost disappeared from the earth.

snakes favor drier areas. Fence lizards, blue-tailed skinks, and slider turtles also live on the refuge.

Endangered loggerhead sea turtles nest on the beach in precarious circumstances. Refuge volunteers patrol the nests and either relocate them or protect them until the new turtles hatch and head for the relative safety of the water.

And, of course, alligators reside in the swamp, but only 50 to 100 of them, not as many as inhabit more southern swamps like Okefenokee—at this latitude, the gator is close to the northern edge of its range.

Invertebrates Mosquitoes, ticks, and deerflies take perverse pleasure in pursuing refuge visitors, but on the beach, greenhead flies make the greatest impression, especially on windless days. The greenheads draw blood with their sharp, sawlike mandibles. Strong winds coming off the ocean keep them away.

The world of crabs is divided between ghost and fiddler crabs on land and hermit, blue, and other crabs living in the water. Ghost crabs are sand-colored (good camouflage), fast on their feet, and never far from their deep holes; big ones catch and eat hatchling sea turtles. Hermit crabs live in mollusk shells; when they want bigger or better shells, they evict other hermit crabs from good shells in a hostile takeover. Beachcombers will find sand dollars and mollusk shells along the shore.

ACTIVITIES

■ **CAMPING:** There is no camping on the refuge, but there is a private campground one mile from the refuge and several others also in the near vicinity.

■ **SWIMMING:** Twelve miles of ocean beach are available for swimming on Pea Island. No swimming is allowed at Alligator River.

■ **WILDLIFE OBSERVATION AND PHOTOGRAPHY:** The North Pond Wildlife Trail on Pea Island has two observation platforms, three with fixed spotting scopes. There is a small photography blind west of NC 12, about 0.5 mile north of the Visitor Center.

■ **HIKES AND WALKS:** Pea Island North Pond Wildlife Trail (4 miles) starts at the Visitor Center, passes an observation platform on New Field Pond, and then ends at a two-story tower where you can see the ocean and the sound. It is the best place to observe waterfowl and other birds in marsh and open water and is handicapped-accessible; the Visitor Center can provide wheelchairs. After the second platform, the trail becomes a service road along a dike and is level walking for 3.5 miles. Cross the road and walk back to the Visitor Center for a 7-mile loop.

Several parking lots provide access to the beach. Across the dunes from the Visitor Center are the rusted remains of the *Orient*, a Civil War battleship. Farther down the beach are the cistern and other remains of the lifesaving station (see sidebar, above).

Alligator River trails and boardwalks (one built with the help of a local high school football team) provide intimate views of the swamp and may be extended in the future.

HUNTING AND FISHING You may fish from March through Sept. In the sounds surrounding the refuge, as well as in East and South lakes, you will find species such as **flounder** and **largemouth bass**. In the canals around the refuge, you are likely to find smaller species such as **bluegill** and **crappie**. **Small game** may be hunted only in Oct., and you may hunt **deer** during the months of Sept. through Nov.

■ **SEASONAL EVENTS:** April through December: Red Wolf Howling Programs (Note: Howling programs meet at entrance to Creef Cut Trail on US 64; no reservation required.); May: International Migratory Bird Day; Mid-June through August: Wildlife programs for children and guided canoe tours; Mid-September through November: Guided bird walks; October: National Wildlife Refuge Week; Howl-o-ween Howlings (also every Wed. night June through August and on Christmas and Earth Day); November: Coastal Wings over Water (3-day celebration of wild lands and wildlife with guided tours and programs); December: Christmas Howling Program

■ **PUBLICATIONS:** Bird lists; maps; leaflets; an audiotape guide to both refuges, including bird songs and wolf howls.

Mackay Island NWR

Knotts Island, North Carolina

Mackay Island NWR

It may lie off the beaten path, but this refuge is well worth a respite from the crowds and highways. Here are snow geese and tundra swans gliding in the bay, osprey nesting along the roadside, and rafts of noisy ducks. Other plusses: a free ferry ride from the south and a drive through a privately owned, undeveloped island with its own old-time general store.

HISTORY

It is reputed that John Mackie, an island settler who died in 1823, was buried here standing up so that he could enjoy the view. The island eventually took on Mackie's good name, or a version thereof. Nearly one hundred years later, another fellow who also liked the view would prove instrumental in helping conserve the island's natural attributes. New Yorker Joseph Knapp built a mansion on Live Oak Point in 1918. He raised ducks, developed and managed habitats to attract migratory waterfowl, paid for local children's college educations, and was one of the original founders of Ducks Unlimited, a conservation organization that is active throughout the country today.

The 8,646-acre refuge was established in 1961. Community groups, including the Tidewater Appalachian Trail Club, Virginia Beach Audubon Society, local girl scouts, and senior citizens groups, help with gardens, environmental education, and an annual peach festival, making Mackay Island Refuge a model of citizen participation.

GETTING THERE

From Virginia Beach, VA, drive south on Princess Anne Rd. to the Virginia–North Carolina border on NC 615; continue 1.3 mi. to refuge sign on right. From the south, from the intersection of NC 158 and NC 168, drive north about 4 mi. to the Currituck–Knotts Island Ferry on right (watch for sign; ferry

MACKAY ISLAND NWR

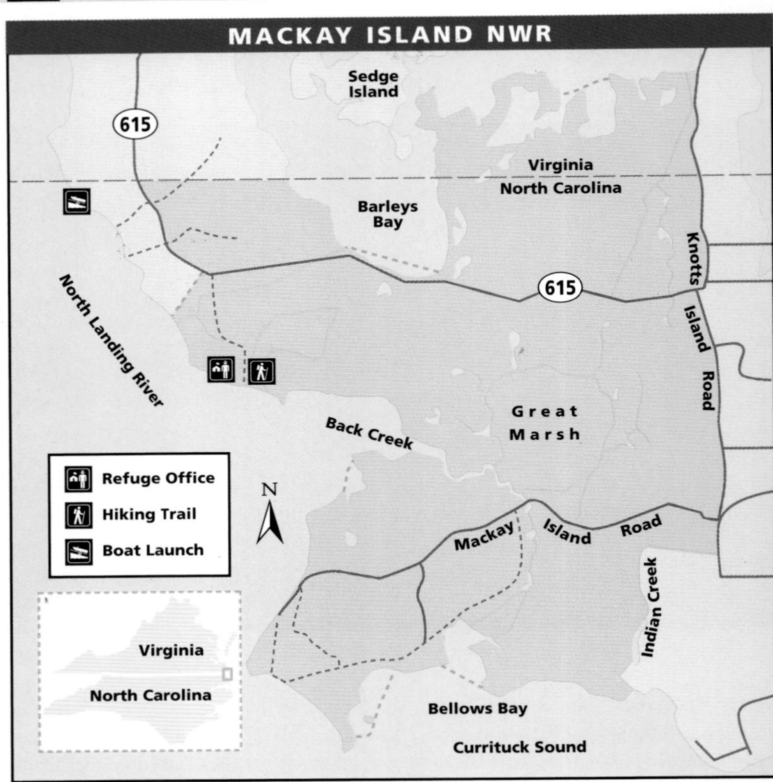

yard is not visible from NC 168). On Knotts Island, drive 8.1 mi. on NC 615 to refuge entrance on left.

■ **SEASON:** Refuge open all year, but portions are closed Nov. through March

■ **HOURS:** Refuge: daylight hours; office: 8 a.m.–4 p.m., weekdays.

■ **FEES:** None.

■ **ADDRESS:** P.O. Box 39, 318 Marsh Causeway, Knotts Island, NC 27950

■ **TELEPHONE:** 252/429-3100

TOURING MACKAY ISLAND

■ **BY AUTOMOBILE:** Mackay Island Rd. from the eastern side of the refuge (off NC 615) goes along a borrow canal (see "Landscape and Climate," below) lined with tall trees. Note: The refuge schedules Open Roads Days; call for details. At other times, the area beyond the end of Mackay Island Rd. may be closed.

■ **BY BICYCLE:** Refuge roads are open to bicycles; also, NC 615 through the refuge and on the causeway toward Virginia could be a good bike route. Dike roads may also be open.

■ **BY FOOT:** The 0.3-mile Marsh Trail and boardwalk, about 2 miles east of the refuge office, is open all year. Dikes in the interior of the refuge offer a 6.5-mile hike or a shorter 4-mile version. The area may be closed to protect nesting bald eagles; call the office.

■ **BY CANOE, KAYAK, OR BOAT:** A boat ramp west of the refuge office allows access to the bay and refuge creeks. Refuge waters are closed to boating from October 16 to March 14.

WHAT TO SEE

■ LANDSCAPE AND CLIMATE Mackay Island NWR, on the northeastern corner of North Carolina, gets cool, rainy weather in winter and hot, occasionally breezy weather in the summer. It is so well sheltered by the Outer Banks that tidal action comes from wind instead of ocean tide and has an irregular schedule. (Normally lunar tides are the primary cause of tidal action, but in southern Currituck Sound lunar tides don't affect tidal activity as much as wind.) Marsh, cultivated fields, impoundments, and sand ridges make up the habitats.

■ PLANT LIFE Marsh with brackish water dominates the refuge, which has an impact on the range of plants that will grow here. Salinity is lower than in many salt marshes because of freshwater from the river and minimal tidal action. Phragmites, a tall, nonnative grass, is battling with native black needlerush and cordgrass for hegemony; refuge staff combat it with herbicides and burning. Other prescribed fires (see sidebar, below) reduce litter and provide new growth for waterfowl food.

Sweet gums, oaks, and maples line ditches and canals, providing some shade for walkers, while loblolly pines grow in small forested areas on sandy low ridges. Planted flowers behind the refuge office attract butterflies.

■ ANIMAL LIFE

Birds Snow geese (10,000 to 12,000 of them) crowd the Mackay Island marsh impoundments and the bay during winter. Large flocks of tundra swans also visit, time-sharing between Mackay Island and the other NWRs. Black ducks, pintails, mallards, gadwalls, wigeons, wood ducks, and other Atlantic Flyway waterfowl dabble for aquatic vegetation.

A pair of bald eagles, the first in 40 years here, is nesting near the beginning of

FIRE ECOLOGY An amphibious vehicle bounces through the marsh of Mackay Island NWR. Gas jets on the side ignite the tall grass, and a line of flames crackles away from the vehicle toward a canal.

Most refuges carry out controlled, or prescribed, burns. In spite of Smokey the Bear's advice, ecologists recognize that fire is a natural part of most wildlife habitats and has many benefits:

1. Fire reduces leaf litter, dead branches, and dry grass. If this material builds up for several years, accidental fires can be catastrophic. Fire is nature's way of keeping things tidy and safe.
2. Some species depend on fire to germinate. For example, many pinecones will not open to release seeds without fire. Tree bark protects many trees from small, periodic fires.
3. Exotic plants that replace native plants can be controlled by fire. At Mackay Island and many other southeastern refuges, a grass called phragmites has invaded the marshes. Native grasses may return if phragmites is burned.
4. Fire returns nutrients to the soil and allows new growth that feeds waterfowl and other wildlife. The primary nutrients returned to the soil are nitrogen and phosphorous. Essentially, burning areas of the forest brings these areas closer to their historical condition. By burning areas of the refuge, certain plants that are not adapted to fire are excluded.

the hike and bicycle tour around the impoundments, which is why that part of the refuge may be closed. But you might spot them soaring overhead in search of prey.

Sandpipers, willets, and dowitchers feed in the marshes, and kingfishers swoop over open water. High in the old trees at the bay overlook, visitors may spot nesting ospreys, and in the same trees, cormorants sometimes perch on dead branches.

Open waters west of the refuge are a proclamation area—waterfowl hunting is not allowed.

Mammals Red foxes den each year in an agricultural field 150 yards from the refuge office. Ask the refuge manager for best times to see them come and go. Rice rats, muskrats, bats, raccoons, and otters are native to the island and the region, but you may also see nutria, a muskrat-sized South American rodent, that is a recent invader. White-tailed deer overgraze grasses and shrubs; to protect the plant life, the refuge schedules an annual managed deer hunt.

Reptiles and amphibians You should have no trouble finding painted, red-bellied, and yellow-bellied slider turtles in the canals. Because there are only a few good basking logs, the sliders simply crawl up on top of each other. The whole precarious pile of turtles crashes back into the water if one slider becomes alarmed.

Venomous snakes (water moccasins and their imitators), plus nonvenomous water snakes, share refuge waters. Keep a sharp eye out, and ask at the office for tips on distinguishing these snakes.

Invertebrates Blue crabs, scuttling in the bay and up into the marshes, are the invertebrates most visitors are likely to see at Mackay Island.

Red fox pup

ACTIVITIES

■ **CAMPING:** There is no camping on the refuge itself, but there is a private campground north of the refuge on NC 615 and others in the area. Inquire at the refuge office for suggestions.

■ **WILDLIFE OBSERVATION AND PHOTOGRAPHY:** Charles Kuralt, the late traveling television raconteur, was from North Carolina, and refuges in the state honor him with a wildlife observation site. At Mackay Island, the site is a bay overlook on NC 615 about 1 mile east of the office. A plaque and other interpretive material will be installed. Cormorants, ospreys, waterfowl, and shorebirds visit the open water near the overlook.

Flocks of waterfowl, including snow geese and tundra swans, can usually be seen from the causeway and boat launch west of the refuge office.

Behind the office is an attractive open area with a butterfly garden overlooking a fine view of the salt marsh.

SATELLITE REFUGE

■ **Currituck NWR** First acquired in 1984, partly from a land donation from The Nature Conservancy, Currituck NWR (4,095 acres) has beach, dune, marsh, scrub, live-oak forest, and impoundment habitats. Currituck has several units north of Corolla (where the Outer Banks road ends). Two units can be reached with a 4WD vehicle or by beach walk from Corolla; the rest are accessible by boat. All vehicles must stay on the beach; foot traffic only beyond the dunes. The refuge is open daily from sunrise to sunset. Some marsh units are closed from October 15 to March 14. Threatened piping plovers and endangered loggerhead sea turtles may nest here, and waterfowl, shorebirds, wading birds, and many other migrants visit. The refuge has plans for a visitor station with information.

Mattamuskeet NWR

Swan Quarter, North Carolina

Wintering tundra swans, Lake Mattamuskeet

Lake Mattamuskeet, the largest natural lake in North Carolina, resembles an ocean bay—a large expanse of water with a just-visible horizon of trees in the distance. But the lake is deceptively shallow, varying from a few inches to 5 feet. Hungry tundra swans and other waterfowl love it because of the abundance of water plants, and the marshes, woods, and swamps around the lake provide varied habitats for other plants and animals. Wildlife observation, fine fishing opportunities, and an unusual hunting lodge/pump station draw visitors to this coastal marshland refuge.

HISTORY

Lake Mattamuskeet formed as the ancient ocean receded and left a basin behind "ridges" of coastal sand just a few feet higher than the flat plain. Fire and other factors may have deepened the basin. Over time, sphagnum moss decayed to form peat, and rain filled the area with freshwater.

In 1915, landowners dug canals to pump water from the lake to develop soybean, rice, barley, corn, and buckwheat fields, and, in the spirit of similar Dutch drainage operations, they built New Holland, a planned community. By 1932, they had streets, houses, stores, and more fields. The world's largest steam-powered pumping station—a three-story building with a lighthouse-sized smoke stack—loomed over the southern edge of the former lake and pumped water into the Outfall Canal, a misnomer in such flat land. The pump house itself formed a barrier to prevent water from flowing back into the lake. Early maps show a semicircular town with symmetrical streets.

Accumulating rain and the expense of pumping (and perhaps lower dikes than would have been built in old Holland) conspired against the project. The U.S. government bought the lake in 1934 and allowed it to refill. The Civilian Conservation Corps converted the pump house into a hunting lodge and the smokestack into an observation tower. Now it really looks like a lighthouse and has a spiral staircase to two observation platforms. Visitors used the lodge for Canada goose hunting trips. In 1972, goose hunting was stopped and the lodge was closed and placed on the National Register of Historic Places in 1980. East Carolina University uses part of the lodge as a research station. Plans are under way to develop the building into a Visitor Center and an environmental-education facility.

GETTING THERE

From Manteo, drive west on US 64/264 for 10 mi. Where the routes split, turn right on US 264 and drive about 25 mi. to Engelhard. Continue on US 264 for about 15 mi. and turn right onto NC 94. In 1.5 mi., turn right at refuge sign and drive 2 mi. on entrance road to refuge office. From the west, Mattamuskeet is about 70 mi. east of Washington (NC) on US 264.

■ **SEASON:** Refuge is open all year.

■ **HOURS:** Refuge: daylight hours; refuge office: 7:30 a.m.–4 p.m., Mon.–Fri. Lodge is open at times for tours; call refuge office for schedule.

■ **FEES:** None.

■ **ADDRESS:** Rte. 1, Box N-2, Swan Quarter, NC 27885

■ **TELEPHONE:** 252/926-4021

TOURING MATTAMUSKEET

■ **BY AUTOMOBILE:** The main entrance road and the 5-mi. Wildlife Drive along the southern edge of the lake are best bets for wildlife observation. NC 94 cuts across the middle of the lake, providing more good views, especially of waterfowl.

■ **BY FOOT:** Refuge roads and dikes are open to hiking. On the western side of the refuge, at the Rose Bay Entrance, there is a shaded dike between pine woods and a canal.

■ **BY BICYCLE:** The dike at Rose Bay Entrance is the best choice for bicycles. Other dikes are open to bicycles but may be bumpy.

■ **BY CANOE, KAYAK, OR BOAT:** Canoes and small boats may explore the lake and canals from March 1 to Nov. 1. Put in at the Rose Bay Entrance for a 9-mile marked canoe trail on a canal to the lake, making two loops.

WHAT TO SEE

■ **LANDSCAPE AND CLIMATE** Lake Mattamuskeet (18 miles long, 6 miles wide) takes up 80 percent of the refuge. February is the coolest month, with occasional frost. Late fall, winter, and early spring are pleasant and provide the best birdwatching. In summer, the area is hot and humid, but some of the canals are shaded for comfortable canoeing and fishing.

Eleven impoundments on the eastern edge of the lake are used to control water levels and to provide more food for birds. Water is pumped, and gates control the flow. Some croplands also provide food, and there is a "greentree" area (a section of oaks, hickories, and other nut-bearing trees, flooded in the fall) lying near the Rose Bay Canal.

■ **PLANT LIFE** Open water, marsh, cypress swamp, and loblolly pine woods make up the habitats of Mattamuskeet Refuge. The most important plants on the refuge—masses of aquatic vegetation supporting vast flocks of waterfowl—are submerged, but in summer, parts of the lake become dry. Maples, oaks, and

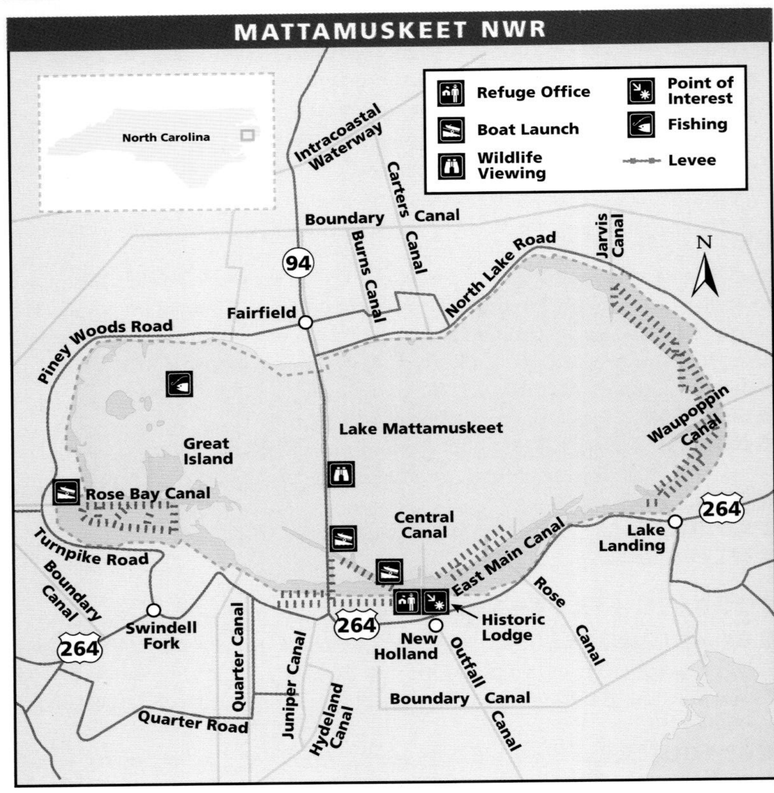

sweet gums take root beside Rose Bay Canal, along with the fragrant rose bay, a type of magnolia. Understory vines include trumpet creeper, greenbrier, and muscadine grapes.

Across the dike from Rose Bay Canal is Salyer Ridge, a National Natural Resource Area. This 157-acre tract, administered by the refuge and by the National Park Service, is one bit of old-growth loblolly forest that survived the logging era. From the dike it hardly looks like a ridge, but compared with the canal bank, it is a few feet higher.

■ ANIMAL LIFE

Birds Can you imagine the sound and sight of 30,000 tundra swans? These elegant white birds with distinctive black bills feed in Mattamuskeet Lake in the winter. Arriving in groups in late fall, many of them leave the refuge during a full moon in March. They take off with a chorus of melodic honking. Contrary to normal flyway patterns, tundra swans migrate *diagonally* across the United States to nest in Alaska or northwest Canada.

Pintail, mallard, black, and other dabbling ducks share the lake with the swans, but they have to upend themselves to get the water plants that the swans reach easily with their long necks. Canvasback and other diving ducks submerge themselves to feed. Coots swim with the ducks, using their lobed toes instead of webbed feet. Diving ducks and coots both run across the water to get airborne. Dabbling ducks are more like helicopters: They just jump up from the water and start flying. Many of the ducks migrate north to the Great Lakes and then turn left to the potholes of the upper Plains.

Canada geese winter over at Mattamuskeet, but in spring some of them head back to Canada and some stay at the refuge to nest. Pileated and red-bellied woodpeckers take up residence in the woods along Rose Bay Canal. To spot an osprey, scan the tops of cypress trees from the NC 94 overlook.

Approximately 400 tundra swans get leg bands each year at this refuge. Wildlife managers use five small rockets to shoot a 100-by-60-foot net over a flock of swans. Then they wade in to band and release the birds, trying not to get scratched by the swans' strong claws.

Mammals River otter, raccoon, deer, bobcat, and nutria (muskrat-sized introduced South American rodents) are common on the refuge. One family of wolves has raised pups here, and black bears are seen occasionally.

Reptiles and amphibians Yellow-bellied sliders, snapping turtles, and other turtles live in the lake and in the canals. Alligators are common at the Swan Quarter satellite refuge (see below), and several species of nonvenomous water snakes slither along the banks of all parts of Mattamuskeet. Venomous snakes here include water moccasins (you might see one fishing in the lake or canals). The Carolina pygmy rattlesnake, a threatened species, has a pretty red back, creamy belly, and the smallest rattle of any rattlesnake (it sounds like an buzzing insect). Keep an eye out for the pygmy in dry loblolly or scrub woods.

Fish Lake Mattamuskeet, despite its shallowness, is a popular fishing area, with striped and largemouth bass, bream, and catfish.

Invertebrates Blue crabs travel up the canals from Pamlico Sound and thrive in freshwater, salt water, and brackish water. Crabbing is good year-round at the lake.

ACTIVITIES

■ **CAMPING:** Camping is not allowed on the refuge, but facilities are available at a private campground, Mattamuskett Campground, less than a mile from the refuge on the south end of NC 94.

■ **WILDLIFE OBSERVATION AND PHOTOGRAPHY:** The best place at Mattamuskeet for close-up views of waterbirds is the entrance road (with its pull-offs), which runs along a strip of land protruding into the lake. The Wildlife Drive serves up lovely views of marsh, woods, and open water. In winter, ask at the refuge office where the greatest concentration of waterfowl is feeding on that day. Warblers and other neotropical migrants are best seen in wooded areas near the refuge office and at the Rose Bay Entrance.

HUNTING AND FISHING **Deer season** runs through the months of Oct., Nov., and Dec. You may fish in the refuge waters from March through Oct. The most commonly found species are **striped** and **largemouth bass, bream,** and **catfish. Blue crabs** travel up the canals from Pamlico Sound and thrive in the refuge waters—crabbing is allowed year-round.

■ **HIKES AND WALKS:** Mattamuskeet doesn't have specific footpaths, but walking on the dikes rewards you with views of the lake. For hot, sunny days, there are sheltered walks along the canals. A 1,500-foot boardwalk starting from the refuge office is being built by young people in a local conservation corps, funded by Friends of Mattamuskeet Lodge and other supporting groups.

■ **SEASONAL EVENTS:** "Swan Days," early December—generally attended by thousands of swans and many tourists. Workshops, lectures, tours of the refuge and the lodge, craft shows, and wildlife exhibits; annual Audubon Christmas bird count; birdwatching tours during spring and fall migrations (inquire at refuge office).

■ **PUBLICATIONS:** Maps; bird lists; brochures; and a pamphlet on the Mattamuskeet Lodge.

SATELLITE REFUGES

■ **Swan Quarter NWR** This refuge occupies 16,000 acres of salt marsh and forested wetlands southwest of Lake Mattamuskeet, bordering on Pamlico Sound. Most of the refuge is open to boat access only. A 1,000-foot fishing pier and two undeveloped trails for walking or biking can be reached on a 2-mile access road from US 264 just west of Swan Quarter. Bears, alligators, bald eagles, and great flocks of waterfowl live in the refuge, part of which is a Wilderness Area. One parcel of the refuge is open to hunting. Waters around the marshes and islands of the refuge are posted as a Presidential Proclamation Area, where hunting is not allowed. A ferry runs between the towns of Ocracoke and Swan Quarter.

Canada geese

■ **Cedar Island NWR** Directly south of Swan Quarter NWR is Cedar Island NWR, also connected to Ocracoke by ferry. NC 12 runs through the refuge and south to Beaufort, NC. Established in 1964, Cedar Island grew by land purchase and donation to 14,000 acres by 1990. It provides the pristine marsh needed by waterfowl, alligators, black bears, and the young of marine vertebrates and invertebrates. It offers a refuge office, two undeveloped trails, crabbing and fishing, and a public waterfowl hunting area.

Pee Dee NWR

Wadesboro, North Carolina

Northern shoveler

One of the best birdwatching sites in North Carolina lies less than 60 miles from the bustling city of Charlotte. Pee Dee NWR offers trails, an observation platform, and more ducks and geese than you can count. Plans are under way for the construction of an Environmental Education Center; for now, however, interpretive trails and easy access to all habitats of the refuge attract wildlife enthusiasts.

HISTORY

Catawba and Pee Dee Indians lived along the Pee Dee River on this lower part of the Piedmont. European settlers planted the fertile hills and riversides with cotton, soybean, and corn. While most farmers drained the wetlands for timber and agriculture and allowed erosion and overgrazing, one farsighted landowner named Lockart Gaddy maintained a private refuge for geese and other wildlife. A goose hunter, Gaddy used decoys to lure Canada geese to his riverside property. In 1934 he gave up hunting and rededicated his land to wildlife observation and protection.

When Gaddy's private refuge closed after his death, waterfowl and other wildlife relocated to 8,843-acre Pee Dee NWR, established at the most opportune of times in 1965. The refuge manages 15 conservation easements in eight surrounding counties and is part of the Savannah–Pee Dee–Santee Ecosystem.

GETTING THERE

From Wadesboro drive 7 mi. north on US 52 to refuge office on right.

■ **SEASON:** Refuge open year-round.

■ **HOURS:** Refuge: daylight hours; office: 8 a.m.–4:30 p.m.

■ **FEES:** None.

■ **ADDRESS:** Rte. 1, Box 92, Wadesboro, NC 28710

■ **TELEPHONE:** 704/694-4424

TOURING PEE DEE NWR

■ BY AUTOMOBILE: A 2.5-mile interpretive auto tour provides fine views of ponds, swamp, fields, and upland pine forest. Signs along the road provide information. Other refuge roads are also open to cars.

■ BY FOOT: Two established trails and woods roads include the 3-mile Prothonotary Warbler Trail and a 0.25 mile handicapped-accessible nature trail.

■ BY BICYCLE: The auto tour and refuge roads are open to bicycles in this easy-to-ride landscape.

■ BY CANOE, KAYAK, OR BOAT: No boating is allowed in the creek—extensive damage from Hurricane Hugo in 1986 made much of it unnavigable.

WHAT TO SEE

■ LANDSCAPE AND CLIMATE The refuge landscape is made up of rolling forested hills, fields, floodplain with bottomland hardwoods, and the Pee Dee River, with its tributary creeks—typical lower Piedmont terrain slowly descending into coastal plain. Impoundments create ponds that support waterfowl. Fall, winter, and spring are the best times to visit, but fishing is good from March 15 through October 15, especially in morning and evening.

Northern pintail

■ PLANT LIFE The refuge contains the largest intact bottomland hardwood tract in the Piedmont section of North Carolina, earning it a designation on the registry of State Natural Heritage Areas, plus extra protection and biological research projects. This large area is important because bottomland hardwood forests are not at allcommon in mountainous areas.

Refuge management includes planting native trees and grasses, burning to promote new growth, and practicing no-till agriculture on open fields, which helps to reduce the erosion and disturbance of native grasses. Early successional habitats of prairie grasses were lost to agriculture over the years and are being replanted because native wildlife and migratory birds depend on the habitat for survival.

■ ANIMAL LIFE

Birds At Pee Dee a few endangered red-cockaded woodpeckers nest in pine uplands; sharp-eyed bird-spotters may spy bald eagles and peregrine falcons. Several species of ducks are regular Pee Dee visitors, including green and blue-winged teal, mallards, wood ducks, pintail, gadwall, and shovelers.

Canada and snow geese also spend the winter on the refuge; one group of Canada geese stays here to nest. Woodland birds, including indigo buntings, blue grosbeaks, scarlet tanagers, prothonotary warblers (yellow head and breast), bluebirds, and red-winged blackbirds nest here.

To monitor populations F&WS biologists at Pee Dee Refuge band migratory songbirds.

Larger birds nesting on the refuge include quail, turkey, barred and screech owls, and several kinds of woodpeckers.

Mammals Deer, foxes, squirrels, and bobcats are permanent residents here. The deer and squirrels are easy to spot; the fox and bobcat, far less cooperative. In meadows with many predators, golden mice somehow manage to build grass-and-leaves nests on plant stalks.

Beavers engineer woodland ponds that are also used by frogs and salamanders to lay eggs in spring. Working beavers are interesting to watch. They may be cutting timber at water's edge or dragging it to a dam or to their lodge. If you frighten them, they will signal danger to one another by slapping the water's surface with their wide, flat tails and then dive for cover.

Reptiles and amphibians Pee Dee's mix of wet and dry habitats suits the turtle realm well. Box turtles live on land, and cooter turtles and sliders live and feed in refuge waters. All need to find dry land for egg laying. Several snake and lizard species live on the refuge.

ACTIVITIES

■ **CAMPING:** Camping is not allowed on the refuge. Uwharrie National Forest, 30 miles north of the refuge, offers modern camping facilities and a swimming lake (704/257-4200).

■ **WILDLIFE OBSERVATION AND PHOTOGRAPHY:** The observation blind near the wildlife drive, overlooking Sullivan's Pond, is a favorite site for watching waterfowl. Other good wildlife viewing sites are the dikes around refuge impoundments. Take a walk and explore. Silent canoes floating on the slow current of the Pee Dee River can bring you close to such wildlife as herons or basking turtles and snakes. Checklists of bird, reptile, and amphibian species are available at the refuge.

■ **HIKES AND WALKS:** The footpath to the observation blind and Prothonotary Warbler Trail both have interpretive signs and take you through all the habitats of the refuge, a good way to see the connections between one habitat and another. Some refuge roads are gated (keeping cars out) and provide peaceful hiking—if you visit in cool, relatively bug-free months.

Pocosin Lakes NWR

Creswell, North Carolina

Nutria, yawning

A pocosin is a curious landform. The name is an old Indian term meaning "swamp on a hill"—the "hill" being 2 feet or so high, resting on wet, spongy peat moss, and perhaps having a slight depression on top. Trees grow better on pocosins than in the surrounding wetlands. A dense, sprawling terrain of natural pocosin is the distinguishing feature at Pocosin Lakes NWR, where canoeing and birdwatching are the main attractions. A spanking new Visitor Center in Columbia provides good access to the refuge and wildlife information.

HISTORY

Before European settlement, the Great Dismal Swamp (in what is today Virginia) extended farther south into what is now North Carolina. Pocosin Lakes was part of the same water system, providing freshwater for Pamlico Sound. Although farming and draining disrupted the larger ecosystem, refuges in North Carolina and Virginia now protect these habitats.

The Pungo Lake Unit was established in 1963, and adjacent units were added in 1990 with help from the Conservation Fund and donations from other private foundations—a good example of government and nongovernmental organizations working together to support wildlife refuges.

GETTING THERE

The new Visitor Center is located in Columbia on the south side of US 64 just east of the Scuppernong River bridge. To reach the Pungo Lake Unit, take NC 45 south from Plymouth. After about 15 mi., look for refuge signs on the left.

To reach Phelps Lake and the original refuge office, drive to Roper on US 64. About 0.5 mi. west of Roper, look for a refuge sign and turn right onto Newland Rd. After 8 mi., turn right at a large concrete grain bin onto Shore Dr. and drive 2.5 mi. to the refuge office on the left.

■ SEASON: Refuge open all year.
■ HOURS: Refuge: daylight hours. Office: 7:30 a.m.–4 p.m., Mon.–Fri.
■ FEES: None.
■ ADDRESS: 3255 Shore Dr., Creswell, NC 27928
■ TELEPHONE: 252/797-4431

TOURING POCOSIN LAKES

■ BY AUTOMOBILE: Several roads are open to vehicles. They may be rough and, in wet weather, very muddy; check with the refuge office.

■ BY FOOT: Many miles of dikes and areas around the lakes are open to hiking except for posted areas. Take a map and a compass—it's easy to get turned about. Behind the new Visitor Center, the Scuppernong Boardwalk winds through a forested wetland.

■ BY BICYCLE: Mountain bikes can be used on dikes and open refuge roads (no paved roads for skinny tires).

■ BY CANOE, KAYAK, OR BOAT: New Lake, Frying Pan Lake, and Phelps Lake are open to canoeing. The network of canals and creeks connecting to Pamlico and Albemarle sounds also provides extensive canoeing or kayaking. Look for "The Albemarle Region Canoe and Small Boat Trails System," a free one-page map and brochure available at the refuge and other locations. Pungo Lake is closed to protect waterfowl.

WHAT TO SEE

■ LANDSCAPE AND CLIMATE Pocosin Lakes NWR (114,000 acres) shares space with two other refuges, a few small towns, and several farms on a bulge of marshy land between Albemarle and Pamlico sounds. It spreads across three different counties, each with diverse habitats: Tyrrell County contains bottomland hardwoods; Hyde County offers upland and freshwater habitats; and Washington County contains mostly agricultural land. The Outer Banks on the Atlantic coast shield this land from the erosion caused by tides and saltwater overwash that would otherwise have a negative impact the plant life. The coastal climate is most pleasant in winter, early spring, and late fall.

■ PLANT LIFE About half of the refuge is pocosin wetland, with pond pine and an understory of scrub oaks, other small trees, and vines. Other habitats include shallow open water, riverside swamp, grassy fields that once were farmed, and pine/ hardwoods. Some fields are leased to farmers who leave parts of their crops for wildlife. The dense growth and the underlying peat (up to 12 feet thick) are highly combustible and catch fire in dry seasons; refuge managers set prescribed burns to improve habitat and to prevent larger fires.

Sweet bay, black willow, and other shrubs line the canals. Atlantic white cedar, once common here, was overharvested; managers are replanting it to reestablish mature stands.

■ ANIMAL LIFE

Birds Pocosin Lakes is a favorite overwintering spot for tundra swans, snow geese, and 20 species of ducks. Many of the birds move from this refuge to Mattamuskeet and Pea Island NWRs and other safe places. Snow geese favor sprouts of winter wheat, whereas tundra swans feed on water plants and field grains. In March migrating birds depart at different times: snow geese, early; swans, usually during a full moon.

Bitterns, great blue herons, black ducks, wood ducks, hawks, owls, buzzards, woodpeckers, and many other nesting birds make good use of Pocosin's varied habitats. Birders can see waves of warblers, wrens, thrushes, and other neotropical migrants passing through in spring and fall.

Mammals The impenetrable cover of brush and thick woodland understory hides black bears and wolves. Some wolves were introduced here from Alligator River NWR, and some came on their own. Mink and otter are common, and deer are sometimes too common—they chew newly planted trees. Bats, shrews, moles, and several rodents (including nutria, a destructive South American species that competes with native animals for food) also use the Pocosin refuge.

Reptiles and amphibians Salamander and frog experts take note: Sixteen species of salamanders and more than 20 kinds of frogs and toads occupy the Pocosin wetlands.

Yellowbelly sliders, other turtles, water snakes, and cottonmouths live in the canals. Garter snakes, corn snakes, fence lizards, and other reptiles favor the drier spots.

ACTIVITIES

■ **CAMPING:** Camping is not allowed on the refuge. Pettigrew State Park, in nearby Creswell, offers campsites and primitive camping opportunities (252/797-4475).

■ **WILDLIFE OBSERVATION AND PHOTOGRAPHY:** At Pungo Lake visitors can take advantage of a bird blind and an observation platform (helpful in a relatively flat landscape).

■ **HIKES AND WALKS:** The dikes are a visitor's best bet for an excellent view of the refuge's lush vegetation. Take a hat and sunscreen, or walk during cooler times of the day.

The Scuppernong Boardwalk, in the town of Columbia, provides a close-up look at forested wetland and peaceful river views. Scuppernong, the name of the river here that flows into the Albemarle Sound, has lent its name to a delicious thick-skinned grape that is a fall delicacy and used to make a sweet white wine. Cypress trees are deciduous conifers with swollen bases and fine, slightly shaggy bark.

■ **SEASONAL EVENTS:** October: National Wildlife Refuge Week; November: Wings Over Water, celebration of wintering waterfowl.

■ **PUBLICATIONS:** Brochures, animal checklists, maps.

Caribbean Islands NWRs

Boqueron, Puerto Rico

Young boy strolling a Caribbean beach

Collectively, the eight Caribbean NWRs protect an astonishing variety of tropical, subtropical, and marine wildlife—often in the face of formidable challenges. On one island refuge, for example, the main threat to wildlife is a troop of introduced rhesus monkeys; rats, goats, and mongooses do their share of mischief at other sites. Two refuges are undergoing restoration after serving as bombing ranges; another is recovering from the overgrazing of cows. Still others are battling the effects of sugarcane runoff. The good news is, the recovery of coral reefs and the revitalized numbers of leatherback turtles, tropic birds, and the critically endangered St. Croix ground lizard tell of a growing success story.

HISTORY

Archaeological evidence has determined that American Indians settled the islands around 800 A.D., leaving piles of conch shells (middens) and other relics of everyday use. Christopher Columbus sailed by three of the present-day refuges in 1493 on his second trip to the New World; records show he didn't stop to look around. Taino Indians, a branch of the Arawakans, lived in Cuba, Puerto Rico, and Hispaniola at the time, but after only 100 years of Spanish occupation and slavery, the Taino, like many Caribbean people, died out completely. Spain controlled the islands and grew sugarcane—importing slaves from other places—until the Spanish-American War (1898).

In 1909 President Theodore Roosevelt proclaimed the islands near Culebra a wildlife refuge, subject to naval use. President Taft designated Desecheo Island a nesting refuge with the same proviso. For many years, the U.S. Navy exercised its option for bombing practice. In 1976 the Navy turned the land over to the U.S. Fish & Wildlife Service to become permanent refuges.

Until recently, the Caribbean National Wildlife Refuges consisted of seven separate parcels of land (totaling less than 4,000 acres) situated on the big island of

Puerto Rico and some of its smaller islands and in the U.S. Virgin Islands. In April 1999, the refuge acquired an eighth parcel: Navassa Island, comprising 300,000 acres, most of which is coral reef.

Recently, hurricanes Hugo (1989) and Marilyn (1995) hit the Caribbean hard, damaging some of the refuges, especially Culebra.

GETTING THERE

The refuge office and Visitor Center are in Boqueron, on the main island of Puerto Rico. From Mayaguez on the western side of the island, drive south on Rte. 2 to Rte. 100. At end of Rte. 100, turn left onto Rte. 101, proceed 0.8 mi., and turn right onto Rte. 301. Look for refuge sign after 3 mi.

Inquire at the Boqueron office about boat and plane travel to the other island refuges open to the public.

■ **SEASON:** Year-round.
■ **HOURS:** Weekdays, 7:30 a.m.–4 p.m. Call refuge for weekend hours
■ **FEES:** None.
■ **ADDRESS:** P.O. Box 510, Boqueron, P.R. 00622
■ **TELEPHONE:** 787/851-7258

WHAT TO SEE IN PUERTO RICO

■ **Cabo Rojo NWR (1974)** This 587-acre refuge has a Visitor Center, a 2-mile interpretive trail, a cactus garden, and 12 miles of hiking on service roads Before 1974 the CIA used the land for a communications monitoring post, and cattle ranching damaged the dry forest around the buildings. The property now attracts such residents as the endangered yellow-shouldered blackbird. A few migratory North American birds spend the winter here, and many warblers pass through on their way to South America. Native birds include Adelaide's Warbler, the Puerto Rican tody, and the Caribbean elaenia (both flycatchers), troupial (an orange-and-black tropical oriole), and bananaquit (a nectar-sipping honeycreeper).

Refuge management includes restoring native plant species and removing exotic plants by haying.

Little blue heron

■ **Laguna Cartegena NWR (1989)** Sugarcane fields, abandoned cow pastures, dry upland forest and a freshwater lagoon make up this 1,059-acre inland refuge. Farming and draining have chased away waterfowl, but with habitat restoration, they are coming back. Cattails and water hyacinths, which choke the lagoon, must be cleared on a regular basis. Herons magnificent frigate birds smooth-billed anis, and migrating waterfowl have been seen on the lagoon Visitors can hike on service roads and trails.

■ Culebra NWR (1909) This 1,568-acre refuge consists of units on Culebra Island and 22 smaller islands. Two islands, Cayo Luis Peña and Isla Culebrita, are open to hiking (boat access only). In spite of bombing practice in past years, seabirds nest on the islands, and leatherback and hawksbill sea turtles nest on the beaches. Habitats include subtropical dry forest, mangrove fringes, grasslands, small parcels of tropical rain forest, and beaches.

Sooty and roseate terns, tropicbirds, and boobies nest here; don't disturb them—the other refuges depend on them for recolonization.

A refuge office on Culebra is open 7:30 a.m.–4 p.m., weekdays (787/742-0115). A ferry runs between Fajardo and Culebra.

WHAT TO SEE IN THE U.S. VIRGIN ISLANDS

■ Sandy Point NWR (1984) A bit of St. Croix (398 acres) was saved from development by a timely FWS purchase. The largest nesting population of the endangered leatherback sea turtle under U.S. jurisdiction uses this small stretch of beach. Migrating birds stop at the refuge, and mangroves, deciduous forest, and scrub provide habitat.

The refuge is open 10 a.m.–4 p.m., Sat.–Sun. Call the office (340/773-4554) to get more information or to volunteer for turtle patrol.

■ Buck Island NWR (1969) Open daylight hours every day, this 45-acre refuge lies two miles south of the island of St. Thomas. Visitors can hike, watch birds, take photographs of the resident lighthouse, or snorkel over the colorful coral reef surrounding the island. Cactus and thorny scrub grow here. A large population of introduced rats has destroyed bird nests; it is hoped that vigilant rat control will eventually bring back nesting birds.

OTHER REFUGES

The following refuges are closed to public use but are of interest to wildlife conservationists.

■ Green Cay NWR (1977) The refuge managers of this 14-acre island just north of St. Croix have a major challenge: to protect the endangered St. Croix ground lizard. Indian mongooses, introduced by sugar farmers, decimated many snake and lizard populations on neighboring islands and cays. It is hoped that the mongoose-free Green Cay will serve as a lizard reserve, and lizards from here may be recruited to recolonize other habitats.

Brown pelicans, little blue herons, American oystercatchers, and other waterfowl stop on the cay. A pile of 33,000 conch shells is evidence of human use.

■ Desecheo NWR Brown boobies once nested on Desecheo, which became a refuge twice: originally in 1912 and again in 1976. The 360-acre rocky island, off the west coast of Puerto Rico, is closed to public use but can be observed from boats. Introduced rhesus monkeys, rats, cats, and goats—plus bombing practice—effectively wiped out seabird nesting colonies, including boobies, sooty terns, frigatebirds, and noddies. Refuge staff are removing invasive animals and plants in the hope that these birds will nest here again.

■ Navassa Island NWR (1999) Three hundred thousand acres of healthy coral reef and a few small islands between Puerto Rico and Haiti have become one of the newest refuges. The new refuge is closed to protect the coral, which has increasingly become a threatened habitat worldwide.

ACE Basin NWR

Hollywood, South Carolina

Wetland, ACE Basin NWR

The South Carolina Low Country is a landscape of coastal marshes and natural estuaries. One particularly rich estuarine ecosystem evolved from the merger of three rivers. Where the Ashepoo, Combahee, and Edisto rivers come together into St. Helena Sound, just south of Charleston, a new refuge has been created to protect this valuable ecosystem. ACE Basin NWR ("ACE" represents the first letters of the three rivers) is part of an ambitious cooperative arrangement among private and public interests. Instead of saving mere sections of good wildlife habitat, the philosophy goes, why not preserve the whole estuary?

Birdwatching and boating are excellent on this new refuge. There are grassy trails along the dikes to wander and view waterfowl; other visitor facilities are in the planning.

HISTORY

Building cities and roads on the vast wetlands of the low country coastal plain proved too challenging for early European settlers, so they grew rice instead. A few owners managed large plantations. After the Civil War, rice farming declined, and sportsmen bought the plantations for hunting. Luckily, both rice planters and hunters practiced smart stewardship over the years, and much of the land remained undisturbed. In the 1980s, conservationists realized the value to wildlife of keeping the area intact, and they devised a land-acquisition plan within reach of conservation funds. They drew a line around the whole estuary and began working to preserve parcels of land within that boundary.

The collaborators include The Nature Conservancy, the U.S. Fish & Wildlife Service, Ducks Unlimited, South Carolina Department of Natural Resources, Westvaco Corp., the philanthropist Ted Turner, and other private landowners. ACE Basin refuge was established in 1990; today at least half of the area within that estuary line is under some sort of protection, with more land acquisition in progress.

The Grove plantation house, built in 1828, was one of the few in this area to survive the Civil War; it now serves as the refuge office, shared with The Nature Conservancy. Restoration has brought back its antebellum elegance. A wide outside staircase leads to an upstairs door. Historic preservationists were reluctant to build the staircase; they were concerned that it was not an authentic part of the original house. But someone discovered a diary entry describing how a resident plantation owner trained his horse to mount the stairs and deliver him to his bedroom when he was drunk; upon reading this, the restorers gladly designed the staircase. The Grove plantation house is on National Register of Historic Places.

GETTING THERE

Take US 17 for 25 mi. south of Charleston. Turn right onto SC 174 and go through Adams Run. At flashing light, turn right onto Willtown Rd. and drive 2 mi. Turn left onto refuge entrance road (Jehossee Island Rd.) , and follow dirt road 2 mi. to office.

■ **SEASON:** Open all year.

■ **HOURS:** Daylight hours.

■ **FEES:** None.

■ **ADDRESS:** ACE Basin NWR, P.O. Box 848, Hollywood, SC 29449

■ **TELEPHONE:** 843/889-3084

TOURING ACE BASIN

■ **BY AUTOMOBILE:** The 2-mile entrance road, sometimes muddy, is a good wildlife observation drive.

■ **BY FOOT:** From the refuge office, you can walk through the gardens and out along dikes. Trails are presently unmarked but will be improved.

■ **BY CANOE, KAYAK, OR BOAT:** Boats can be launched in many parts of the estuary, but there are no rentals at the refuge.

Swallow-tailed kite

WHAT TO SEE

■ **LANDSCAPE AND CLIMATE** Cool in winter, this South Carolina region is hot and muggy from late spring to early fall. People who visit nearby ocean beaches in summer find the refuge pleasant for touring in early morning or late evening. The coastal landscape hereabouts is flat, with diked areas that attract birds. Water levels in ponds are raised and lowered to improve food and habitat for waterfowl.

■ **PLANT LIFE** ACE Basin's varied overlapping habitats include tidal marshes, fresh water wetlands, bottomland hardwoods, pine and hardwood uplands, barrier islands, and beaches. The tidal marshes are distinct in that they flood twice a day

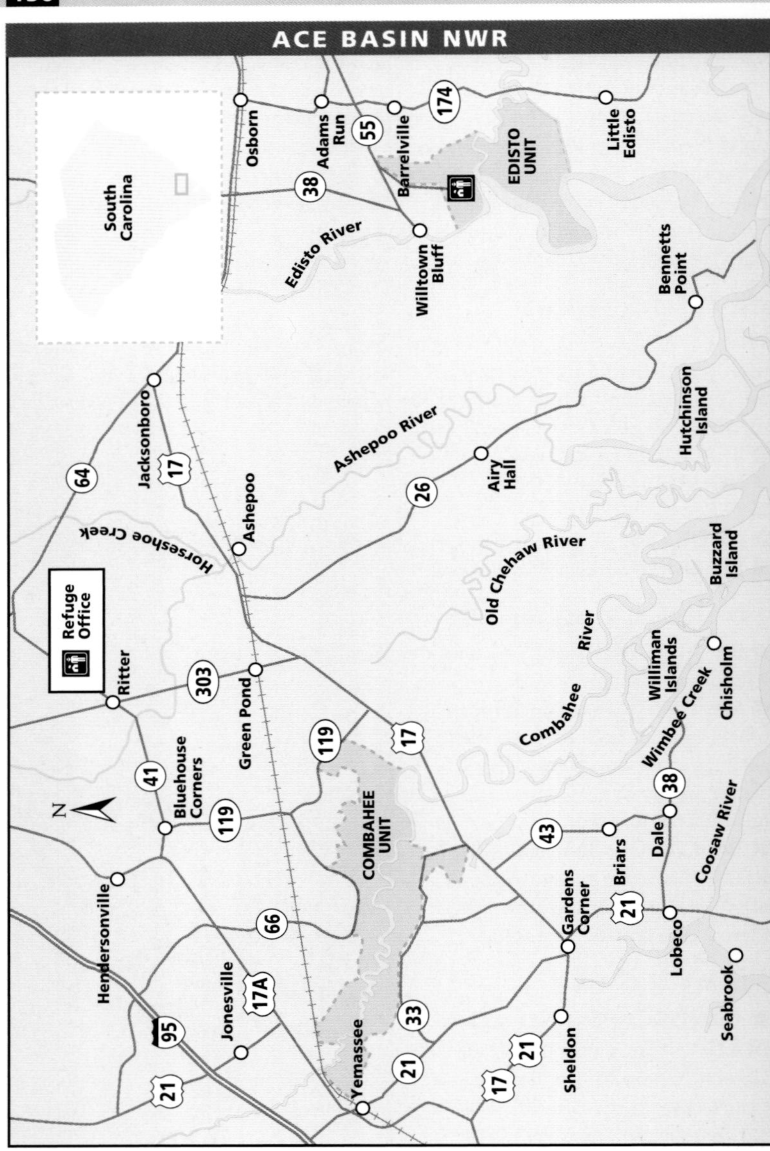

with the tides and produce organic matter that supports more wildlife than most other habitats here.

Huge live oaks (an evergreen oak prized for the radius of its crown, abundant shade, and durability) surround the plantation house, and vibrant azaleas fill the garden. Aficionados of lilies strike it rich here: spider lilies, Easter lilies, and surprise lilies (also known as naked ladies) all bloom in spring at ACE Basin.

Swamp trees, including cypress, tupelo, maple and black gum, grow in the fresh water wetlands. The waterways are often lined by tall oaks and maples.

■ ANIMAL LIFE

Birds Directly under the Atlantic Flyway, ACE Basin is a popular stop for birds

Wood stork

and birders. Wood storks feed on the refuge and bring their young, hatched in Florida, here in summer. Take a boat out on the Combahee River to see bald eagles nesting in tall trees. Both Mississippi and swallow-tailed kites hunt large insects, reptiles, and rodents. Visitors exploring the wetlands and marshes will probably spot ducks, herons, loons, grebes, both white and glossy ibis, and many other shorebirds. Neotropical migrants such as warblers and thrushes pass through. Painted and indigo buntings (both are residents) are easy to see in various habitats, and the diversity of habitats here attracts many other permanent residents (ask for a bird list at headquarters).

Mammals Mammals at ACE Basin are typical of eastern forests and coastal plains. The biggest are white-tailed deer. Some others are familiar to many visitors, such as raccoons, gray squirrels, and fox squirrels. More elusive mammals also live here: otters, bobcats, red foxes, and opossums. Inquire at headquarters for good locations. Learning to read tracks in the mud may help.

Reptiles and amphibians Alligators bask out in the open and build their mound nests in the swamps. These nests consist of piles of gathered grasses, mud, and other organic matter. Female alligators lay their eggs deep in the mound and guard them while the composting heat of the mound incubates the eggs. The abundant wetlands also support fish-eating water snakes and venomous cottonmouths, as well as many amphibians; the drier areas, such as the pine and hardwood uplands, are home to rat snakes, pine snakes and fence lizards.

Invertebrates The salt marshes serve as nurseries for crustaceans and mollusks. Look for crabs, shrimp, and oysters.

Live oak with Spanish moss

ACTIVITIES

■ **CAMPING:** There is no camping on the refuge, but a private campground in nearby Hollywood offers camping facilities.

■ **WILDLIFE OBSERVATION AND PHOTOGRAPHY:** There is, as yet, no wildlife observation tower at ACE Basin. Canoe along tidal creeks and the river to find the most promising sites where wildlife may appear in a variety of habitats. Take a map, compass, lens filter, bug repellent, and sunscreen.

■ **HIKES AND WALKS:** Grassy paths along the dikes offer the best chances to see waterfowl in the impoundments. Ask at the Visitor Center about trails under development.

■ **SEASONAL EVENTS:** The refuge celebrates National Wildlife Refuge Week in October with special events.

HUNTING AND FISHING
The refuge allows **waterfowl** and **white-tailed deer** hunting on the refuge. The deer-hunting season runs from Sept. through Nov. The refuge follows the state seasons for waterfowl. For information on current license requirements, seasons, and bag limits, consult the refuge office.

Fishing is also permitted on the refuge. The season runs from March through Sept.

Cape Romain NWR

Awendaw, South Carolina

Bobcat

Cape Romain provides development-free beachfront property for the birds—but visitors are welcome too; just take a 3-mile boat trip from busy US 17 to peaceful Bulls Island. The rewards are miles of beach and shaded trails under live oak trees. A day at Cape Romain may include hiking, beachcombing, watching egrets, waterfowl, and nesting wood storks, stepping around basking alligators, or possibly glimpsing a red wolf.

If you miss seeing a wolf at the island, there's another chance at Sewee Visitor and Environmental Education Center, run cooperatively by Cape Romain NWR and Francis Marion National Forest. The center features nature programs, exhibits, a nature trail, a raptor rehabilitation project, and a red-wolf enclosure.

HISTORY

Cape Romain refuge covers a 20-mile coastal section north of Charleston. The 64,229-acre property was established in 1932; 28,000 acres today comprise a National Wilderness Area. The entire refuge is included in the South Atlantic Biosphere Reserve. Its location between Charleston and Myrtle Beach and its proximity to US 17 make this refuge accessible to millions of people, many of them winter and spring vacationers.

An elbow-shaped barrier island, Cape Romain is smaller than Cape Cod and Cape Hatteras (on the Outer Banks) but has a similar geological history. The coast of North America extends east as a shallow continental shelf of sand, and a warm river—the Gulf Stream—runs north just a few miles offshore. Water displaced by the Gulf Stream peels off in eddies and carries masses of sand back toward the coast, which creates a barrier island sheltering the coastline. Hurricanes take sand from one part of a barrier island, and other storms bring it back, so the islands shift constantly, no matter what beachfront owners do to prevent it. The Cape Romain barrier islands are allowed to shift in the natural pattern.

It is thought that Blackbeard and other pirates hid their ships in the salt marshes, and another outlaw, the Swamp Fox, Francis Marion, used the densely vegetated Lowcountry to carry out successful guerrilla raids against British troops during the American Revolution. Before the war Marion served in the Provincial Congress; after the war he served in the U.S. Congress.

In 1989 Hurricane Hugo flattened large areas of forest and damaged dikes and other structures. Massive live oaks and old magnolias on Bulls Island fell; replacements are slowly growing.

GETTING THERE

From Charleston, South Carolina, drive 20 mi. north on US 17 to Sewee Nature Center and refuge office on the right.

■ **SEASON:** Refuge and visitor center open all year.

■ **HOURS:** Refuge: daylight hours; Sewee Visitor and Environmental Education Center: 9 a.m.–5 p.m., Tues.–Sun.; refuge office: 8 a.m.–4 p.m. weekdays.

■ **FEES:** None.

■ **ADDRESS:** 5821 Hwy. 17 North, Awendaw, SC 29429

■ **TELEPHONE:** Refuge Office: 843/928-3264; Sewee Visitor and Environmental Education Center: 843/928-3368

TOURING CAPE ROMAIN

■ **BY AUTOMOBILE:** There are no wildlife drives on the refuge, but several scenic roads go through Francis Marion National Forest.

■ **BY FOOT:** At Visitor Center: short trails through forest and red-wolf areas and a 1-mile interpretive loop. On Bulls Island: National Recreational Trail (2.0 miles) and 16 miles of road and beach. On Raccoon Key, part of the Wilderness Area, beach hiking is allowed. Francis Marion National Forest has more than 120 miles of well-marked trails.

■ **BY CANOE, KAYAK, OR BOAT:** The islands and salt-marsh creeks of the refuge can be reached by private boat, sea kayak, or passenger ferry service from Moores Landing or McClellanville. The ferries reach Bulls Island (3 miles).

Painted bunting

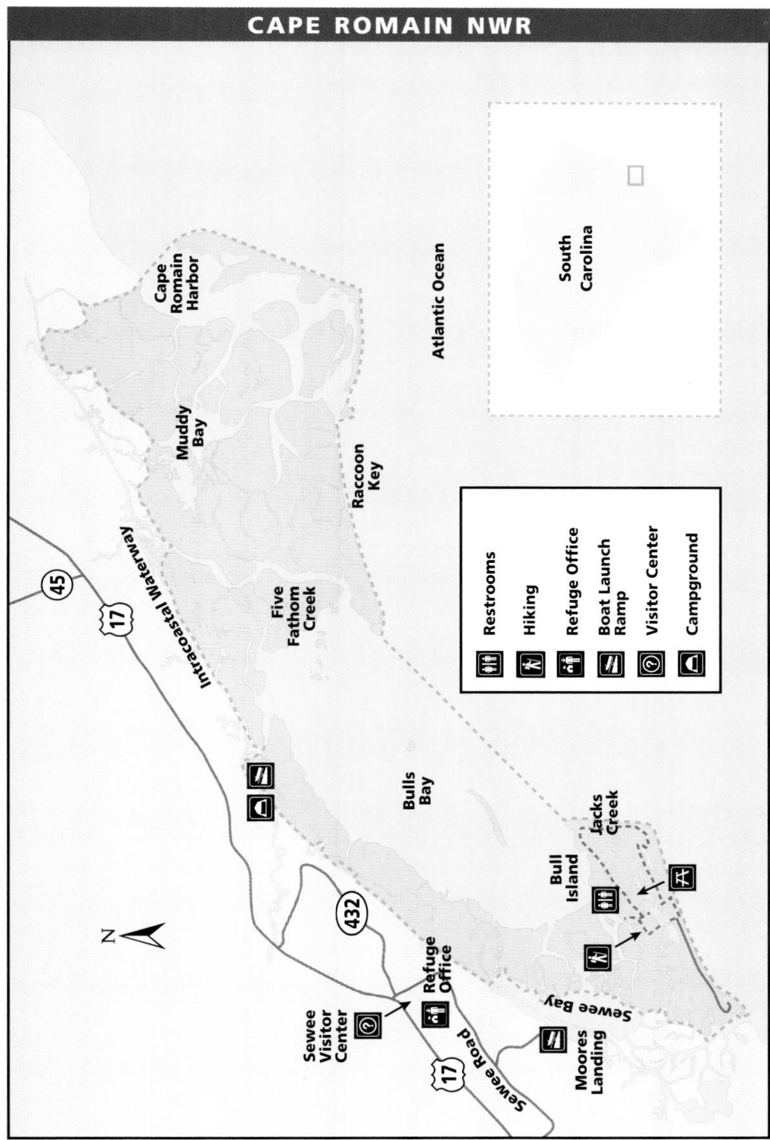

Guided expeditions also explore the salt-marsh creeks. For schedule and reservations, call Coastal Expeditions (843/881-4582). Before launching private boats, check with the refuge office for tide and current information.

WHAT TO SEE

■ **LANDSCAPE AND CLIMATE** Cape Romain and its associated islands are flat with occasional forested sand ridges. Ocean breezes moderate summer heat; still, it can get intensely hot inland from the dunes, so cooler months may be better times for hiking and birdwatching. Late summer and fall are hurricane season, and other storms may come quickly; keep track of local weather forecasts. Wave action generally moves sand from north to south on the barrier islands in this region, a process that was accelerated by Hurricane Hugo in 1989.

On Bulls Island old dikes hold shallow ponds with vegetation for waterfowl. Cape Island and Lighthouse Island have two old lighthouses that are no longer in use and not open to the public.

Cordgrass, also called Spartina

■ **PLANT LIFE** Cordgrass (*Spartina*) dominates the salt marshes and contributes to their high productivity; the marsh, in turn, supports diverse wildlife food chains. The cordgrass is so tall in some places that boaters can get lost in a maze of tidal creeks, although patches of trees can serve as landmarks. New sprouts of cordgrass grow from rhizomes when old stems fall and decay in the black mud. Sedges and rushes live around the edge of the salt marsh.

Deep-rooted sea oats, pennywort, wax myrtle, and other tough salt-tolerant plants hold the barrier island dunes together—without them, the dunes would simply blow away. Another dune stabilizer is the innocent-looking sand spur, with sand-colored barbed burrs that can work their way into the skin of bare feet. Bulls Island has the largest maritime forest on the refuge. Live oaks—decorated in Spanish moss and resurrection ferns—and southern magnolias arch over the roads behind the dunes, and red cedars, cabbage and saw palmettos, and yaupon holly (*Ilex vomitoria*) form the understory.

Banana water lilies, with bright yellow flowers and large oval leaves, bloom in freshwater ponds. Though not native, they provide food for waterfowl. The blue flag iris and pickerelweed also blossom here.

Native grasses favor the freshwater marshes, but cattails, which are not useful as wildlife food, invade open water and choke out grass and submerged aquatic vegetation. Refuge staff work to remove cattails and other exotics that displace native plants.

Skeletons of dead trees, mostly live oaks and palmettos, decorate Boneyard Beach, on the northeastern part of Bulls Island, where the sea has overtaken the land. This is barrier island shifting in action.

■ **ANIMAL LIFE**

Birds Seabirds, beach birds, salt-marsh birds, maritime forest birds, pond birds—all flock to the large and varied undisturbed habitats on Cape Romain. Atlantic Flyway migrants stop here, and many others nest. The greatest variety of birds is found on Bulls Island.

Royal and sandwich terns, sporting black, swept-back crests, lay eggs right on the beach. The eggs and chicks have the same sand-and-pebble camouflage; they require isolated beaches for breeding colonies. Camouflage works well against predators—but doesn't save birds from foot traffic.

Other shorebirds include several gull species, sandpipers, sanderlings, dowitchers, plovers, yellowlegs, willets, turnstones, knots, godwits, and dunlins. Unless you are a dedicated birder, you may need the refuge's bird list and a bird identification book to tell them all apart.

Brown pelicans, herons, and egrets fish offshore or in the marshes and build chaotic rookeries in the treetops. Specialty feeders at Cape Romain include black skimmers, which catch fish or crustaceans by flying just above the water surface with their lower beaks cutting through the water; and oystercatchers, which spend their whole lives at a raw bar, slipping their flattened beaks into the shells of unwary oysters and clams, extracting the soft stuff.

Clapper rails, with remarkably unmusical voices, and smaller herons hide in the tall marsh grasses and eat small mollusks and crustaceans. The marshes also provide shelter for bobolinks, red-winged blackbirds, grackles, and meadowlarks.

These islands are prime nesting grounds for painted buntings, ruby-throated hummingbirds, bluebirds, and many other small birds; many warblers and other small birds stop here during migration. Cedar waxwings and yellow-rumped warblers (formerly called myrtle warblers) digest wax and eat the seeds of the wax myrtle (bayberry) bushes on the dunes. Tanagers, wrens, grosbeaks, and kinglets migrate north in April.

Migrant waterfowl include tundra swans and enough species of ducks—including teal, mallard, shoveler, gadwall, wigeon, scaup, scoter, goldeneye, bufflehead, mergansers (which dive and catch fish with saw-toothed bills), and more—to keep any duck fancier entertained for days.

Mammals Red wolves—believed to be extinct in the wild—raise pups on Bulls

Red fox with fresh kill

MAKING THE BEACH SAFE FOR TURTLES A hatchling sea turtle climbs out of the sand and races for the sea while ghost crabs, raccoons, sea gulls, herons, and terns snatch its nest mates. Once in the sea, the little turtle faces other dangers: shrimp and fish nets, dredgers, oil rigs, and pieces of plastic that look like food.

Five species of sea turtles nest on our coasts, and all are threatened or endangered. Little turtles have always had to run a gauntlet of predators, but human activity adds more hazards—nesting habitat destruction, vehicles on the beach, lights on the beach that confuse the hatchlings, and increased populations of raccoons.

Southeastern coastal refuges increase the chances of sea turtle survival through the protection of dunes and beaches. Refuge workers cover nests with wire frames or relocate the eggs—a complicated procedure because turtle embryos attach to the inside of the shell and must be relocated in the same position that the female deposited them. The temperature of the nest determines the sex, and mother knows best how to maintain a proper balance.

Researchers have shown that the threats of the open sea contribute most to population declines, but refuges can give the turtles a head start and increase their chances of survival.

Island. Biologists and refuge staff released the wolves here in 1987 from captive-bred groups to track them to see whether captive wolves could relearn survival skills in the wild. The wolves passed the test. They were recaptured and returned to the captive breeding project; their relatives are now permanent residents in the wild. The red wolves live on three islands and on one mainland refuge, as well as in many zoos. Every one of these animals came from a core population of 14 wolves captured in Louisiana and Texas. The education center has a red-wolf enclosure and a display about the recovery program.

Dolphins and right whales swim by the beach, and a manatee might enter the bay in summer. Raccoons, fox squirrels, opossums, bobcats, otters, and deer also all live on the Cape Romain islands.

Reptiles and amphibians Big alligators enjoy freshwater ponds and marshes behind the dunes; they can put on surprising bursts of speed and should be observed only from a distance. Several kinds of nonvenomous water snakes also slither about here, and some of them can tolerate salt or brackish water. Fat, slow-moving venomous cottonmouths, or water moccasins, are refuge residents, as well.

More loggerhead sea turtles nest at Cape Romain than on any other beach north of Florida, and refuge staff and volunteers patrol the beach either to protect or relocate turtle eggs. Some eggs from this refuge have been relocated to other nearby beaches where turtles used to nest, in the hopes that the hatchlings will think of those places as home and return there for nesting.

Invertebrates Crabs reign at Cape Romain. Ghost crabs run on tiptoe all over the beaches but dash into their holes when chased. They eat almost anything, including small or weak hatchling sea turtles. Horseshoe crabs wash up in the surf, and blue crabs swim offshore, in lagoons, ponds, and salt marshes. Fiddler crabs process mud from their burrows, eat the organic matter, and deposit little balls of sand near their holes. The males have one brightly colored claw almost as large as their body, which they use to wave off rivals. The female fiddler crabs are brown

Sea turtle researcher tagging a loggerhead turtle

and have two normal claws, which allows them to eat twice as much as the males can. Crabbing for tasty blue crabs is good at Moores Landing.

Each tide brings in more mollusk shells and whelk egg cases and other treasures. Many shells have a neat round hole where a moon snail drilled in with its toothed tongue to suck out the contents.

Salt-marsh mud and warm shallow water foster larvae of shrimp, crabs, clams, oysters, mussels, and many other marine invertebrates. Without salt marshes in refuges and other coastal preserves, there would be no shrimp or fishing industries.

ACTIVITIES

■ **CAMPING:** There is no camping on the refuge, but adjacent Francis Marion National Forest has several campgrounds on the inland side of US 17.

■ **WILDLIFE OBSERVATION AND PHOTOGRAPHY:** Wading birds and waterfowl display themselves obligingly at Moores Landing, which has a fine view over the marsh. Ponds and rookeries on Bulls Island provide a chance to see young birds—just be careful not to disturb them. Alligators laze about as if willing to pose, but for close-up, detailed observations, use binoculars or a telephoto lens.

Boneyard Beach (about 0.5 mile long), where twisted trees resemble standing driftwood, makes for interesting photo opportunities, especially if a fish crow deigns to land on a tree branch.

HUNTING AND FISHING Hunting for **deer** is allowed only in Nov. and Dec. You may fish in the refuge waters year-round; you are likely to find **redfish, speckled trout, flounder,** and **tarpon**.

Look for snowy egrets for a shot of the long plumes that were so popular for women's hats a century ago.

■ **HIKES AND WALKS:** A 1-mile trail at the newly completed Visitor Center will lead past the red-wolf enclosure and ponds with alligators and onto a boardwalk through a shallow tupelo swamp.

On Bulls Island, a 2-mile National Scenic Trail traverses all the habitats of the island. Interpretive signs identify plants and animals likely to be seen, remind people to respect alligators, and explain management issues such as the invasion of cattails.

■ **SEASONAL EVENTS:** February: Southeastern Wildlife Expo; April: Earth Day Observation; May: International Migratory Bird Day; June: National Trails Day; October: National Wildlife Refuge Week.

■ **PUBLICATIONS:** Bird, mammal, and reptile and amphibians lists; Cape Romain maps, environmental education manuals for teachers.

SATELLITE REFUGE

■ **Waccamaw NWR** Managed by Cape Romain, Waccamaw is relatively new (1997) and consists of only 219 acres of bottomland swamp along the Great Pee Dee, Little Pee Dee, and Waccamaw rivers. Nearly 50,000 additional acres have been approved for acquisition, and public-use opportunities will be developed.

NEARBY REFUGE

■ **Santee NWR** Santee is on Lake Marion, in the upper coastal plain just above the Francis Marion National Forest. This 15,095-acre refuge, established in 1942, is 8 miles south of Summerton on US 15/SC 301. Exit 102, off I-95, is less than 0.5 mile from the refuge entrance.

Managed impoundments and cultivated fields attract Atlantic Flyway migrants, including raptors, shorebirds, neotropical songbirds, swans, ducks, and geese.

Four units make up the refuge and include shoreline, mixed hardwood and pine forests, fields, marshes, and other wetlands. A Visitor Center (open Thurs.-Sun., 8 a.m.-5 p.m.), a hiking trail (Wrights Bluff Nature Trail, with a boardwalk and observation tower), and Fort Watson are all located on Bluff Unit. Other refuge roads and trails are open to hiking and biking from March through October.

Fort Watson, near an Indian mound, was the site of a Revolutionary War battle in which Francis Marion and Light Horse Harry Lee (father of Robert E. Lee) surprised sleeping British soldiers and took the fort.

Carolina Sandhills NWR

McBee, South Carolina

Lake scene, Carolina Sandhills NWR

Walking through the gently rolling Carolina Sandhills is a trip through America's past. Species and habitats that have disappeared from a thousand-mile band of pine forests flourish here. The rounded hills abound with rare plants and wildlife with intriguing, unfamiliar names.

Well's pixie moss, for example, flowers in March; the white wicky blooms in late April. These two rare plants are from the same botanical family as rhododendron, and both thrive at Sandhills NWR. Pine barrens tree frogs—as brightly colored as sugar candy—use sticky toe pads to cling to tree branches. Maturing longleaf pine stands support more than a hundred colonies of the endangered red-cockaded woodpecker. Other rare bird species, such as Bachman's sparrow, attract birdwatchers working on life lists. Carnivorous pitcher plants digest insects in collected rainwater, while wintering waterfowl rest in nearby ponds.

HISTORY

Established in 1939, this 45,000-acre refuge protects habitats that once ran parallel to the coastline from New Jersey to Texas. The Sandhills *were* the coastline, but as the Atlantic Ocean receded eastward, the dunes remained to mark its former boundary. Longleaf pine and wire grass grew on the southern sandy ridges, and wetlands developed between them. Resident plants and animals adapted to the frequent lightning fires—and even came to depend on them. European settlers found longleaf pine valuable and easy to harvest, especially because they could navigate most rivers to the fall line (see below). In the process, old-growth stands were all but destroyed. At this and other southeastern refuges, the coastal plain forests are now recovering.

GETTING THERE

From McBee, drive 4 mi. north on US 1 to refuge office on left.

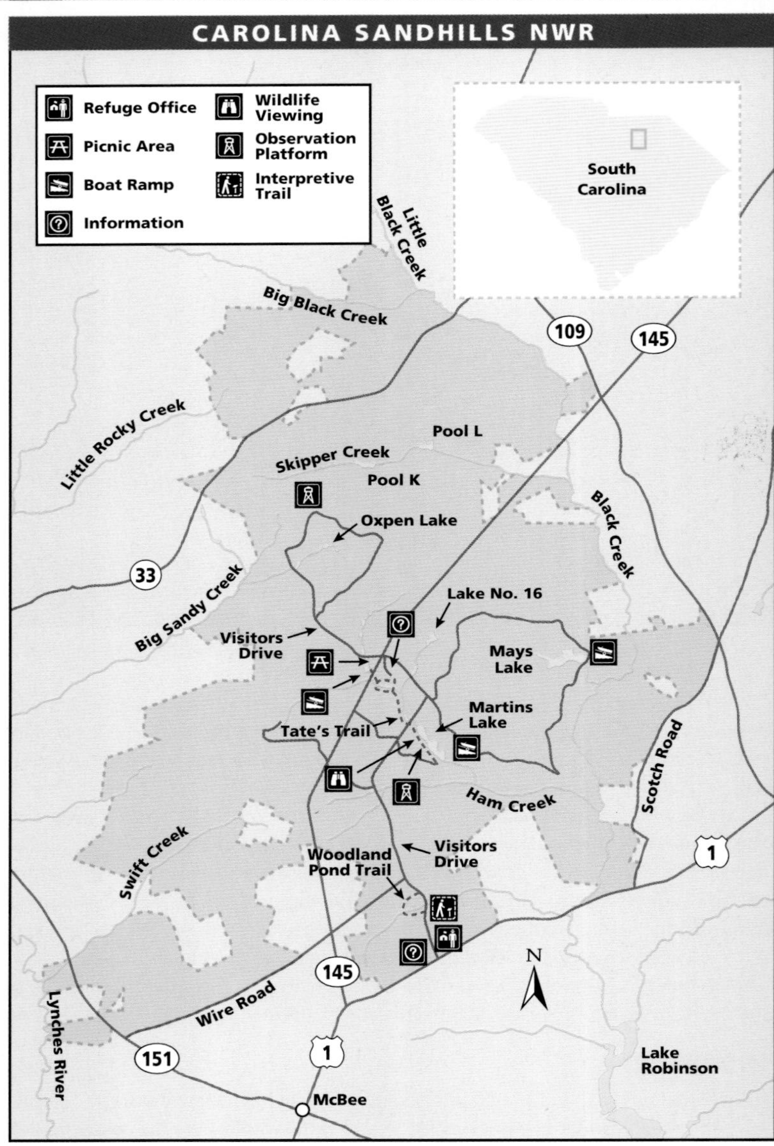

■ **SEASON:** Refuge open all year.
■ **HOURS:** Refuge: daylight hours; office: 8 a.m.–4:30 p.m., Mon.–Fri.
■ **FEES:** There are no fees.
■ **ADDRESS:** Carolina Sandhills NWR, Rte. 2, Box 100, McBee, SC 29101
■ **TELEPHONE:** 843/335-8401

TOURING CAROLINA SANDHILLS

■ **BY AUTOMOBILE:** A 9-mile paved auto tour loops through the middle of the refuge, and gravel roads lead to lakes in other areas. Sand roads on the refuge are also open to cars and provide good opportunities for wildlife observation, but check with office on road conditions.

■ **BY FOOT:** Woodland Pond Trail (1 mile) starts about 1 mile past the refuge office. Tate's Trail (3.5 miles) crosses the auto-tour road and can be accessed either from Lake Bee picnic area or from another refuge road at the far end. Gravel roads in the refuge are open to hiking unless posted.

■ **BY BICYCLE:** The auto tour (skinny tires) and gravel roads (fat tires) in the refuge are open to bicycles. But take care: The gravel roads may be too sandy or muddy in spots to maneuver; check with the refuge office.

■ **BY CANOE, KAYAK, OR BOAT:** Mays Lake, Martins Lake, and Lake Bee all offer boat launches. Several ponds and a few creeks through wetland forest provide good canoeing opportunities (take a map and compass), and electric motorboats can be used for fishing.

WHAT TO SEE

■ **LANDSCAPE AND CLIMATE** These rounded hills were scarred over time by erosion gullies and barren, sandy earth. They occupy the fall line (the last place where rivers lose elevation before flowing sedately toward the ocean) between the foothills and the coastal plain.

Autumn and spring weather provide the best wildlife watching, but mornings and evenings in summer reveal the activities of deer, resident birds, and swamp animals. January and February may be cold with an occasional freeze. But mild, sunny winter days can be excellent for birdwatching on any of the several ponds the refuge manages for waterfowl.

■ **PLANT LIFE** Longleaf pine and wiregrass, with an understory of oaks and shrubs, dominate the uplands, while wetlands and pocosins occupy the valleys. Scrub oaks and other shrubs thrive in porous sandy soil, providing dense cover for wildlife. Plant diversity, including several rare and endangered species, is high at Carolina Sandhills. Pixie moss, most closely related to galax of the higher Blue

Ghost crab on the beach

Ridge mountains, is not really a moss at all but a low-growing laurel that was so named for its small stature. Called a subshrub by botanists, this pink flower is seen only in the Sandhills. White wicky is found nowadays in only a few South Carolina counties.

Early spring brings the vibrant colors of trailing arbutus and butterwort. Pitcher plants bloom in summer, and blazing star and lobelia add more color to fall. Grains and other crops are grown on the refuge by local farmers, who leave a portion of the harvest for birds and mammals.

■ ANIMAL LIFE

Birds Carolina Sandhills NWR supports the largest number of red-cockaded woodpeckers of any refuge in the system, and visitors have opportunities here to observe these endangered birds as long as they keep a good distance and do not disturb the nests. The woodpeckers need century-old pine trees, and wildlife management includes putting in artificial nest cavities and protecting roost and nest trees. The woodpeckers eat wood borers and other insects; in turn, other birds and some mammals depend on abandoned woodpecker cavities. Climbing rat snakes prey on the woodpeckers and their eggs, but the birds protect their cavities from scaly intruders with sticky pitch around the entrance.

Wood ducks, great horned owls, turkeys, bluebirds, and other birds nest year-round on the refuge, and spring migrants pass through in May.

Loggerhead shrike

Mammals As the forest naturally restored the eroded gullies characteristic of unsustainable farming in the 1930s, beaver and deer were restocked. Flying squirrels, fox squirrels, foxes, bobcats, raccoons and other mammals now also thrive at Carolina Sandhills.

Reptiles and amphibians The pine barrens tree frog, whose picture graces the cover of the third edition of *Peterson's Reptile and Amphibian Guide*, is bright green with a lavender or purple stripe the length of its body. It lives in the New Jersey Pine Barrens and in a few boggy spots in the Carolinas, though it may have ranged as far as the virgin pine forests once did. You'll need a sharp eye to see this elegant little frog; more likely, you may hear its nasal "*quonk, quonk*" and have the satisfaction that it finds protection in these woods. Other treefrogs join the (mating call) chorus in spring.

Salamanders (including mud-loving two-toed amphiumas and dwarf mudpuppies), turtles, and several kinds of snakes inhabit the refuge's ponds and wetlands, while slimy salamanders, lizards, nonvenomous black racers, rat snakes, and pine snakes live in the drier uplands.

CAROLINA SANDHILLS HUNTING AND FISHING SEASONS

Hunting	Jan	Feb	Mar	Apr	May	Jun	Jul	Aug	Sep	Oct	Nov	Dec
(Seasons may vary)												
white-tailed deer										■	■	
wild turkey				■								
quail											■	
mourning dove									■			
small game		■										
Fishing			■	■	■	■	■	■	■	■		

For information on current fishing regulations, license requirements, seasons, and bag limits, consult refuge office.

ACTIVITIES

■ **CAMPING:** No camping is allowed on the refuge, but full and primitive camping facilities are available 5 miles away at Sandhills State Forest (843/498-6478).

■ **WILDLIFE OBSERVATION AND PHOTOGRAPHY:** The 9-mile paved auto route passes several ponds and gives access to trails, an observation tower, and red-cockaded woodpecker nesting areas. Martins Lake Trail leads to a photography blind near the observation tower.

Old fields and other open areas are maintained by prescribed burning and cultivation to help feed turkeys, deer, and large birds. Along the auto route, wood ducks and bluebirds use nesting boxes. Strolling in the forest or near shrub edges, you may see migrating birds flitting about. During cool times of day beavers feed or work industriously in ponds; turtles, less ambitious, bask on logs all day.

■ **HIKES AND WALKS:** Woodland Pond Trail— known for songbird observations in spring and vigorous horseflies in summer—starts just beyond the visitor station and goes 1 mile around Pool A.

Tate's Trail is 3.5 miles long but has three access points for shorter hikes and offers much variety, passing by three lakes and the observation tower (at the Martins Lake end of Tate's Trail). At the other end of Tate's trail is a picnic area on Lake Bee (restrooms). Wood ducks (watch for mothers with ducklings), red-cockaded woodpeckers, and brown-headed nuthatches can be seen along this trail.

Other footpaths, such as the grassy pond banks and trails leading to the observation tower, provide shorter walks and are good places to see waterfowl such as the great blue heron, the tallest wading bird of the refuge. Wintering ducks gather in the lakes to dive or dabble for water weeds.

■ **SEASONAL EVENTS:** The refuge celebrates National Wildlife Refuge Week in October with special events.

■ **PUBLICATIONS:** Brochures, bird and amphibian/reptile lists, maps and trail information. Leaflets on sandhill ecology and the endangered red-cockaded woodpecker also available.

Pinckney Island NWR

Hilton Head, South Carolina

Black-crowned night-heron

Every day thousands of people drive right past the entrance to Pinckney NWR on their way to immensely popular and busy Hilton Head Island, one of the premier East Coast resorts. They may glance left and see hundreds of white ibises wheeling in for a landing or a tricolored heron standing statue-still on the edge of a marsh. Those who drive into the refuge will be glad they did: They'll get to see alligators and ducks swimming in ponds and osprey taking fish to their nestlings. Pinckney Island NWR is a good place to slow down, stroll in the shade of live oaks, or watch a painted bunting flash by. Good trails lead to rookeries, live oak forests, and close-up views of salt-marsh life.

Pinckney Island NWR is administered by the Savannah Coastal Refuges, but it is described separately here because of its large visitation and its proximity to Hilton Head.

HISTORY

Humans have lived on Pinckney Island for some 10,000 years, but Charles Pinckney didn't arrive until 1734. He bought the islands from an Indian trader and passed them on to his son, Charles Cotesworth Pinckney, who attended the Continental Congress, signed the Constitution, ran twice (unsuccessfully) for president of the United States, and then returned home to manage his cotton plantation. After cutting down maritime forest and draining marshes, more than 200 slaves grew cotton—the valuable sea island cotton notable for its longer fibers and a higher profit margin.

The Civil War changed all that. Union troops occupied the island; there was even a skirmish with 14 casualties. The Pinckneys tried to start over, but cotton was no longer king, and, as the crop diminished, forest and birds slowly returned. Plantation impoundments collected freshwater in ponds where ducks and geese could feed.

In 1937, the Pinckney family sold out, and the new owners planted trees and grains to attract more wildlife.

Since World War II, the tourism business has grown rapidly on Hilton Head, bringing with it an incentive to allow the preplantation vegetation and wildlife to return to the islands of the refuge. In 1975 private ownership of the land ended when James Barker and Edward Starr donated the land to the U.S. Fish & Wildlife Service as a 4,073-acre refuge.

GETTING THERE

From Bluffton, SC, take US 278 east for 5 mi. Turn left at refuge sign and drive about 0.5 mi. to parking area. From Hilton Head Island, drive 0.5 mi. west on US 278 and turn right at refuge sign.

■ **SEASON:** Refuge open year-round.

■ **HOURS:** Daylight hours.

■ **FEES:** None.

■ **ADDRESS:** c/o Savannah Coastal Refuges, 1000 Business Ctr. Dr., Suite 10, Parkway Business Ctr., Savannah, GA 31405

■ **TELEPHONE:** 912/652-4415

TOURING PINCKNEY ISLAND

Pinckney Island is the only one of several islands in the refuge open to public use.

■ **BY AUTOMOBILE:** Only the entrance road and C.C. Haigh Landing at Last End Point are open to auto traffic. This is a place to walk.

■ **BY FOOT:** There are approximately 14 miles of trails on Pinckney Island that can provide loops and out-and-back hikes. A trail guide, available from the refuge office, shows the hiking options—from 2 miles or less to 7.8 miles, including White Point on Port Royal Sound.

■ **BY BICYCLE:** Refuge trails are open to bicycles, but some are sandy.

Crayfish

■ **BY CANOE, KAYAK, OR BOAT:** A boat launch and fishing pier on Last End Point (across from refuge entrance) gives access to refuge waters and Skull Creek, the Intracoastal Waterway, Port Royal Sound, and the Chechesse River. Some areas are posted no entry, and landing on any of the other refuge islands is not allowed.

WHAT TO SEE

■ **LANDSCAPE AND CLIMATE** Corn, Big Harry, Little Harry, Buzzard, and Pinckney islands are mostly salt marsh laced with tidal creeks. Hilton Head Island shelters Pinckney Refuge from ocean waves but not tidal changes. Hilton Head absorbs most of the sea breezes also, which makes Pinckney Island hot and humid in summer; the cooler months are excellent times to visit. Early spring is the best season to observe rookeries, and April brings a concentration

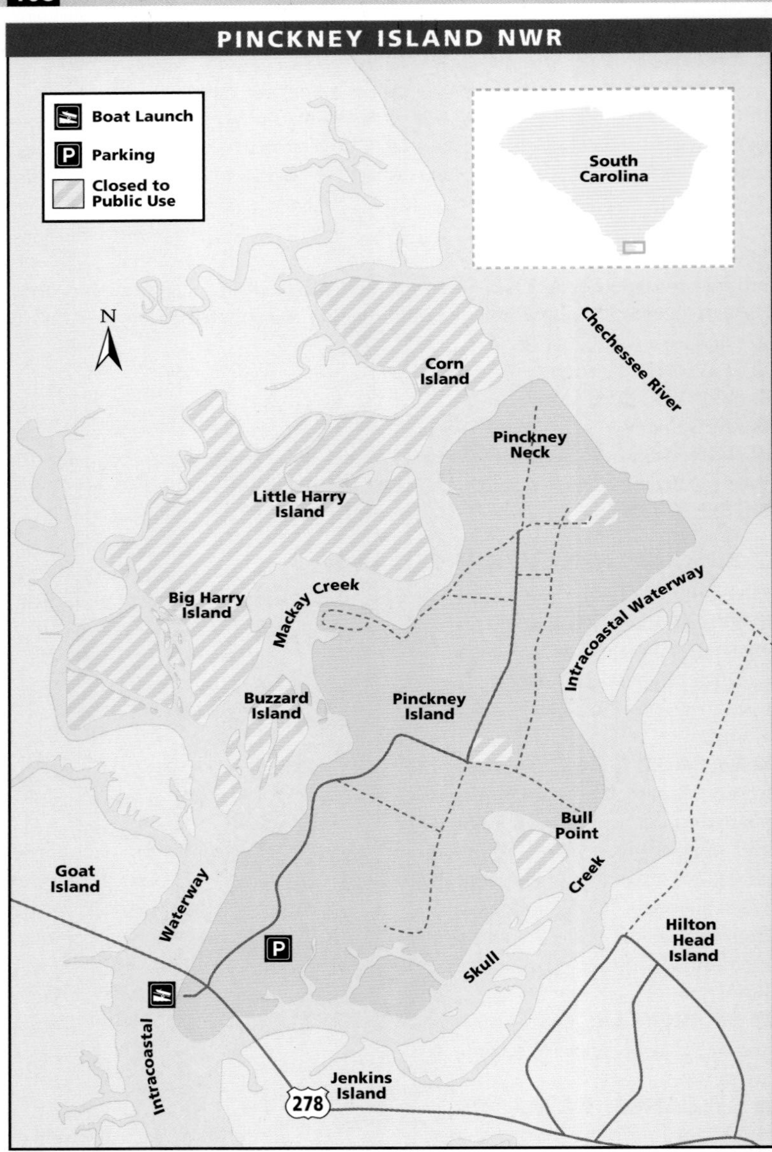

of migrating birds. During winter months waterfowl are in residence, but some areas may be closed to protect them from disturbance. (See the sidebar on barrier islands in Eufala [AL] refuge.)

■ **PLANT LIFE** Cordgrass (*Spartina*) dominates the salt marsh and is the primary anchor in most of the refuge's food chains. Algae grow on cordgrass; snails, zooplankton, and invertebrates feed on the algae; fish and birds eat the snails; and carnivores like hawks, owls, otters, and raccoons feed on fish and birds. Exposure to full sun, ability to live in saltwater, and an efficient rate of photosynthesis allow the cordgrass to make nutritious carbohydrates and proteins. Needlerush, glasswort, marsh elder, and sea ox-eye live between the marsh and solid land.

Grassland and cultivated fields provide food for waterfowl, and aquatic vegetation grows in shallow ponds. Other food comes from a greentree reservoir—a field of trees flooded in fall by refuge managers and then drained before the next growing season. Ducks and geese feed on the softened acorns and nuts.

Forest on hammocks or ridges includes live oaks, water oaks, hickories, southern magnolias, red cedars, sweet gums, and maples. A few sandy places support loblolly and longleaf pines and cabbage palmettos. Evergreen wax myrtle (bayberry) grows in brushy areas.

As with many refuges, managed fires in winter reduce dry vegetation and allow new growth.

■ ANIMAL LIFE

Birds White ibises, herons, and egrets build rookeries on the treetops with piles of sticks. Their nests are not as tight as sea island baskets (an old, admirable craft, much prized hereabouts), but they manage to hold eggs and fuzzy nestlings successfully year after year. These long-legged predators stalk the marsh searching for food; ibises prefer shrimp and minnows; herons eat fish almost too big to swallow; and egrets love crayfish. Because crayfish prey on fish eggs, the egrets help to maintain a food supply (more fish are hatched), a boon to other birds.

Endangered wood storks nest farther south on the coast but spend time at Pinckney Island feeding in pools. Peregrine falcons, another rare bird, come down from northern nesting areas to fly above the marshes in search of prey.

Both eagles and ospreys also eat fish but each uses a different strategy to catch them: Ospreys snag fish by plunging into the water feet first. Short spines on the bottoms of osprey toes help their talons keep a grip on the slippery victim. The bald eagle is not a well-mannered diner—it usually steals fish from the ospreys or scavenges for dead ones. Populations of both birds suffered from DDT poisoning (it weakened their eggs shells), but the eagles came closer to extinction partly because of their feeding habits: many dead fish contained higher loads of pesticides.

American egret

Painted buntings, bluebirds, and hummingbirds (which weigh less than a

Pair of Atlantic bottle-nosed dolphins

penny and make nests out of nearly weightless lichens and spider webs) are at home on the refuge. Warblers, tanagers, sparrows, wrens, thrushes, and other migrants stop to feed and rest on their journeys.

Mammals If you wander the mudflats in the mornings after a low tide, you may see the telltale tracks of such nocturnal mammals as river otters, gray foxes, raccoons, and opossums that have been out hunting crabs. Grey and fox squirrels eat acorns; red foxes in turn eat squirrels and other rodents.

Most of the wild predators that long controlled white-tailed deer populations the natural way are long gone, however, and the refuge allows a managed deer hunt for one day in November. During the hunt, the refuge is closed to other uses.

In summer, West Indian manatees swim around the island while grazing on underwater plants; they surface to breathe every few minutes. (See Crystal River NWR [FL] for more about manatees.)

Reptiles and amphibians The important duties of mouse and rat control fall to copperheads and diamondback rattlesnakes, as well as to several nonvenomous constricting snakes such as rat, corn, black racer, and king snakes. Water snakes and venomous water moccasins keep track of fish and frog populations. Fast-paced racerunner and anolis lizards catch wasps, beetles, and other small prey. Keep an eye out for snakes on the trails and give them a wide berth.

Invertebrates The salt marshes serve as nurseries for oysters, clams, mussels, crabs, and shrimp. Above them, trying hard to keep their shells dry, pea-sized snails crawl up the grass stems as the tide rises and then climb down to the mudflats to eat organic matter at low tide. Fiddler crabs also feed at low tide and wait out the high tide in their burrows.

Dragonflies are one of a hiker's best friends. They catch mosquitoes and lay their eggs on the surface of freshwater ponds; their larvae eat mosquito larvae.

Ticks wait on grass stems, their front legs outstretched to grab onto anything that brushes past and smells good. Wear long pants and check your legs after walking through tall grasses here.

ACTIVITIES

■ **CAMPING:** Camping is not permitted except during scheduled hunts. Nearby camping facilities are available at private campgrounds on Hilton Head Island and the town of Pritchardville.

■ **WILDLIFE OBSERVATION AND PHOTOGRAPHY:** The network of trails on Pinckney Island improves your chances of seeing a variety of wildlife. Rookeries with young birds can be observed with binoculars or telephoto lenses, and birds in the ponds can be photographed from dikes and walkways. A little patience yields views of painted buntings in the live oaks or scrub forest and a little more patience may provide a glimpse of basking lizards. View alligators with caution and at a distance: Big ones can bite quickly or swat with their tails, and little ones usually have big ones nearby.

HUNTING A managed white-tailed deer hunt to control the local population is open to the public by drawing. Call the refuge for scheduled times.

■ **HIKES AND WALKS:** Only Pinckney Island is open to hiking; Corn, Big Harry, Little Harry, and Buzzard Islands are heavily vegetated and closed to public access. The Hilton Head Audubon Society funds an excellent map showing hiking trails and mileages between points and suggesting trips of various lengths and durations. Access to trailheads is 0.9 mile on the gravel road from the parking lot. The longest hike (7.8 miles round-trip) goes to White Point, which has a view of Port Royal Sound. Shorter hikes explore ponds and other points with views over salt marsh and mudflats.

There are no toilets, drinking water, or shelters on the island. Bring plenty of water and insect repellent and keep track of weather conditions.

■ **SEASONAL EVENTS:** May: Migratory Bird Day; October: National Wildlife Refuge Week.

■ **PUBLICATIONS:** Hiking trail map, brochures.

Reelfoot NWR

Union City, Tennessee

Boardwalk, Reelfoot NWR

The largest earthquake in recorded history formed Reelfoot Lake. Beneath the shallow waters—5 feet, on average—lie the ghostly remnants of a full-grown forest, upended by the violent tremors of the quake. The shallow water, the submerged trees, and nutrient-rich waters combine to make the fishing fine at Reelfoot. Visitors come to this refuge, which lies in a corner of land where Missouri, Kentucky, and Tennessee merge, to fish for largemouth bass and catfish, to see bald eagles and cypress swamps, and to canoe on tranquil waters. Migratory birds on the Mississippi Flyway zero in on the 14-mile-long lake and surrounding rich forest. Most species pause or spend the winter here, to the delight of birdwatchers from all over.

HISTORY

From 1811 to 1812 the New Madrid earthquakes rearranged western Tennessee and eastern Missouri. It caused the Mississippi River to flow backwards and form waves and waterfalls. Floodplains became hills, and forested hills ended up under water. Aftershocks were felt for several months and as far away as New York. The village of New Madrid, Missouri, thought to be the quake's epicenter, was forced to relocate. The passengers aboard the first steamboat on the Mississippi, the *New Orleans*, got quite a surprise on the boat's maiden voyage from Pittsburgh to New Orleans in January 1812. Coming into the New Madrid area, the boat was greeted with whirlpools, collapsing river banks, floating forests, and violent currents. Astonishingly, the *New Orleans* made it through, but many other ships did not.

The 10,428-acre wildlife refuge, established in 1941, covers the northern part of Reelfoot Lake, including some wetlands and forests in Kentucky. A state park and a wildlife management area occupy the southern part of the lake.

GETTING THERE

From Union City, TN, take TN 22 north for about 15 mi. (this part of TN 22 runs east-west, so you actually drive west). Turn right (north) onto TN 157 and drive 1 mile to refuge entrance sign on left.

To get to the Long Point Unit in Kentucky, continue north on TN 157 for 2.5 mi. to the Kentucky border, where the route becomes KY 311. In 2 mi., turn left at refuge sign onto KY 1182.

■ **SEASON:** March 15 through Nov. 15 for Long Point auto tour. Lake access and Grassy Point auto tour available year-round.

■ **HOURS:** Visitor Center: 8 a.m.–4 p.m.; daily Jan. through March; weekdays rest of year.

■ **FEES:** None.

■ **ADDRESS:** 4343 Highway 157, Union City, TN 38261

■ **TELEPHONE:** 901/538-2481

TOURING REELFOOT

■ **BY AUTOMOBILE:** The gravel Grassy Island Auto Tour (2.5 miles, not a loop) runs across the northern edge of the Grassy Island Unit. Other refuge roads and those at Lake Isom (see Satellite Refuges, below) can be used if not gated. The gravel Long Point Auto Drive is 15 miles. Both drives are open from March 15 to November 15.

■ **BY FOOT:** Refuge roads and dikes are open to hiking. Short, wheelchair-accessible walks cross the Backyard Habitat Showcase behind the Visitor Center. A boardwalk leads from the end of the auto tour to an observation tower.

■ **BY BICYCLE:** Refuge roads are open to bicycles.

■ **BY CANOE, KAYAK, OR BOAT:** Canoes and small boats (under 10 hp.) can be launched on or near the refuge.

EARTHQUAKE! *I was jogging along one afternoon . . . on Barro, when a sudden, strange darkness rose from the western horizon. Used to thunder and rain, I took no more notice of it. I thought the speed of my horse would enable me to reach shelter beneath the roof of a friend not far distant. A mile further on I heard distant rumbling as of a violent tornado. I spurred my steed into a gallop toward shelter. The animal, however, knew better than I what was coming. Instead of going faster, he nearly stopped. He put one foot down after another with such measured caution that he might have been walking on ice, and seemed to founder. . . . Then all of a sudden he began a piteous groaning, hung his head, spread his four legs to brace himself, and stood stock still. . . . The ground rose and fell in billows like ruffled waters of a lake. Bewildered, I nonetheless discerned that all this awful commotion in Nature was the result of an earthquake. . . .*

I found myself rocking on my horse and I moved to and fro with him like a child in a cradle, expecting the ground to open at any moment and reveal an abyss to engulf me and all around me. The fearful convulsion lasted only minutes, however. The heavens brightened as quickly as they had darkened. Burro drew up, raised his head, and galloped off, as if loose and frolicking without a rider.

—John James Audubon, *Reminiscences* (1812)

WHAT TO SEE

■ LANDSCAPE AND CLIMATE The Mississippi River deposited alluvial mud and glacial rock flour on the wide, flat floodplain over millions of years. An earthquake occurring beneath this type of material, which is sedimentary but not compacted, causes waves across the landscape, as Audubon experienced (see sidebar, previous page). Reelfoot Lake, 14 miles long and 5 miles wide, is a depression between land waves, as are many of the other 200-year-old lakes in this area. Soil lining the lake was fertile to start with and hasn't had enough time to lose its minerals and nutrients; as a result Reelfoot has lush plant life and an unusual variety of fish.

■ PLANT LIFE Some of the more interesting plants of Reelfoot Lake are dead. A healthy pre-earthquake forest suddenly found itself under water, and the resulting snags (good for eagle perches) and submerged trunks (good for fish shelters) help increase habitat diversity. The dead forest has even inspired the invention of a special kind of fishing boat to navigate over sunken logs and branches. Tall grasses grow in the shallows around the lake. Thick forests of oaks, cottonwoods, pecans, and persimmons occupy the drier land and produce bright fall colors. Bald cypress, some of which survived the earthquake, are now huge, with wide buttresses and moss-covered knobby knees. Unlike most conifers, the cypresses are deciduous and their needles turn bronze before falling. When cypresses die, they create even more snags for eagles and ospreys.

The woodland's wildflowers, such as violets, phlox, and buttercups, come out in spring, and yellow lotus and water lilies bloom in summer. The local farmers lease fields to cultivate both grains and soybeans. They leave 25 percent of the crops for winter food for migratory birds.

■ ANIMAL LIFE

Birds Up to 200 bald eagles spend the winter at Reelfoot, more than anywhere else in Tennessee. Until 1963 eagles nested here, but then they succumbed to DDT contamination. Today, the bald eagles are back, thanks to release and hacking (raising eaglets on site with minimal human contact) programs in the 1980s.

American wigeon

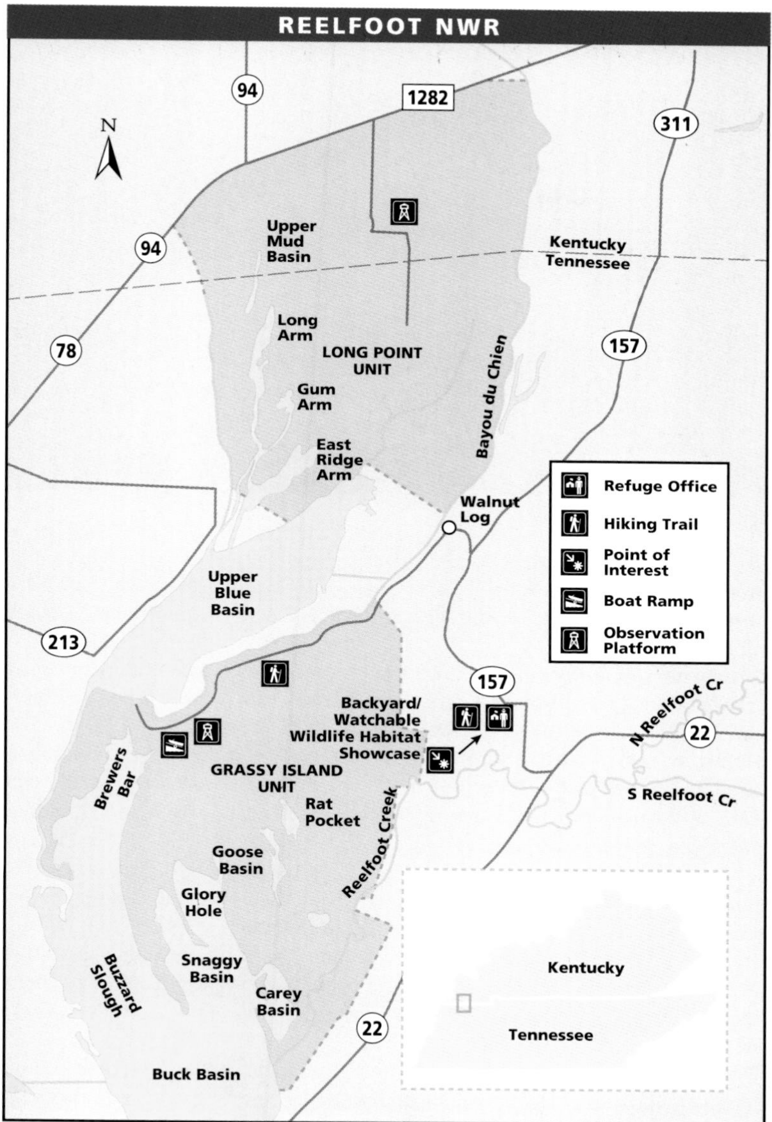

The Mississippi Flyway brings Canada geese, ruddy ducks, wigeons, coots, gadwalls, and many other American waterfowl that birdwatchers need for their life lists—sometimes 250,000 birds in mixed-species flocks (good for keeping the birders guessing). Plovers, sandpipers, terns, and gulls feed on mudflats. Fish-eating birds, including mergansers, herons, and grebes, do well here.

Nesting birds at Reelfoot include eight kinds of herons, Mississippi kites (which migrate to southern South America for the winter!), six kinds of woodpeckers, and crowds of warblers, vireos, thrashers, wrens, and goatsuckers. Goatsuckers—so named because it was once believed that they sucked goat milk—are also called nightjars (they make jarring noises at night) or frogmouths

Bald eagle

(their wide mouths have sensitive bristles, the better to catch insects). Other nesters include whip-poor-wills and chuck-will's-widows (because that's what they say)—weird names for strange birds that feed on flying insects and squawk all night.

Mammals Mammals include foxes, bobcats, raccoons, beavers, deer, opossums, muskrats, and bats. Coyotes established themselves from the west. The question is, did they swim across the Mississippi or use the bridge?

Reptiles and amphibians Though birds get most of the attention at Reelfoot, the wetlands support a variety of amphibians, including intriguingly named salamanders (lesser siren, two-lined salamander, three-toad amphiuma, and zigzag salamander).

The biggest reptile is the alligator snapping turtle—which grows up to 150 pounds; the turtles most likely to be seen are the sliders and painted turtles that bask on logs, sometimes piled one on top of the other when basking space is scarce. Snakes thrive here, 26 species in all; many are harmless water snakes. The prettiest is the scarlet snake, with its red snout and bright red splotches along the back. Venomous snakes include copperheads, cottonmouths, and canebrake rattlesnakes.

Fish Fifty-seven species of fish live in great abundance in Reelfoot Lake, and the number of people trying to catch them is pretty big, too. The strangest may be the paddlefish, a bottom feeder that can weigh up to 200 pounds, has no scales, and grows a long, flexible paddle from its snout. It looks like swordfish with paddle-shaped rubber swords; indeed, its eggs make good caviar.

Another remarkable fish is the alligator gar, which may reach 12 feet, including the snout, which resembles an alligator's except that it has more teeth. If reeling in a 12-footer seems a bit much to you, you can also go for bream, bass, or crappie.

Invertebrates Mosquitoes and deerflies feed voraciously in summer. Crayfish and many other crustaceans live in the water, and aquatic insect larvae such as mayflies and dragonflies are eaten by the fish as part of the food chain. Butterflies visit the demonstration garden near the Visitor Center.

ACTIVITIES

■ **CAMPING:** There is no camping on the refuge, but Reelfoot State Resort Park offers camping facilities both at the south end of Reelfoot Lake and 14 miles away on the Tiptonville side of the lake (901/253-7756).

■ **SWIMMING:** Although the lake has no open beaches per se, visitors can swim in a beach-type area on the washout on the south end of the lake.

■ **WILDLIFE OBSERVATION AND PHOTOGRAPHY:** The two observation towers (one at the end of the auto tour on Grassy Island Unit and the other in Long Point Unit) provide waterfowl views. Wildlife in open water, swamp, and forest habitats can be seen from a car on Grassy Island Wildlife Drive, which has Reelfoot Lake on one side and seasonally flooded bottomland forest on the other. Long Point tower overlooks planted fields and wetlands, offering views of waterfowl feeding. Grassy Island tower has a short boardwalk leading to it and looks out over a secluded pocket of Reelfoot Lake with dense water vegetation and large cypress trees. Wading birds are common here in summer.

HUNTING AND FISHING Fishing season is year-round. **Deer-hunting season** is during Oct. and Nov. Small game can be hunted from Aug. through Oct. **Wild turkey season** is April.

From Jan. to March, many bald eagles fish and perch photogenically on snags, but you will likely need a telephoto lens to see them well.

■ **HIKES AND WALKS:** The butterfly garden near the Visitor Center and the boardwalk (0.25 mile) are handicapped accessible. Refuge roads provide longer hikes.

■ **SEASONAL EVENTS:** April: The adjacent state park may be one of the few places in the world with a "Crappiethon," where people compete to catch tagged crappie (a sunfish-type pan fish). May: Migratory Bird Day; June: National Fishing Day; October: National Wildlife Refuge Week.

■ **PUBLICATIONS:** Bird list, amphibian and reptile list.

SATELLITE REFUGES

■ **Lake Isom NWR** Comprised of 1850 acres, Lake Isom lies a few miles south of Reelfoot Lake on TN 22. It was established in 1938 and has most of the same wildlife as that found on Reelfoot NWR, including bald eagles living on open water, wetlands, and woodlands. Fishing, hiking, boating, and dry-weather road access are available.

■ **Chickasaw NWR** Established in 1985, Chickasaw (22,376 acres) formerly belonged to a timber company. The refuge borders a loop of the Mississippi River and contains bottomland hardwood forest, cropland, bluffs, and several oxbow lakes. Migrating waterfowl and bald eagles use the wetlands, and neotropical migrants stop to rest and feed.

Hunting, fishing, and boating are favorite activities, and old logging roads and trails provide good cool-weather hiking. Seasonal flooding occurs, so visitors should call the refuge before visiting.

The entrance to Chickasaw NWR is on Sand Bluff Rd. about a mile north of Edith, TN. The closest large town is Ripley, on US 51. Call 901-635-7621 for more information.

■ **Lower Hatchie NWR**

Lower Hatchie (7,394 acres), established in 1980, lies farther south on the

Mississippi along the twisting course of the Hatchie River. Wildlife and visitor opportunities are similar to those of Chickasaw NWR. These two refuges help to stabilize the Mississippi River banks and restore water cycles and wildlife habitats. Snowmelt from northern states and spring rains cause frequent flooding. The entrance to Lower Hatchie NWR is about 20 mi. west of Henning on TN 87.

NEARBY REFUGE

■ Hatchie NWR

Comprised of 11,556 acres and established in 1964, Hatchie NWR is farther up the Hatchie River, where creeks and streams split off from the contorted waterway and rejoin as they snake through swamp and marsh. From Brownsville, take TN 76 for 4 miles south to the refuge sign and office.

Wood ducks and hooded mergansers nest at Hatchie, and many species of ducks, shorebirds, and wading birds spend the winter here. Thick woods shelter migratory birds, such as scarlet tanagers, blue jays, warblers, goldfinches, and kinglets, while many kinds of woodpeckers, including red-headed, nest here. Red-shouldered hawks catch snakes, lizards, and rodents; barred owls call at night or on cloudy days and prey on rodents, small birds, frogs, and crayfish. If crows find the owl during the day, they mob it and torment it until it finds another hiding place.

Hatchie Refuge designed Project Fish, a demonstration program to make fishing available to visitors with disabilities.

Agricultural runoff and windblown soil present management challenges for the refuge and surrounding farms. Hatchie Pride, a cooperative group of landowners, conservation groups, and agencies, was formed to alleviate river siltation and damage to forest habitats.

A year-round wildlife drive is planned and should increase visitation to the Hatchie National Scenic River. Parts of the refuge are closed from November 15 through March 15, and roads my be closed due to flooding; check with refuge office (901/772-0501).

Tennessee NWR

Paris, Tennessee

Wetlands, Tennessee NWR

As the Tennessee River flows north from Alabama to Kentucky, in central western Tennessee, it passes through three units of the Tennessee NWR. Rivers and creeks from the Cumberland Plateau join in, creating a wide wetland interrupted by forested rolling hills. About 100 miles away, the Mississippi River flows south; carrying water from the Tennessee and Ohio rivers. To the birds, it's all part of the Mississippi Flyway—the fact that the two great rivers run in opposite directions just means more wetlands.

Here you can see expanses of unbroken forest, more than 600 species of plants, swamp lands and lake, and waterfowl stocking up on energy to fly north and nest in the upper prairie states and Canada.

Cross Creeks NWR, located northeast of the Big Sandy Unit of Tennessee NWR, has similar wildlife and habitats and is also described here.

HISTORY

Kentucky Dam, built on the Tennessee River in 1944, is the longest (though not the highest) Tennessee Valley Authority (TVA) dam. With 2,300 miles of shoreline, Kentucky Lake, behind the dam, is one of the largest man-made lakes in the world. In 1945 President Harry Truman signed an executive order to establish the 51,358-acre Tennessee NWR. Under an agreement with TVA, U.S. Fish & Wildlife administers the refuge, while TVA manages water levels of Kentucky Lake.

Chickasaw Indians lived here and may have met the Spanish explorer Hernando De Soto in 1540. Sites along creeks and rivers were favored places of European settlers and traders as they had been for the Chickasaws. In 1834 the 5,000 Chickasaws east of the Mississippi were forced to march on the infamous and deadly Trail of Tears to present-day Oklahoma where, as one of the Five Civilized Tribes, they were given land and the right to govern themselves with documents patterned after the U.S. Constitution. At the time of Oklahoma

TENNESSEE NWR

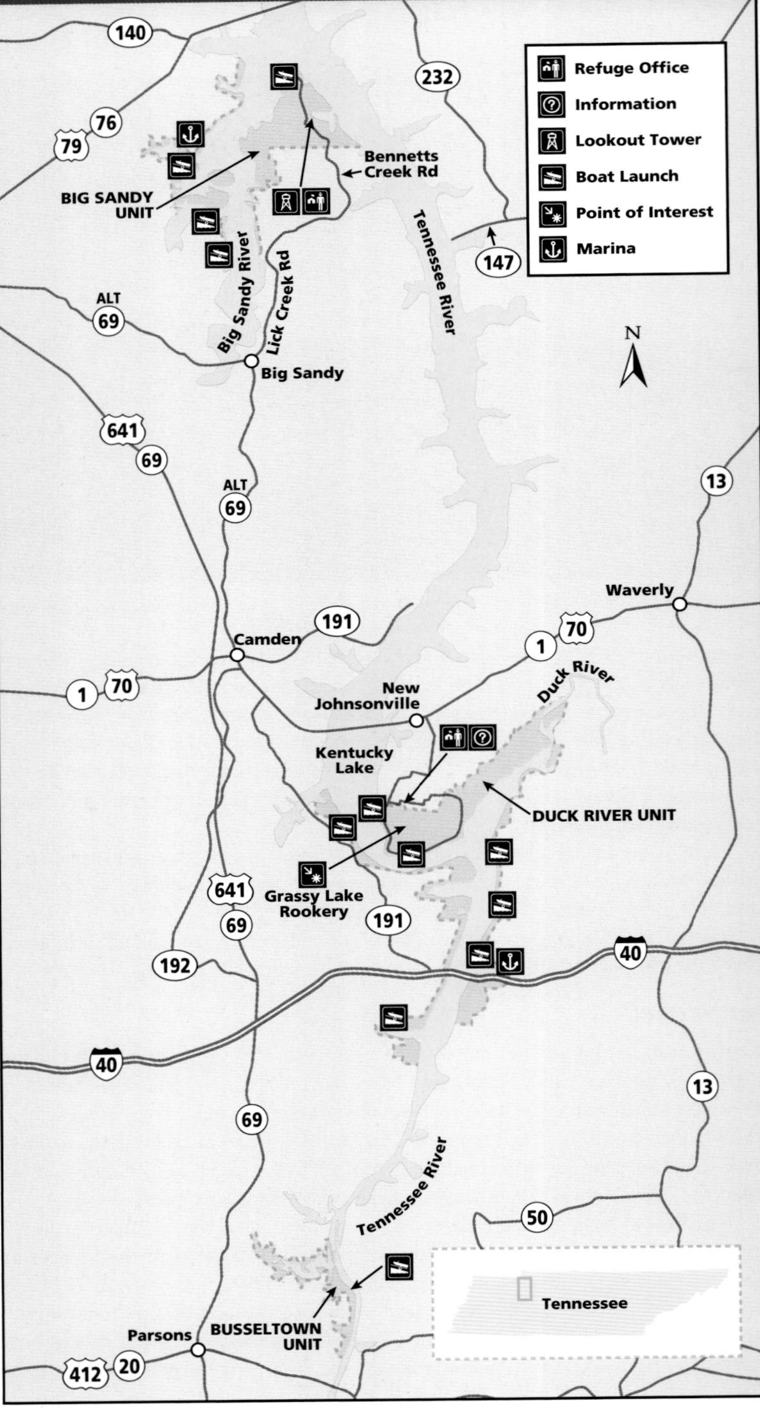

Refuge Office
Information
Lookout Tower
Boat Launch
Point of Interest
Marina

140
232
76
79
BIG SANDY UNIT
Bennetts Creek Rd
Tennessee River
147
Big Sandy River
Lick Creek Rd
ALT 69
Big Sandy
N
641
69
ALT 69
13
Waverly
191
Camden
70
1
1
70
New Johnsonville
Duck River
Kentucky Lake
DUCK RIVER UNIT
Grassy Lake Rookery
641
69
191
192
40
40
13
69
Tennessee River
50
Tennessee
Parsons
BUSSELTOWN UNIT
412
20

statehood in 1906, however, their land was opened to a frenzy of homesteading, so they lost much of that, too.

Before TVA bought the land for the lake, erosion and overgrazing had damaged the farms, and wildlife populations were in danger of disappearing. Refuge management now involves restoring habitats and leasing fields to local farmers who grow wheat, soybeans, milo, and other grains beneficial not only to people but also to birds. They use sustainable methods, such as no-till planting, and they leave 25 percent of the crop for wildlife. Managed seasonal flooding, burning, and draining also increase food supplies for wintering migrants.

The three units of the refuge—Big Sandy, Duck River, and Busseltown—are strung along about 60 air miles, but many more driving miles are required in this geographically complex wetland area.

GETTING THERE

The refuge headquarters are in Paris, Tennessee, at 810 East Wood Street, Suite B. The three units of the refuge are large and spread out, with several points of access. Call the headquarters for detailed directions. However, each unit has subheadquarters. Subheadquarters for the largest unit, Duck River, are south of Hustburg. Take US 70 from Camden (on the west) or from Waverly (on the east) to New Johnsonville. Turn south onto Long Rd. to Hustburg (about 2 mi.) and then follow refuge signs 1.5 mi. to refuge entrance. Big Sandy Unit: From Paris take Alt. TN 69 east to Big Sandy. Turn left (north) onto Lick Creek Rd. and drive 12 mi. to refuge entrance. Busselton Unit: from Parsons, go 2 mi. east on US 412. Turn left onto Mousetail Rd. and drive 3 mi. to refuge entrance.

Dogwood

■ **SEASON:** Refuge is open year-round; some parts are closed in winter to protect migrant waterfowl.

■ **HOURS:** Refuge: daylight hours; office: 7 a.m.–3:30 p.m. Each of the three refuge units has an information station.

■ **FEES:** None.

■ **ADDRESS:** 810 East Wood St., Suite B, P.O. Box 849, Paris, TN 38242

■ **TELEPHONE:** 901/642-2091

TOURING TENNESSEE

■ **BY AUTOMOBILE:** Many miles of refuge roads in all three units are open to cars. Some roads may be seasonally flooded; current road conditions are provided by a recorded message at the refuge office.

■ **BY FOOT:** Refuge roads and trails are available for hiking.

■ **BY BICYCLE:** Bicyclists may use any of the refuge roads.

■ **BY CANOE, KAYAK, OR BOAT:** All parts of Kentucky Lake are open to boats, and there are boat launches both on the refuge and nearby at commercial sites.

WHAT TO SEE

■ **LANDSCAPE AND CLIMATE** About half of the refuge is the open water of

Kentucky Lake (formed from Big Sandy, Tennessee, and Duck rivers and their tributaries), streams, creeks, and ponds. Along the water are seasonally flooded bottomland forests. Hills and river bluffs support upland hardwood and pine forests, and about 3,000 acres of old fields and farmland occupy level spots. Winter can be cold and wet, but it is the best time to observe waterfowl. Spring provides good shows of wildflowers and neotropical migrants. Summer is a good time for boating and water sports, and this part of Tennessee is temperate enough to display good fall colors.

■ **PLANT LIFE** Upland hardwoods include red and white oaks, maples, hickories, sassafras, and flowering dogwood. Many of these deciduous trees contribute red and yellow fall colors to decorate the hillsides.

The refuge is surrounded by thousands of acres of wooded and natural areas providing habitat for many species, but still there is shortage of appropriate food for waterfowl. Local farmers and refuge managers collaborate to provide extra feed for the birds. Winter wheat covers the fields in fall, ready for geese to forage as they arrive in winter. Moist-soil management—flooding of shallow ponds to develop a crop of aquatic plants needed by dabbling ducks—provides more winter food.

Bottomland hardwoods include bald cypress, a deciduous conifer that turns bronze before it carpets woods and swamps with its fernlike leaves.

■ ANIMAL LIFE

Birds In 1962 Rachel Carson published *Silent Spring*, detailing how DDT and other pesticides were killing birds, especially predatory birds high on the food chain. Twenty-two years after DDT was banned, bald eagles (especially hard-hit by the toxic pesticides) began returning to this area and built the first successful nest in Tennessee near Cross Creeks NWR. Today several bald eagle nests on the refuge produce young, and golden eagles, rare in the south, are seen on the Tennessee refuge, too.

Cottontail rabbit

Mallards, black ducks, wigeons, blue-winged teal and 20 other species of ducks spend the winter here, along with Canada geese. Bluebirds and wood ducks, both of which had suffered reduced populations because of a shortage of old trees with nesting holes, are increasing with the help of nest boxes and protected woods with maturing trees.

The refuge attracts most migratory birds using the Mississippi Flyway, as well as birdwatchers to spy on them—the refuge's most popular wildlife observation activity.

White-tailed deer

Mammals Mammals typical of this latitude, elevation, and woodland enjoy a protected life at Tennessee refuge. Beaver (especially well suited to the wetlands), raccoons, foxes, many species of mice, voles, and shrews, and deer are common here. A red-wolf reintroduction was attempted on Land Between the Lakes (on the Tennessee River, near the Kentucky border), which might have provided wolves for Big Sandy, the northern unit of this refuge; but the plan failed. Coyotes, however, have moved into the refuge on their own.

Reptiles and amphibians These wetlands are good for salamanders, frogs, and toads, all of which lay eggs in refuge wetlands. Slimy salamanders and other lungless woodland salamanders live under moist logs and moss, and they venture out on rainy nights to eat insects. Their young develop in the eggs and hatch as fully formed salamanders with no larval stage.

King snakes, corn snakes, black racers, and rat snakes catch rats and mice; while green snakes eat insects and garter snakes eat worms—all part of the well-organized food chain. Venomous snakes include copperheads and timber rattlesnakes, mainly in refuge forests, and cottonmouths in the wetlands.

ACTIVITIES

■ **CAMPING:** There is no camping on the refuge. Mouse Tail Landing State Park, Land Between the Lakes, and Nathan Bedford Forrest State Park have campgrounds in the area. When planning a visit, remember that this refuge and these campgrounds are spread out over many miles up and down the Tennessee River.

■ **WILDLIFE OBSERVATION AND PHOTOGRAPHY:** Boating on Kentucky Lake and canoeing on creeks and other wetlands provide the best opportunities for viewing wildlife here. Others include an observation platform and photography blinds. Inquire at the refuge offices for suggestions and local maps.

■ **SEASONAL EVENTS:** The refuge celebrates National Wildlife Week in October with special events.

NEARBY REFUGES

■ **Cross Creeks NWR** Established in 1962, Cross Creeks NWR consists of

8,862 acres along Barkley Lake and the Cumberland River. Rolling hills and rocky bluffs line part of the river, and bottomland hardwoods and creeks make up wetland habitats along the lake. Plant and animal diversity is similar to that of Tennessee NWR. Call the refuge at 615/232-7477 for more information

From Dover, TN, drive 3 miles east on TN 49 to entrance sign on left. Address: 643 Wildlife Rd., Dover, TN 37058.

The entire refuge is open from March 15 to October 31; during the winter many areas may be closed to protect waterfowl. The lake is open to boating all year, but refuge ponds and creeks may be closed in winter.

Wood ducks nest here, and thousands of other birds spend the winter. Among raptors, bald eagles and peregrine falcons may be seen, and neotropical migrants are abundant in spring and fall. Interpretive Rattlesnake Trail (1 mile) is open March 15 through October 31. Other refuge roads are open to hiking. The Visitor Center is open 7 a.m. to 3:30 p.m. weekdays.

Nearby Fort Donelson National Military Park commemorates the first Union victory of the Civil War, in 1862. An as yet unknown general, Ulysses S. Grant, surrounded two Confederate forts to gain river access to Nashville. The battle, fought partly on refuge land, ended when two Confederate generals retreated and the third agreed to Grant's demand of unconditional surrender. He and his soldiers spent the rest of the war in prison; after the war, Grant resumed his friendship with the defeated general. Lt. Colonel (later General) Nathan Bedford Forrest refused to surrender, however, and escaped with his cavalry to fight again at Shiloh and other battles.

■ **Clarks River NWR** Clarks River, in Paducah, was established in 1997. It has several creeks and ponds and a free-flowing river and will provide habitat for neotropical songbirds and the endangered peregrine falcon, among other wildlife. When land acquisition is complete, the refuge will consist of 18,000 acres of forest and wetland, and visitor facilities will be developed.

Appendix

NONVISITABLE NATIONAL WILDLIFE REFUGES

Below is a list of other national wildlife refuges in the southeastern states. These refuges are not open to the public.

Crocodile Lake NWR
P.O. Box 370
Key Largo, FL 33037
305/451-4223

Florida Panther NWR
3860 Tollgate Blvd., Suite 300
Naples, FL 34114
941/353-8442

Lake Wales Ridge NWR
c/o Merritt Island NWR
P.O. Box 6504
Titusville, FL 32782
407/861-0667

Passage Key NWR
c/o Chassahowitzka NWR
1502 S.E. Kings Bay Dr.
Crystal River, FL 34429
352/563-2088

Pinellas NWR
c/o Chassahowitzka NWR
1502 S.E. Kings Bay Dr.
Crystal River, FL 34429
352/563-2088

Bond Swamp NWR
c/o Piedmont NWR
Rte. 1, Box 670, Juliette Rd.
Round Oak, GA 31038
912/986-5441

Tybee NWR
c/o Savannah Coastal Refuges
1000 Business Center Dr., Suite 10
Savannah, GA 31405
912/652-4415

Wolf Island NWR
c/o Savannah Coastal Refuges
1000 Business Center Dr., Suite 10
Savannah, GA 31405
912/652-4415

Desecheo NWR
c/o Caribbean Islands Refuges
P.O. Box 510
Boqueron, PR 00622
787/851-7258

Green Cay NWR
c/o Sandy Point NWR
Federal Building
3013 Estate Golden Rock, Suite 167
Christiansted, VI 00820-4355
809/773-4554

FEDERAL RECREATION FEES

Some—but not all—NWRs and other federal outdoor recreation areas require payment of entrance or use fees (the latter for facilities such as boat ramps). There are several congressionally authorized entrance fee passes:

■ ANNUAL PASSES

Golden Eagle Passport Valid for most national parks, monuments, historic sites, recreation areas and national wildlife refuges. Admits the passport signee and any accompanying passengers in a private vehicle. Good for 12 months. Purchase at any federal area where an entrance fee is charged. The 1999 fee for this pass was $50.

Federal Duck Stamp Authorized in 1934 as a federal permit to hunt waterfowl and as a source of revenue to purchase wetlands, the Duck Stamp now also serves as an annual entrance pass to NWRs. Admits holder and accompanying passengers in a private vehicle. Good from July 1 for one year. Valid for *entrance* fees only. Purchase at post offices and many NWRs or from Federal Duck Stamp Office, 800/782-6724, or at Wal-Mart, Kmart or other sporting good stores.

■ LIFETIME PASSES

Golden Access Passport Lifetime entrance pass—for persons who are blind or permanently disabled—to most national parks and NWRs. Admits signee and any accompanying passengers in a private vehicle. Provides 50 percent discount on federal use fees charged for facilities and services such as camping, or boating. Must be obtained in person at a federal recreation area charging a fee. Obtain by showing proof of medically determined permanent disability or eligibility for receiving benefits under federal law.

Golden Age Passport Lifetime entrance pass—for persons 62 years of age or older—to federal lands including national parks and NWRs. Admits signee and any accompanying passengers in a private vehicle. Provides 50 percent discount on federal use fees charged for facilities and services such as camping, or boating. Must be obtained in person at a federal recreation area charging a fee. One-time $10 processing charge. Available only to U.S. citizens or permanent residents.

For more information, contact your local federal recreation area for a copy of the *Federal Recreation Passport Program* brochure.

VOLUNTEER ACTIVITIES

Each year, 30,000 Americans volunteer their time and talents to help the U.S. Fish & Wildlife Service conserve the nation's precious wildlife and habitats. Volunteers conduct Fish & Wildlife population surveys, lead public tours and other recreational programs, protect endangered species, restore habitat, and run environmental education programs.

The NWR volunteer program is as diverse as are the refuges themselves. There is no "typical" Fish & Wildlife Service volunteer. The different ages, backgrounds, and experiences volunteers bring with them is one of the greatest strengths of the program. Refuge managers also work with their neighbors, conservation groups, colleges and universities, and business organizations.

A growing number of people are taking pride in the stewardship of local national wildlife refuges by organizing nonprofit organizations to support individual refuges. These refuge community partner groups, which numbered about 200 in 2000, have been so helpful that the Fish & Wildlife Service, National Audubon Society, National Wildlife Refuge Association, and National Fish & Wildlife Foundation now carry out a national program called the "Refuge System Friends Initiative" to coordinate and strengthen existing partnerships, to jump start new ones, and to organize other efforts promoting community involvement in activities associated with the National Wildlife Refuge System.

For more information on how to get involved, visit the Fish & Wildlife Service Homepage at http://refuges.fws.gov/ or contact one of the Volunteer Coordinator offices listed on the U.S. Fish & Wildlife General Information list of addresses below or the U. S. Fish & Wildlife Service, Division of Refuges, Attn: Volunteer Coordinator, 4401 North Fairfax Drive, Arlington, VA 22203 703/358-2303.

U.S. FISH & WILDLIFE GENERAL INFORMATION

Below is a list of addresses to contact for more information concerning the National Wildlife Refuge System.

U.S. Fish & Wildlife Service
Division of Refuges
4401 North Fairfax Dr., Room 670
Arlington, Virginia 22203
703/358-1744
Web site: fws.refuges.gov

F & W Service Publications:
800/344-WILD

U.S. Fish & Wildlife Service
Pacific Region
911 NE 11th Ave.
Eastside Federal Complex
Portland, OR 97232-4181
External Affairs Office: 503/231-6120
Volunteer Coordinator: 503/231-2077
The Pacific Region office oversees the refuges in California, Hawaii, Idaho, Nevada, Oregon, and Washington.

U.S. Fish & Wildlife Service
Southwest Region
500 Gold Ave., SW
P.O. Box 1306
Albuquerque, NM 87103
External Affairs Office: 505/248-6285
Volunteer Coordinator: 505/248-6635
The Southwest Region office oversees the refuges in Arizona, New Mexico, Oklahoma, and Texas.

U.S. Fish & Wildlife Service
Great Lakes-Big Rivers Region
1 Federal Dr.
Federal Building
Fort Snelling, MN 55111-4056
External Affairs Office: 612/713-5310
Volunteer Coordinator: 612/713-5444
The Great Lakes-Big Rivers Region office oversees the refuges in Iowa, Illinois, Indiana, Michigan, Minnesota, Missouri, Ohio, and Wisconsin.

U.S. Fish & Wildlife Service
Southeast Region
1875 Century Center Blvd.
Atlanta, GA 30345
External Affairs Office: 404/679-7288
Volunteer Coordinator: 404/679-7178
The Southeast Region office oversees the refuges in Alabama, Arkansas, Florida, Georgia, Kentucky, Louisiana, Mississippi, North Carolina, South Carolina, Tennessee, and Puerto Rico.

U.S. Fish & Wildlife Service
Northeast Region
300 Westgate Center Dr.
Hadley, MA 01035-9589
External Affairs Office: 413/253-8325
Volunteer Coordinator: 413/253-8303
The Northeast Region office oversees the refuges in Connecticut, Delaware, Massachusetts, Maine, New Hampshire, New Jersey, New York, Pennsylvania, Rhode Island, Vermont, Virginia, West Virginia.

U.S. Fish & Wildlife Service
Mountain-Prairie Region
P.O. Box 25486
Denver Federal Center
P. O. Box 25486
Denver, CO 80225
External Affairs Office: 303/236-7905
Volunteer Coordinator: 303/236-8145, x 614
The Mountain-Prairie Region office oversees the refuges in Colorado, Kansas, Montana, Nebraska, North Dakota, South Dakota, Utah, and Wyoming.

U.S. Fish & Wildlife Service
Alaska Region
1011 East Tudor Rd.
Anchorage, AK 99503
External Affairs Office: 907/786-3309
Volunteer Coordinator: 907/786-3391

NATIONAL AUDUBON SOCIETY WILDLIFE SANCTUARIES

National Audubon Society's 100 sanctuaries comprise 150,000 acres and include a wide range of forest habitats. Audubon managers and scientists use the sanctuaries for rigorous field research and for testing wildlife-management strategies. The following is a list of 24 sanctuaries open to the public. Sanctuaries open by appointment only are marked with an asterisk.

EDWARD M. BRIGHAM III ALKALI LAKE SANCTUARY*

c/o North Dakota State Office
118 Broadway, Suite 502
Fargo, ND 58102
701/298-3373

FRANCIS BEIDLER FOREST SANCTUARY

336 Sanctuary Rd.
Harleyville, SC 29448
843/462-2160

BORESTONE MOUNTAIN SANCTUARY

P.O. Box 524
118 Union Square
Dover-Foxcroft, ME 04426
207/564-7946

CLYDE E. BUCKLEY SANCTUARY

1305 Germany Rd.
Frankfort, KY 40601
606/873-5711

BUTTERCUP WILDLIFE SANCTUARY*

c/o New York State Office
200 Trillium Lane
Albany, NY 12203
518/869-9731

CONSTITUTION MARSH SANCTUARY

P.O. Box 174
Cold Spring, NY, 10516
914/265-2601

CORKSCREW SWAMP SANCTUARY

375 Sanctuary Rd. West
Naples, FL 34120
941/348-9151

FLORIDA COASTAL ISLANDS SANCTUARY*

410 Ware Blvd., Suite 702
Tampa, FL 33619
813/623-6826

EDWARD L. & CHARLES E. GILLMOR SANCTUARY*

3868 Marsha Dr.
West Valley City, UT 84120
801/966-0464

KISSIMMEE PRAIRIE SANCTUARY*

100 Riverwoods Circle
Lorida, FL 33857
941/467-8497

MAINE COASTAL ISLANDS SANCTUARIES*

Summer (June–Aug.):
12 Audubon Rd.
Bremen, ME 04551
207/529-5828

MILES WILDLIFE SANCTUARY*

99 West Cornwall Rd.
Sharon, CT 06069
860/364-0048

NORTH CAROLINA COASTAL ISLANDS SANCTUARY*
720 Market St.
Wilmington, NC 28401-4647
910/762-9534

NORTHERN CALIFORNIA SANCTUARIES*
c/o California State Office
555 Audubon Place
Sacramento, CA 95825
916/481-5440

PINE ISLAND SANCTUARY*
P.O. Box 174
Poplar Branch, NC 27965
919/453-2838

RAINEY WILDLIFE SANCTUARY*
10149 Richard Rd.
Abbeville, LA 70510-9216
318/898-5969 (Beeper: leave message)

RESEARCH RANCH SANCTUARY*
HC1, Box 44
Elgin, AZ 85611
520/455-5522

RHEINSTROM HILL WILDLIFE SANCTUARY*
P.O. Box 1
Craryville, NY 12521
518/325-5203

THEODORE ROOSEVELT SANCTUARY
134 Cove Rd.
Oyster Bay, NY 11771
516/922-3200

LILLIAN ANNETTE ROWE SANCTUARY
44450 Elm Island Rd.
Gibbon, NE 68840
308/468-5282

SABAL PALM GROVE SANCTUARY
P.O. Box 5052
Brownsville, TX 78523
956/541-8034

SILVER BLUFF SANCTUARY*
4542 Silver Bluff Rd.
Jackson, SC 29831
803/827-0781

STARR RANCH SANCTUARY*
100 Bell Canyon Rd.
Trabuco Canyon, CA 92678
949/858-0309

TEXAS COASTAL ISLANDS SANCTUARIES
c/o Texas State Office
2525 Wallingwood, Suite 301
Austin, TX 78746
512/306-0225

BIBLIOGRAPHY AND RESOURCES

Aquatic Biology

Morgan, Ann Haven. *Field Book of Ponds and Streams: An Introduction to the Life of Fresh Water*, New York: G. P. Putnam's Sons, 1930.

Audio recordings

Peterson, Roger Tory. *Field Guide to Bird Songs—Eastern/Central North America*, Boston: Houghton Mifflin, 1999.

Voices of the Night: The Calls of the Frogs & Toads of Eastern North America, Ithaca, N.Y.: Cornell Laboratory of Ornithology, 1982.

Walton, Richard K. and Robert W. Lawson. *Birding by Ear: Guide to Bird Song Identification*, Boston: Houghton Mifflin, 1989.

Walton, Richard K. and Robert W. Lawson. *More Birding By Ear: Eastern and Central*, Boston: Houghton Mifflin, 1994.

Birds

(See Field guides for other titles)

Ehrlich, Paul R., David S. Dobkin, and Darryl Wheye. *The Birder's Handbook, A Field Guide to the Natural History of North American Birds*, New York: Simon & Schuster, 1988.

Georgia Birds: An Introduction to Familiar Species, Ellicott City, Md.: Pocket Naturalist, Waterford Press, 1999.

Botany

Grimm, William Carey. *The Illustrated Book of Trees*, Mechanicsburg, Pa.: Stackpole Books, 1983.

Newcomb, Lawrence. *Newcomb's Wildflower Guide*, Boston: Little, Brown, 1977.

Radford, Albert et al. *Manual of the Vascular Flora of the Carolinas*, Chapel Hill, N.C.: Chapel Hill Press, 1968.

Sutton, Ann and Myron. *National Audubon Society Nature Guides, Eastern Forests*, New York: Alfred A. Knopf, 1985.

Field guides

Cobb, Boughton. *Peterson Field Guides: Ferns*, Boston: Houghton Mifflin, 1963.

Conant, Roger. *Peterson Field Guides: Eastern and Central Reptiles and Amphibians*, Boston: Houghton Mifflin, 1975.

Field Guide to the Birds of North America, 3rd Edition, Washington, D.C.: National Geographic Society, 1999.

Gosner, Kenneth L. *Peterson Field Guides: Atlantic Seashore*, Boston: Houghton Mifflin, 1978.

Griggs, Jack. *American Bird Conservancy's Field Guide, All the Birds of North America*, New York: Harper Perennial, 1997.

Kale, Herbert and David Maehr. *Florida's Birds*, Sarasota, Fla.: Pineapple Press, 1990.

Kricher, John C. *Peterson Field Guides: Eastern Forests*, Boston: Houghton Mifflin, 1988.

Opler, Paul A. and Vichai Malikul. *Peterson Field Guides: Eastern Butterflies*, Boston: Houghton Mifflin, 1992.

Peterson, Roger Tory. *Peterson Field Guides: Eastern Birds*, Boston: Houghton Mifflin, 1980.

Peterson, Roger Tory and Margaret McKenny. *Peterson Field Guides: Wildflowers*, Boston: Houghton Mifflin, 1968.

Petrides, George A. *Peterson Field Guides: Trees and Shrubs*, Boston: Houghton Mifflin, 1972.

Stokes, Donald W. *Stokes Nature Guides: A Guide to Animal Tracking and Behavior*, Boston: Little, Brown, 1998.

Stokes, Donald W. *Stokes Nature Guides: A Guide to Bird Behavior*, Boston: Little, Brown, vol. 1, 1983; vol. 2, 1985; vol. 3, 1989.

Stokes, Donald W. *Stokes Nature Guides: A Guide to Nature in Winter*, Boston: Little, Brown, 1979.

Stokes, Donald W. *Stokes Nature Guides: A Guide to Observing Insect Lives*, Boston: Little, Brown, 1983.

Tyning, Thomas F. *Stokes Nature Guides: A Guide to Amphibians and Reptiles*, Boston: Little, Brown, 1990.

General background

Allport, Susan. *Sermons in Stone*, New York: W. W. Norton, 1990.

Douglas, Marjory Stoneman. *Voice of the River*, Sarasota, Fla.: Pineapple Press, 1987.

Hollingsworth, John and Karen. *Seasons of the Wild: A Journey through our National Wildlife Refuges*, Bellevue, Colo.: Worm Press, 1994.

Laycock, George. *The Sign of the Flying Goose*, Garden City, N.Y.: The Natural History Press, 1965.

Riley, Laura and William. *Guide to the National Wildlife Refuges*, New York: Collier Books, Macmillan, 1992.

Geology

Luther, Edward. *Our Restless Earth: The Geological Regions of Tennessee*, Knoxville, Tenn.: The University of Tennessee Press, 1977.

Pellant, Chris. *Rocks and Minerals*, New York: DK Publishing, 1992.

Sorrell, Charles A. *A Guide to Field Identification, Rocks and Minerals*, New York: Golden Press, 1973.

Mammals

Gingerich, Jerry. *Florida's Fabulous Mammals*, Tampa, Fla.: World Publications, 1994.

Regional and state guides

Bowen, John. *Adventuring Along the Southeast Coast: The Low Country, Beaches, and Barrier Islands of North Carolina, South Carolina, and Georgia*, San Francisco: Sierra Club Books, 1999.

Cerulean, Susan and Ann Morrow. *Florida Wildlife Viewing Guide*, Helena, Mont.: Falcon Publishing, 1993.

Jewell, Susan. *Exploring Wild South Florida*, Sarasota, Fla.: Pineapple Press, 1997.

McGinnis, Helen. *Hiking Mississippi*, Jackson, Miss.: University Press of Mississippi, 1994.

Perry, John and Jane Greverus Perry. *Sierra Club Guide to the Natural Areas of Florida*, San Francisco: Sierra Club Books, 1992.

Stall, Chris. *Animal Tracks of the Southeast States*, Seattle: Mountaineers Books, 1990.

Strutin, Michael et al. *The Smithsonian Guides to Natural Areas—The Southeast*, Washington, D.C.: Smithsonian Books, 1997.

Reptiles and amphibians

Bartlett, Richard et al. *A Field Guide to Florida Reptiles and Amphibians*, Houston: Gulf Publishing Field Guides, 1998.

Mount, Robert. *The Reptiles and Amphibians of Alabama*, Tuscaloosa, Ala.: University of Alabama Press, 1996.

Palmer, William and Alvin Braswell. *Reptiles of North Carolina*, Chapel Hill, N.C.: University of North Carolina Press, 1995.

GLOSSARY

4WD Four-wheel-drive vehicle. *See also* ATV.

Accidental A bird species seen only rarely in a certain region and whose normal territory is elsewhere. *See also* Occasional.

Acre-foot The amount of water required to cover one acre one foot deep.

Alkali sink An alkaline habitat at the bottom of a basin where there is moisture under the surface.

Alligators and crocodiles Alligators—wide, rounded snouts, no teeth showing when mouth is closed; fairly common, usually in freshwater, range from Everglades to coastal North Carolina, have young that are yellowish with brown patterns; alligators bellow and roar. Crocodiles—tapered snouts, a tooth on each side that fits into a notch outside the skin; relatively rare, prefer salt water, range mostly south of Miami, have greenish young with black crossbands or spots; crocodiles grumble and grunt. Both species lay eggs in mounds of vegetation; female alligators guard nests, help the young hatch, and protect them for up to a year; female crocodiles visit nests only occasionally.

Alluvial Clay, sand, silt, pebbles, and rocks deposited by running water. River floodplains have alluvial deposits, sometimes called alluvial fans, where a stream exits from mountains onto flatland.

Aquifer Underground layer of porous water-bearing sand, rock, or gravel.

Arthropod Invertebrates, including insects, crustaceans, arachnids, and myriapods, with a semitransparent exoskeleton (hard outer structure) and a segmented body, with jointed appendages in articulated pairs.

ATV All-terrain vehicle. *See also* 4WD and ORV.

Barrier island Coastal island produced by wave action and made of sand. Over time the island shifts and changes shape. Barrier islands protect the mainland from storms, tides, and winds.

Basking The habit of certain creatures such as turtles, snakes, or alligators of exposing themselves to the pleasant warmth of the sun by resting on logs, rocks, or other relatively dry areas.

Bayou Term used along central coast of Gulf of Mexico for a usually slow-moving stream or watercourse in a swamp or marsh.

Biome A major ecological community such as a marsh or a forest.

Blowout A hollow formed by wind erosion in a preexisting sand dune, often due to vegetation loss.

Bog Wet, spongy ground filled with sphagnum moss and having highly acidic water.

Bottomland Low-elevation alluvial area, close by a river. Sometimes also called bottoms.

Brackish Water that is less salty than seawater; often found in salt marshes, mangrove swamps, estuaries, and lagoons.

Brake Term used along lower Mississippi River for a crescent-shaped lake formed from an abandoned river course that became blocked from the main channel. *See also* Oxbow.

Breachway A gap in a barrier beach or island, forming a connection between sea and lagoon.

Bushwhack To hike through territory without established trails.

Cambium In woody plants, a sheath of cells between external bark and internal wood that generates parallel rows of cells to make new tissue, either as secondary growth or cork.

Canopy The highest layer of the forest, consisting of the crowns of the trees.

Carnivore An animal that is primarily flesh-eating. *See also* Herbivore and Omnivore.

Chiggers Larval form of some species of mites. Chiggers burrow into the skin of humans and other vertebrates (usually in warm, moist parts of the body), feed off blood and cells, and then drop off to continue their development.

Climax In a stable ecological community, the plants and animals that will successfully continue to live there.

Colonial birds Birds that live in relatively stable colonies, used annually for breeding and nesting.

Competition A social behavior that organizes the sharing of resources such as space, food, and breeding partners when resources are in short supply.

Conifers Trees that are needle-leaved or scale-leaved; mostly evergreen and cone-bearing, such as pines, spruces, and firs. *See also* Deciduous.

Cordgrass Grasses found in marshy areas, capable of growing in brackish waters.

Crust The outer layer of the earth, between 15 to 40 miles thick.

Crocodiles *See also* Alligators.

Crustacean A hard-shelled, usually aquatic, arthropod such as a lobster or crab. *See also* Arthropod.

DDT An insecticide (C14H9Cl5), toxic to animals and human beings whether ingested or absorbed through skin; particularly devastating to certain bird populations, DDT was generally banned in the United States in 1972.

Deciduous Plants that shed or lose their foliage at the conclusion of the growing season, as in "deciduous trees," such as hardwoods (maple, beech, oak, etc.). *See also* Coniferous.

Delta A triangular alluvial deposit at a river's mouth or at the mouth of a tidal inlet. *See also* Alluvial.

Dominant The species most characteristic of a plant or animal community, usually influencing the types and numbers of other species in the same community.

Ecological niche An organism's function, status, or occupied area in its ecological community.

Ecosystem A mostly self-contained community consisting of an environment and the animals and plants that live there.

Emergent plants Plants adapted to living in shallow water or in saturated soils such as marshes or wetlands.

Endangered species A species determined by the federal government to be in danger of extinction throughout all or a significant portion of its range (Endangered Species Act, 1973). *See also* Threatened species.

Endemic species Species that evolved in a certain place and live naturally nowhere else. *See also* Indigenous species.

Epiphyte A type of plant (often found in swamps) that lives on a tree instead of on the soil. Epiphytes are not parasitic; they collect their own water and minerals and perform photosynthesis.

Esker An extended gravel ridge left by a river or stream that runs beneath a decaying glacier.

Estuary The lower part of a river where freshwater meets tidal salt water. Usually characterized by abundant animal and plant life.

Evergreen A tree, shrub, or other plant whose leaves remain green through all seasons.

Exotic A plant or animal not native to the territory. Many exotic plants and animals displace native species.

Extirpation The elimination of a species by unnatural causes, such as overhunting or overfishing.

Fall line A line between the piedmont and the coastal plain below which rivers flow through relatively flat terrain. Large rivers are navigable from the ocean to the fall line.

Fauna Animals, especially those of a certain region or era, generally considered as a group. *See also* Flora.

Fledge To raise birds until they have their feathers and are able to fly.

Floodplain A low-lying, flat area along a river where flooding is common.

Flora Plants, especially those of a certain region or era, generally considered as a group. *See also* Fauna.

Flyway A migratory route, providing food and shelter, followed by large numbers of birds.

Forb Any herb that is not in the grass family; forbs are commonly found in fields, prairies, or meadows.

Frond A fern leaf, a compound palm leaf, or a leaflike thallus (where leaf and stem are continuous), as with seaweed and lichen.

Glacial outwash Sediment dropped by rivers or streams as they flow away from melting glaciers.

Glacial till An unsorted mix of clay, sand, and rock transported and left by glacial action.

Gneiss A common and rather erosion-resistant metamorphic rock originating from shale, characterized by alternating dark and light bands.

Grassy bald A summit area devoid of trees due to shallow or absent soil overlying bedrock (ledge).

Greentree reservoir An area seasonally flooded by opening dikes. Oaks, hickories, and other water-tolerant trees drop nuts (mast) into the water. Migratory birds and other wildlife feed on the mast during winter.

Habitat The area or environment where a plant or animal, or communities of plants or animals, normally live, such as an "an alpine habitat."

Hammock A fertile spot of high ground in a wetland that supports the growth of hardwood trees.

Hardwoods Flowering trees such as oaks, hickories, maples, and others, as opposed to softwoods and coniferous trees such as pines and hemlocks.

Herbivore An animal that feeds on plant life. *See also* Carnivore and Omnivore.

Heronry Nesting and breeding site for herons.

Herptiles The class of animals including reptiles and amphibians.

Holdfast The attachment, in lieu of roots, that enables seaweed to grip a substrate such as a rock.

Hot spot An opening in the earth's interior from which molten rock erupts, eventually forming a volcano.

Humus Decomposed leaves and other organic material found, for instance, on the forest floor.

Impoundment A man-made body of water controlled by dikes or levees.

Indigenous species Species that are native to a certain area.

Inholding Private land surrounded by federal or state lands such as a wildlife refuge.

Intertidal zone The beach or shoreline area located between low and high tide lines.

Introduced species Species brought to a location by humans, intentionally or accidentally; also called nonnative or alien species. *See also* Exotic.

Key A small low island, such as Key West, FL. Term used mostly in Florida and the Caribbean.

Lichen A ground-hugging plant, usually found on rocks, produced by an association between an alga, which manufactures food, and a fungus, which provides support.

Loess Deep, fertile, and loamy soil deposited by wind, the deepest deposits reaching 200 feet.

Magma Underground molten rock.

Management area A section of land within a federal wildlife preserve or forest where specific wildlife-management practices are implemented and studied.

Marsh A low-elevation transitional area between water (the sea) and land, dominated by grasses in soft, wet soils.

Mast A general word for nuts, acorns, and other food for wildlife produced by trees in the fall.

Meander A winding stream, river, or path.

Mesozoic A geologic era, 230-65 million years ago, during which dinosaurs appeared and became extinct, and birds and flowering plants first appeared.

Midden An accumulation of organic material near a village or dwelling; also called a shell mound.

Migrant An animal that moves from one habitat to another, as opposed to resident species that live permanently in the same habitat.

Mitigation The act of creating or enlarging refuges or awarding them water rights to replace wildlife habitat lost because of the damming or channelization of rivers or the building of roads.

Moist-soil unit A wet area that sprouts annual plants, which attract waterfowl. Naturally produced by river flooding, moist-soil units are artificially created through controlled watering.

Moraine A formation of rock and soil debris transported and dropped by a glacier.

Neotropical New world tropics, generally referring to central and northern South America, as in *neotropical* birds.

Nesting species Birds that take up permanent residence in a habitat.

Occasional A bird species seen only occasionally in a certain region and whose normal territory is elsewhere.

Oceanic trench The place where a sinking tectonic plate bends down, creating a declivity in the ocean floor.

Old field A field that was once cultivated for crops but has been left to grow back into forest.

Old-growth forest A forest characterized by large trees and a stable ecosystem. Old-growth forests are similar to precolonial forests.

Omnivore An animal that feeds on both plant and animal material. *See also* carnivore and herbivore.

ORVs Off-road vehicles. *See also* 4WD and ATV.

Oxbow A curved section of water, which was once a bend in a river that was severed from the river when the river changed course. An oxbow lake is formed by the changing course of a river as it meanders through its floodplain.

Passerine A bird in the *Passeriformes* order, primarily composed of perching birds and songbirds.

Peat An accumulation of sphagnum moss and other organic material in wetland areas, known as peat bogs.

Petroglyph Carving or inscription on a rock.

Photosynthesis The process by which green plants use the energy in sunlight to create carbohydrates from carbon dioxide and water, generally releasing oxygen as a by-product.

Pictograph Pictures painted on rock by indigenous people.

Pit-and-mound topography Terrain characteristic of damp hemlock woods where shallow-rooted fallen trees create pits (former locations of trees) and mounds (upended root balls).

Plant community Plants and animals that interact in a similar environment within a region.

Pleistocene A geologic era, 1.8 million to 10,000 years ago, known as the great age of glaciers.

Pocosin Area in a swamp that is slightly higher than the surroundings and is spongy enough to retain water and to support hardwood growth. Term used mostly in the Carolinas.

Prairie An expansive, undulating or flat grassland, usually without trees, generally on the plains of midcontinent North America. In the southeast, prairie refers to wet grasslands with standing water much of the year.

Prescribed burn A fire that is intentionally set to reduce the buildup of dry organic matter in a forest or grassland, to prevent catastrophic fires later on or to assist plant species whose seeds need intense heat to open.

Proclamation area An area of open water beside or around a coastal refuge where waterfowl are protected from hunting.

Rain shadow An area sheltered from heavy rainfall by mountains that, at their higher altitudes, have drawn much of the rain from the atmosphere.

Raptor A bird of prey with a sharp curved beak and hooked talons. Raptors include hawks, eagles, owls, falcons, and ospreys.

Rhizome A horizontal plant stem, often thick with reserved food material, from which grow shoots above and roots below.

Riparian The bank and associated plant life zone of any water body, including tidewaters.

Riverine Living or located on the banks of a river.

Rookery A nesting place for a colony of birds or other animals (seals, penguins, others).

Salt marsh An expanse of tall grass, usually cordgrass and sedges, located in sheltered places such as the land side of coastal barrier islands or along river mouths and deltas at the sea.

Salt pan A shallow pool of saline water formed by tidal action that usually provides abundant food for plovers, sandpipers, and other wading birds.

Scat Animal fecal droppings.

Scrub A dry area of sandy or otherwise poor soil that supports species adapted to such conditions, such as sand myrtle and prickly pear cactus, or dwarf forms of other species, such as oaks and palmettos.

Sea stack A small, steep-sided rock island lying off the coast.

Second growth Trees in a forest that grow naturally after the original stand is cut or burned. *See also* Old-growth forest.

Seeps Small springs that may dry up periodically.

Shell mound A mound of shells built by coastal native Americans who ate shellfish and disposed of shells in a pile. Most shell mounds are now covered with trees and other vegetation. *See also* Midden.

Shorebird A bird, such as a plover or sandpiper, frequently found on or near the seashore.

Shrub-steppe Desertlike lands dominated by sagebrush, tumbleweed, and other dry-weather-adapted plants.

Slough A backwater or creek in a marshy area; sloughs sometimes dry into deep mud.

Spit A narrow point of land, often of sand or gravel, extending into the water.

Staging area A place where birds rest, gather strength, and prepare for the next stage of a journey.

Successional Referring to a series of different plants that establish themselves by territories, from water's edge to drier ground. Also, the series of differing plants that reestablish themselves over time after a fire or the retreat of a glacier.

Sump A pit or reservoir used as a drain or receptacle for liquids.

Swale A low-lying, wet area of land.

Swamp A spongy wetland supporting trees and shrubs (as opposed to a marsh, which is characterized by grasses). Swamps provide habitat for birds, turtles, alligators, and bears and serve as refuges for species extirpated elsewhere. *See also* Extirpated.

Test The hard, round exoskeleton of a sea urchin.

Threatened species A species of plant or animal in which population numbers are declining, but not in immediate danger of extinction. Threatened species are protected under the Endangered Species Act of 1973. *See also* Endangered species.

Tuber A short, underground stem with buds from which new shoots grow.

Understory Plants growing under the canopy of a forest. *See also* Canopy.

Vascular plant A fern or another seed-bearing plant with a series of channels for conveying nutrients.

Vernal pool Shallow ponds that fill with spring ("vernal") rains or snowmelt and dry up as summer approaches; temporary homes to certain amphibians.

Wader A long-legged bird, such as a crane or stork, usually found feeding in shallow water.

Wetland A low, moist area, often marsh or swamp, especially when regarded as the natural habitat of wildlife.

Wilderness Area An area of land (within a national forest, national park, or a national wildlife refuge) protected under the 1964 Federal Wilderness Act. Logging, construction, and use of mechanized vehicles or tools are prohibited here, and habitats are left in their pristine states. Designated Wilderness is the highest form of federal land protection.

Wrack line Plant, animal, and unnatural debris left on the upper beach by a receding tide.

INDEX

ACKNOWLEDGEMENTS

Refuge personnel arranged tours, provided documents, answered questions, returned phone calls even when they were busy, and showed me how much they loved the refuges. They also made sure I saw swans, snow geese, manatees, a black bear in a refuge cornfield, a prescribed burn, gumbo-limbo, a live-oak arbor, a rocket-launched net for catching birds for banding programs, a stand of white cedars, and more.

For refuges that I could not visit, staff members described trails and refuge features in detail. They convinced me to visit those refuges as soon as I have time, and I will.

Refuge volunteers and friends groups helped also. Thank you. I thank Norwood Gove, Ruth Gove, and Laura Mellor for making a long, wonderful trip around Florida with me.

Ginna and Bob Mashburn also helped by visiting ACE Basin NWR and bringing back notes and a video.

I'd also like to thank David Emblidge, the editors and designers at B&F, and those at Audubon who helped move the book along.

—Doris Gove

ABOUT THE AUTHOR

Doris Gove, a zoologist and biology instructor, has directed an Audubon Nature Center and curated a museum of natural history. She wrote *Exploring the Appalachian Trail: Hikes in the Southern Appalachians.*

PHOTOGRAPHY CREDITS

We would like to thank the U. S. Fish & Wildlife Service for letting us publish photos from their collection, as well as the other contributing photographers for their wonderful imagery. The pages on which the photos appear are listed after each contributor.

f-stop fitzgerald: 14, 53, 54, 72, 73, 79, 83, 84, 106, 108, 145, 152, 163, 166, 169, 170, 182

Dan Gibson: 5

John & Karen Hollingsworth: 4, 6, 18, 21, 24-25, 34, 39, 43, 46, 48, 51, 56, 59, 60, 65, 66, 69, 75, 86, 88, 99, 115, 122, 126, 129, 132, 134, 142, 148, 159, 161, 164, 172, 179

Gary Kramer: xii, 7, 8, 22, 44, 62, 71, 118, 138, 139, 140, 146, 153, 154, 174

Omni-Photo: 32

U.S. Fish & Wildlife Service: ii-iii, 20, 23, 26, 28, 35, 36, 80, 91, 93, 96, 102, 108, 110, 120. 151, 157, 176, 183

f-stop fitzgerald at Balliett & Fitzgerald, Inc. would like to thank Angela Herndon at Hilton Head Island Chamber of Commerce, Mike Overton at Outside Hilton Head, Allan Flock and Pat Metz at the Savannah Coastal Refuge Office of U.S. Fish & Wildlife Service, Kim Washok of the Coastal Discovery Museum, and especially Page Mulhollan, President of the Audubon Society of Hilton Head Island.

NATIONAL AUDUBON SOCIETY
Mission Statement

The mission of National Audubon Society, founded in 1905, is to conserve and restore natural ecosystems, focusing on birds, other wildlife, and their habitats for the benefit of humanity and the earthís biological diversity.

One of the largest, most effective environmental organizations, Audubon has more than 560,000 members, numerous state offices and nature centers, and 500+ chapters in the United States and Latin America, plus a professional staff of scientists, lobbyists, lawyers, policy analysts, and educators. Through our nationwide sanctuary system we manage 150,000 acres of critical wildlife habitat and unique natural areas for birds, wild animals, and rare plant life.

Our award-winning Audubon magazine, published six times a year and sent to all members, carries outstanding articles and color photography on wildlife and nature, and presents in-depth reports on critical environmental issues, as well as conservation news and commentary. We also publish Field Notes, a journal reporting on seasonal bird sightings continent-wide, and Audubon Adventures, a bimonthly childrenís newsletter reaching 500,000 students. Through our ecology camps and workshops in Maine, Connecticut, and Wyoming, we offer professional development for educators and activists; through Audubon Expedition Institute in Belfast, Maine, we offer unique, traveling undergraduate and graduate degree programs in Environmental Education.

Our acclaimed World of Audubon television documentaries on TBS deal with a variety of environmental themes, and our children's series for the Disney Channel, Audubonís Animal Adventures, introduces family audiences to endangered wildlife species. Other Audubon film and television projects include conservation-oriented movies, electronic field trips, and educational videos. National Audubon Society also sponsors books and interactive programs on nature, plus travel programs to exotic places like Antarctica, Africa, Australia, Baja California, Galapagos Islands, Indonesia, and Patagonia.

For information about how you can become an Audubon member, subscribe to Audubon Adventures, or learn more about our camps and workshops, please write or call:

National Audubon Society
Membership Dept.
700 Broadway
New York, New York 10003
212/979-3000
http://www.audubon.org/audubon